BL 625.9 .S53 A63 2003
Anderson, Megory.
Sacred dying

WITHDRAWN

JAN   2014

journey has given her the grace to venture ......
Mystery."

—MADELINE L'ENGLE, author, *A Wrinkle in Time*

"If death is part of God's plan for us, there must be a sacred
dime........... ......ess."

—........ ...., author,
When Bad Th...... .....*d People*

"In dying, we pass through a narrow gate at the threshold
between the known and the unknown. This passage can be done
with meaning and dignity or else done blindly, or with nothing
but pain, fear, and regret. This book is an invaluable resource
written to guide all of us who will, or should, one day keep vigil
at the deathbed of someone we love."

—TOM F. DRIVER, author, *Liberating Rites: Understanding the
Transformative Power of Ritual*

"In this culture we have stripped dying of meaning, often reducing
it to a purely medical event. This book helps reclaim death's sacred
ground and provides practical tools and rituals to help caregivers
use the time of dying and grieving as a path to wholeness."

—FRANK OSTASESKI, founder, Zen Hospice Project

"If you are mortal, read this book. It is moving and beautifully
written. More than that, you will know what to do for the passing
of a loved one, and you will have the strength to do it."

—STEPHEN KIESLING, executive editor, *Spirituality & Health*

"One of the most important and eloquent books available on
tending to the dying. . . . Anderson offers a lovely book that covers
everything you need to know to help a dying person feel deeply
cared for, whether you choose to read poems aloud from the final
chapters or simply sit in silence, holding the hand of a loved one."

Parkland College Library
2400 West Bradley Avenue
Champaign, IL 61821

—Amazon.com

WITHDRAWN

Sacred Dying

MEGORY ANDERSON

Sacred Dying

Creating Rituals for
Embracing the End of Life

Foreword by Thomas Moore

Parkland College Library
2400 West Bradley Avenue
Champaign, IL 61821

Marlowe & Company
New York

SACRED DYING:
Creating Rituals for Embracing the End of Life

Copyright © 2001, 2003 by Megory Anderson
Foreword copyright © 2000 by Thomas Moore

Published by
Marlowe & Company
An Imprint of Avalon Publishing Group Incorporated
245 West 17th Street · 11th Floor
New York, NY 10011-5300

Originally published in hardcover format by Prima Publishing.

Sacred Dying® is a registered trademark of the Sacred Dying Foundation

All rights reserved. No part of this book may be reproduced in whole or
in part without written permission from the publisher, except by reviewers
who may quote brief excerpts in connection with a review in a newspaper,
magazine, or electronic publication; nor may any part of this book be
reproduced, stored in a retrieval system, or transmitted in any form or by
any means electronic, mechanical, photocopying, recording, or other,
without written permission from the publisher.

Library of Congress Cataloging-in-Publication Data

Anderson, Megory.
   Scacred dying : creating rituals for embracing the end of life / Megory
Anderson.--[Rev. and expanded ed.]
      p. cm.
   Includes bibliographical references (p.) and index.
   ISBN 1-56924-434-0
      1. Terminally ill--Religious life. 2. Death--Religious aspects. 3. Rites
and ceremonies. I. Title.

BL625.9.S53A63 2004
203'.8--dc22

                                                            2003061522

9 8 7 6 5 4 3 2 1

Designed by Simon M. Sullivan
Printed in the United States of America
Distributed by Publishers Group West

*This book is dedicated with special love
and immense gratitude to:*

KAREN ABRAMS, CAROLYN KELLOGG, AND YO-YO MA

*Three people who have profoundly and irrevocably
changed my life.*

Contents

Acknowledgments

.S. ELIOT WRITES that the end is where we start from. *Sacred Dying* is a book about endings, and in it, I have tried to honor the final hours of a person's life. As I express my gratitude to all the people who helped make this book a reality, I must first thank all those, named and unnamed, whose stories I tell. Their journeys and their experiences are the heart of this book.

Many people have had an instrumental role in the creation of this work. My thanks to Doug Abrams, who was the very first person to read a few pages and say, "Megory, this is a book that needs to be written. Let me call my agent, Heide Lange."

And to Heide Lange, who has become more than just an extraordinary agent. She has become my advocate and truest supporter, seeing possibilities I never knew existed. I cannot begin to express my gratitude to Heide and her colleagues at Sanford Greenburger Associates. Thank you, Heide, for everything.

I am also grateful to Matthew Lore at Marlowe *&* Company for his vision in seeing that *Sacred Dying* needed to be out in the world, and thank you, Matthew, for patiently waiting for it. Thank you also to Peter Jacoby for handling all the minutiae it has taken to make everything absolutely perfect.

Special thanks to Rachel Carlton Abrams, MD, for her help with medical information, and to Mrs. Wendy Han and Valerie Han Veimau for their help with all things Korean. Thank you, Trish Butler, for finding the perfect words for our subtitle. Thank you also, Macha NightMare, for both friendship and a shared vision of being with the dying. I am also grateful to the University of San Francisco Gleeson Library for allowing me the generous use of their facilities.

Friends of the heart: I am gifted with a wonderful community of friends, all of whom deserve appreciation and thanks for their support and encouragement throughout the process of writing this book. My gratitude goes to Sarah Campbell for her faithful friendship; to Nancy Pyzel for her constant prayers; to Jill Singer for her treasured friendship as well as her editing advice during a difficult transition; to Shannon and Toni Mallory for believing in me throughout my journey. Special appreciation goes to my 'Easy Bay families': Doug, Betsy, Philip and Katy Gentry; and Murray, Cindy, Ellen, Donald and Andrew Towle Kephart. And of course to Karen, who knows me better than I know myself.

I am grateful to Con and Patsy Goddard for the constant support when things were hard; and to Tony Cornellier, Peter Sluglett, Steve Kiesling, John Ryan, Father Dan Adams, and Robin Brooksby for their much appreciated help and encouragement. Many thanks to Professor Fred White of Santa Clara University for taking my writing to a deeper level, and a very special thank you to both Daniel Brewbaker and Carter Brey for allowing Beth's story to happen.

Three people deserve the highest accolades for all they have done to help during the writing, especially in the final days. Norma Butler lived with the process day after day, sacrificing the dining room table as stacks of manuscript pages grew and multiplied. Her calm and steady encouragement was in direct proportion to the rising frenzy. She has no idea what a difference her presence made. Part of this book belongs to her. Michele Radford offered her time and her diligence day after day in going over the minutiae needed to make things right. Thank you, Michele. And David Robinson, SJ. David painstakingly read each page, making invaluable comments and corrections, and for that I am grateful. Even more so, I am thankful for the bond of our friendship. His open heart and passion for the journey has been not only a strength in my life, but also an absolute joy.

Finally, I would like to honor two people who died before this book was completed: my cousin Karen Chick and my beloved Rabbi Ze'ev Falk. I know their blessings are on every page.

Foreword

by Thomas Moore

I T ISN'T EASY to live and die meaningfully in a society that has forgotten its natural religious roots. We think we're smart and sophisticated because we have outgrown the need for ritual and prayer. We have vanquished religion intellectually and are therefore surprised when, faced with our own death or illness or with the dying of a loved one, we don't have the answers to the basic questions. And so we have to learn all over again, remembering our traditions, if we're lucky enough to have had them, and looking for someone to help us deal with mysteries we've ignored.

Over the years I have met many thoughtful and courageous people who have stepped into this wasteland to offer their wisdom and insight. I have met physicians and nurses who know that their technical training has given them only half the skill they need. I have met volunteer workers at hospices everywhere who spend their days and nights living from the intelligence of their hearts and giving themselves to the point of exhaustion to families and to men, women, and children at the edge of death. I don't understand why, mortals all, we don't spend our communal money, otherwise known as taxes, training and supporting a million times the number of people now helping us die and deal with death. Although the situation seems to be improving, I don't see why we don't initiate our doctors and medical professionals in the mysteries that surround illness and dying. All it takes is a little depth, some serious reflection, an easing of our defensiveness, and an intelligent approach to the spirit.

These lessons and much more, thankfully, are all to be found in this wise and useful book by Megory Anderson. What I appreciate most in her teaching is her understanding that spirituality and life are inseparable, indeed indistinguishable. For me, one of the first stories is the key to the book and to the work of healing body, soul, and spirit. A dying woman, confused when told to remember her baptism, has the luck to have Megory Anderson nearby to wash her hair slowly and luxuriously. Afterward she can say, "That was my baptism." The spiritual life is not restricted to what goes on in church or to the traditional language and ceremonies. The soul knows what it needs, and a major part of spiritual care is to pay close attention to the deep desires of those who are dying, even if those wishes are plain and apparently insignificant.

I'm reminded of a story I often tell, which made such an impression. I was speaking at a large hospital at a conference on care of the dying. Several experts appeared with slides full of data on the biology of dying. I was the last speaker and the only one without a laser pointer, and I felt somewhat naïve in my lack of technical display. But I talked of the kinds of things you will read about in this book. In the discussion session following the presentations, a hospice worker stood up and told about a man she cared for shortly before he died. He said he didn't want prayers or priests or ceremonies or even family interactions. She asked what he would like. A piece of banana-nut bread, he said. The next day she brought him the bread that she herself had baked and he died peacefully. If this isn't communion, then nothing is.

Megory Anderson covers most of the difficult questions associated with the act of dying and attendant care, and her recommendations are intelligent, inventive, and mercifully humane. She tells us not to shock a relative by holding a drumming session at the deathbed if the relative wasn't into drumming. The basic principle here is very important: Don't confuse your own needs and enthusiasms (more often, neuroses) with the needs of the dying person. Megory is someone who obviously has a background in ritual and has spent enough years at it, with sufficient attention and skepticism, to know the real thing from the merely sentimental. I always get nervous when people talk about making up rituals, but this book, I'm happy to say, is a solid guide.

She also walks a broad and colorful line between the spiritual traditions. She recognizes the importance of the simplest objects and words that might be part of a person's religious upbringing. You don't have to give up your hard-won spiritual sophistication, slipping back into naïve and childish beliefs, but you can reconnect with those simple things that carry the spiritual emotions and help deal with the threshold experience of death.

When I read this advice, I thought about the rosary that I have said thousands of times in my life and that has been such a central part of my mother's religious life. What could be more meaningful to me, not to my intellectual positions on the nature of things, but to my experience of meaning, my memories, my emotions, and my sensitivities.

As a musician, I appreciate the importance Megory gives to music and sound in making a sacred place. Music is a ladder between heaven and earth, perhaps a bridge between life and death. We don't have to think much about it as we listen, and we don't have to attend to it too closely. It can carry us, and to the weak, surrendering, dying person, it's terribly important to be carried along and assisted. It can transform our immediate world from a place of practicality to a revelation of the sublime. The other things she mentions, too—aroma, color, cleanliness, poetry, and prayer—are simple and physical and yet speak directly to the soul.

I've read quite a few books on dying, and one of the remarkable things that impresses me about them is how they teach me to live with care and appreciation. They are not at all morbid, and they are not for someone else. They speak to me, as this book will speak to you. You can put its wisdom into practice today. After reading it for today, you can do what I have already done: Place it on a special shelf with a few other books that you can reach for easily when the angel of death passes close. This is one book to keep at hand, because you can be sure that one day you will need it.

Preface

SACRED DYING LOOKS closely at the rituals we have created to help us as well as our dying loved ones make the transition between life and death. This is not a book about mourning and how to handle grief; it is not about the mythology of death; it is not about funeral planning. It is about bringing spirituality, through ritual, into the physical act of dying.

Sacred Dying is intended for those who face the death of a loved one and want to bring a spiritual yet personal presence into the dying experience. Rituals help heal the pain of letting go, offering reconciliation and peace, while at the same time connecting us with the divine. It has been my experience that end-of-life rituals can help a person die not only a peaceful death, but also a sacred death, bringing reconciliation and acceptance to both the loved ones and to the person dying.

Sacred Dying is meant to be both a testimonial and a handbook. It grows out of the wealth of experiences and challenges

I have encountered in being with those on the verge of dying, a process I call "vigiling." This book tells many stories of people who are faced with dying and all the emotions and fears that dying produces. Family members often ask me, "What can I do to help my loved one die peacefully?" When I vigil with the dying, I sometimes use formal religious rites from specific faith traditions—the last rites—but more often I create rituals of my own, drawing from the circumstances of each situation. Rituals are meant to be ageless and timeless, bringing the needs of the participants into the present situation. But, all too often, traditional religious rituals fail to provide satisfying closure, either because clergy are not always available to assist in these rites or the rites themselves have lost significance for the participants.

These rituals, however, are not meant to take the place of medical, palliative, or hospice care. They assume that the physical needs of the dying person are well attended to and that pain management is under control. It is when the body is freed from pain and physical concerns that the spiritual can truly come to the forefront.

Sacred Dying's most important role is taking the attention from those survivors who are going through grief and loss and placing it onto the person who is at the point of death. The focus here is on the dying experience itself, as the last of life's great transitions. *Sacred Dying* attempts to reclaim death and dying for the person going through it.

I find that the people who understand this concept the best are those families with children who are dying. They instinctively know what is best for their children, that they have to put their own feelings of fear and sadness aside so their babies can get through this without additional worries. I have heard many times, "I have to be brave for her. I can't let her see how afraid I am." It makes an enormous difference for the children not to carry their parents' anxieties and fears with them as they die.

Mourning and grief come for the survivors, regardless. I

do not try to diminish the agony of anyone watching a loved one die; it is often the hardest thing we have to face. My hope is that, in spite of our fears and sadness, we can offer our loved one an opportunity to experience death as it should be, with honor, respect, and sacredness.

Sacred Dying

CHAPTER 1

Journey with the Dying

*There is no greater gift of charity you can give
than helping a person to die well.*
—SOGYAL RINPOCHE
The Tibetan Book of Living and Dying

The Beginning Story

THE PHONE RANG.

"Megory," the voice said. "It's Laura." My longtime friend.

"I've decided to bring my brother to San Francisco to die." Her voice was flat. "L.A. isn't the place for him. With Steve dead now, there is no one to take care of him. They were together for ten years, but AIDS got him too. Tom deserves to have someone who loves him take care of him. Mom can't do it, so I'm going down this weekend to get him."

There was silence. I didn't know what to say. "What can I do to help?" I finally asked.

"I don't know yet," Laura said. "I'll have to see when we get back. He doesn't have long; the doctors said maybe a couple of weeks. I'm bringing him home and putting him in the guest room."

Three days later Laura arrived with her younger brother and

tenderly settled the AIDS-frail man in her guest room. All the necessary hospital equipment had been rented and put into place. It was now just a question of trying to make him comfortable and helping him to die peacefully.

Laura learned about all the medical procedures from a hospice worker, and her activities fell into a rhythm of nights and days. She called her parish priest, who promised to help in whatever way he could; he would bring over communion after church on Sunday.

"Megory," she asked me, "you know all about these things. You're a theologian and a good Episcopalian. What does the church do when someone dies?"

I thought for a moment. "Well, there are several sacraments that are used; communion, of course, and then there are the 'last rites,' which are basically confession and absolution and anointing with holy oil."

"Is anointing the same thing that's done when someone asks for physical healing?"

"Yes," I said. "Although, at the point of death, it's more for sanctifying the body, making it ready for death."

I wasn't entirely certain where the distinction lay between using the oil for physical healing and using it for a death ritual, but in Tom's case, it was a bit too late for prayers for recovery. We were both worried that his death would drag out and Tom would have to suffer more than was necessary.

It was Thursday afternoon when Laura called to say she did not think Tom would last the night. She was beginning to panic. Tom wanted a priest with him when he died, but she'd only been able to reach an answering machine at the church office, and there was no one home at the rectory.

I knew that I needed to help, but at first I was not exactly sure what I could do. I certainly knew plenty of clergy—I had worked in churches all my life. Perhaps I would have better luck. I got out my address book and began making calls, but to no avail. When I reported back to Laura, she was in tears.

"Can you come over?" she asked hesitantly. "Maybe we can figure something out between the two of us."

Laura was clearly distraught when I arrived at her home. Tom seemed frailer and whiter than he'd been just a few days before. Laura was right; he wasn't going to last the night. I sat down on the bed and took his hand. He opened his eyes a bit and recognized me. A small smile appeared on his face.

I asked Tom how he was feeling and what he needed.

He was quiet a moment and then whispered, "I want to go. I'm tired."

Laura told him that we were trying to reach a priest and assured him that we would find someone soon.

At that moment the doorbell rang. "Maybe that's Father Peters," Laura said.

Instead, standing at the door was a rather elderly woman clutching a covered dish with two bulky potholders.

"Hello there, I'm Mabel Johnson from St. Paul's," she said. "I'm on the shut-in committee, and I got a message that you had someone ill here. I brought a turkey casserole."

Laura and I looked at each other, speechless. After an uncomfortable silence, we invited her in, took the casserole, and led the small woman into the kitchen.

"My brother is dying," Laura explained hesitantly. "I wanted a priest to bring the last sacraments."

Mabel said that she didn't know anything about that. "I just help out when I can," she explained. "Maybe the casserole will help."

I couldn't quite believe this was happening.

As Mabel walked out the door, she said, "I'll see you in church on Sunday. I hope your brother feels better."

Laura turned to me as she shut the door and asked, "Megory, will you take over? You do all those rituals with your women's groups. This is what you're about. Please help. I don't know what else to do."

I thought a moment. I had spent four years as an Anglican

nun in a monastic order. I had been on the staff of so many churches I could barely remember them all. I had begun working on a doctoral dissertation in theology. But the past few years had changed my life radically. Stricken with a chronic illness, I had been living in a very different reality.

At the start of my illness, when it was at its worst, I contracted meningitis and had come within inches of dying. In fact, the experience was so powerful that to this day I remember what it was like to move closer and closer into that place where the darkness takes over. I vividly remember the moment when I was sure that death would come. It was what I have since termed the "in-between place."

Something within me changed irrevocably after that experience. Having gone to the brink of death and come back from it, it was no longer something foreign to me or even feared. It was awe-filled, and I think it always will be. There was no comfort or ease in that in-between space, but I am not afraid of it anymore.

"All right, Laura," I said with resolve. "Let's do it. I think I know what to do."

Feeling bold even in my insecurity, I told Laura to get candles and some oil, and I went into the kitchen and got some bread and wine.

"We can't celebrate the Eucharist without a priest, but we can certainly gather around the breaking of the bread."

We needed some music—something calm and soothing, strong but not distracting. I found a few things, kind of New Age and meditative.

I glanced through Laura's book shelves, found a Bible and some poetry, and added those to the pile.

I met Laura near the guest room, she with her stack and I with mine. We looked at each other with a bit of fear and trembling, but mostly with reassurances and determination to do what was ahead of us.

"Are you ready?" I asked her. She nodded. "All right. Let's go to Tom."

We went to the bed where Tom was dozing off. Laura touched his arm.

"Tom," she whispered. He opened his eyes and looked at her. "Megory is here, and we're going to help you through this. She knows about ritual, and I think she can help us with what to do."

He nodded, his eyes brimming with tears.

"Let's start," I said, "with a few minutes of being quiet. Let's try to ready our inner selves, preparing for what we are about to do. Let's ask God to help us with this."

HAVING GONE TO *the brink of death and come back from it, it was no longer something foreign to me or even feared.*

The three of us, finding a comfortable place to be, sat in the quiet room. I listened to my breathing, in and out, and to Tom's. I regulated my breath and then attempted to match it with Laura's. I tried to quiet my thoughts and focus on the stillness. I asked God to be with us and guide us in what we were about to do. When I opened my eyes, I saw a lovely peacefulness on Laura's face, and Tom showed an even calmer look than before. I began to pray out loud, once again asking for God to be with us in all ways.

As I closed the prayer, I began placing the candles around the room. I explained, "It's important, as we begin to do ritual, to create a space around us that contains the sacredness. We need this room and this space to hold a lot of powerful things for us. So let's make this room holy. Let's make it comfortable. Let's make it inviting—for us and for God."

We had at least ten candles, and I put them in a circle around the room. The sun was going down, so the light in the room was soft and flickering. Laura worked on straightening up the clutter around the sick bed, removing cups and paper and anything that wasn't needed. She then began attending to Tom, pulling the sheets together and fluffing his pillow. I found the CD player and put on soft, relaxing music. Laura got a bouquet of flowers and added them to our space. Tom was alert and looked at us with anticipation.

"Tell me what it's like to die," he asked. Laura and I caught each other's eye. Silence.

"Tom," I ventured. "We don't know. Maybe that's the reason we're all so afraid of it. Are you scared?" He nodded. "Well, then let's talk about God, because I think God is the one in charge of it all. And the one waiting for you on the other side."

Laura reached for the Bible and began leafing through it.

"Tom, remember all those stories from Sunday School? Let me see if I can find some of them." She took a few minutes, then smiled and said, "Here's one I remember. It talks about Jesus on the Sea of Galilee with his disciples when a huge storm came up. The boat began filling with water and the fishermen were all afraid. The storm got worse and worse, so the disciples woke up Jesus, who was sleeping through it all, and cried to him to save them.

TOM WAS ALERT *and looked at us with anticipation. "Tell me what it's like to die," he asked.*

"Then what did Jesus do but turn to the disciples and say, 'Where is your faith? You should have known better. Don't be afraid.' And it says that the disciples were still frightened, but they marveled at what he did."

"I wonder, Tom," I said, "at how many times the Lord needs to tell us again and again not to be afraid. But we still are. I guess it's human to be afraid. And worried. And filled with all kinds of questions. But the Scriptures say that God loves us. No matter what we have done; no matter how hard it has been; no matter what we think we deserve. My favorite passages when it feels too hard for me are in Isaiah:

Fear not, for I have redeemed you;
I have called you by name and you are mine.
When you pass through the waters, I will be with you;

and through the rivers, they shall not overwhelm you;
when you walk through fire you shall not be burned,
and the flames shall not consume you.
Because you are precious in my eyes, and honored,
and I love you. (43:1B–2, 4)

I could barely keep my voice steady as I read that, thinking how very much I needed to hear it for myself. I looked up and found I was not alone. Both Laura and Tom were in tears.

"Tom," I asked, "do you feel as if something is holding you back? Is there something you've done or said that we can help with?"

He nodded. His voice was scratchy.

"There are things I've done," he said, "and shouldn't have." He went on to talk about the things in his life that pained him, all the little things building up over a lifetime.

As I sat and listened to him, I realized how very small the things are that weigh us down. But they do get in the way, and over time they become too heavy to carry. It was time for Tom to put them down. When he got to things about family and about Laura, I walked over to the window. This was between the two of them. They held each other, sobbing, and saying, "I'm sorry, I'm sorry," over and over. All those years of pain and separation, and now was their chance to come together and experience forgiveness and healing. I don't know how long we were there. Time was forgotten. But the sun went down and the shadows around the candles became deeper.

When words were finished, I returned to the bed. We sat in silence. "I know that God loves us as much as we can possibly imagine," I eventually said, "and when you love, you forgive. Tom, please know that whatever you did or said or were, God sees you only in love, and we do too. That is the only way we can be with God. In love."

I had a thought. "Your inner soul has been cleaned this afternoon. Why don't we help you clean your outer body?

Remember when Jesus was about to die, at the Last Supper he washed his disciples' feet? Why don't you let Laura and me wash you now? It will make you feel so much better."

His tearful eyes lit up and he said, "Yes, that would feel good."

Laura went into the bathroom to find a basin and some cloths. When she returned we organized it so that we each had a side of the bed. Very, very gently, we began washing Tom's arms and legs and then his face and hair. All the while, there was a look of joy on his face, almost like a baby, pure and gentle. Laura began humming to herself and then singing out loud, no particular tune, just a quiet chant. I joined her, and we continued adding words about being clean and pure and ready to begin the journey. It was lovely. I have no idea where the melodies came from; they were just there.

We must have washed him for over an hour. He didn't want us to stop. But finally he became tired and we let him sleep. We waited and watched, the candles still flickering in the dark.

Some time later, in the night, Tom awoke. He appeared to be peaceful. I asked him if he would like to break bread. He said yes. I brought the bread and wine to the bed. I began talking about this being the central ritual for Christians everywhere. Bread and wine. Fellowship. Communion. Being with each other and with God.

"At the Last Supper, Jesus and the disciples celebrated the Passover festival. He knew that it was time for him to die. He looked around the room at all the people he loved and told them not to be afraid, that he was going on ahead of them. Jesus told them how much he loved them and, because of that, they should know how much God the Creator loved them.

"But for now, until he comes back for us, or until we go to be with God in heaven, we have each other. And we have God's peace, so our hearts won't be troubled.

"This bread represents the bread that Jesus offered, when he told us that it was his Body." I held out the piece of bread. And then I poured some wine from the bottle into the wine glass.

"And this wine, he told us, is his Blood.

"When we're together and when we break bread, God is here with us. This is how we can be a part of God and God a part of us, here on earth. And pretty soon, Tom, you are going to experience being with God in a much fuller way. A more complete way. But for now this is how we can share God's fullness on earth."

We broke the bread and we ate it. And we shared the cup. And we knew that God was with us.

As we sat in the quiet and thought about God's presence and the future, I walked over to the dresser where Laura had put the oil. I opened the bottle and put a few drops on my fingertips. I went over and sat at Tom's side.

"I would like to anoint you, Tom. It is an ancient ritual, going back to biblical times. The Israelites used oil to sanctify. Remember when the kings were crowned? King David? King Solomon? They were anointed to prepare them for great things. And the priests too. They were anointed to sanctify their bodies and their souls.

"Christians use oil too, for healing as well as for readiness for death. We want to prepare you, Tom. We want to sanctify your body as it gets ready to give itself up to God."

I made the sign of the cross on his forehead and then on his hands and on his feet. We prayed for blessing on Tom's journey to God. Laura stood at my side and I poured some oil in her hands.

"Take some, Laura, and rub his arms," I said.

She seemed surprised, but followed my instructions. The move seemed easy, from anointing the extremities to a massage of his arms and legs. Tom had endured a lot with this disease, and his body must have suffered horribly. Perhaps this was a way we could help ease the pain so that he could begin to let go.

We rubbed his arms, his legs, his back, his feet. He sighed with pleasure. Little by little, I watched all his pains and stiffness ease. We would stop for a bit, and Laura, resting his head in her lap, would rub his forehead. The evening had turned into night, and we could sense that Tom was losing strength, but he asked again and again to have his back rubbed, his feet massaged, his forehead stroked.

Finally, he slipped into unconsciousness, his breathing growing more shallow. We covered him with his blanket. I brought a candle, the largest one we had, and put it near Tom's head. Laura and I sat on either side of the bed. I listened quietly to the rhythm of his breathing. With my hand on his chest, I tried to match his breath with my own, to make it smoother. He was gasping, making noises as he fought for air. Laura was crying quietly, and I began praying softly that Tom's soul would be wrapped in God's arms. Time passed. And Tom's breathing stopped.

I think I must have stopped breathing myself. It all seemed to be so still. I felt warmth, though, and a very, very strong presence of God. There was no doubt that God was in that room and that Tom's soul was being received by the Light. Every nerve inside me was electric with that Light.

I asked Laura to take Tom's arm, as I held the other, and we prayed that Tom's soul would find peace and joy as it moved into his place with God. And I also prayed that we could find strength as we dealt with Tom's body and prepared it for burial, knowing it was only a shell. Laura stroked the body once more and then she covered him with the sheet. We blew out the candles, except for the one at his head, turned off the music, and left the room.

How many hours had passed? I don't know. Maybe seven or eight, but it didn't matter. Time was fluid. I went home after being assured that Laura was all right, and that she had some other friends to be with her and take care of some of the details for the burial. I crawled into bed exhausted but strangely invigorated.

The experience of vigiling with Tom haunted me. For days, I kept thinking about what had happened. It was the first time I had ever seen a person die, and I knew that dying was much more than the process of the physical body shutting down. I also knew that I instinctively understood what was happening to Tom spiritually and emotionally.

About a month later, I received a call from someone who knew about Tom's death. Would I please come and help his partner when it was time? "Just do the same sort of thing you did when Tom died," the man said. I agreed. And once again, I sat vigil and helped with the spiritual process of letting go.

My name got passed around, and soon I had calls coming from people asking for the same help. Then someone left my name with a hospital nurse, and I began going to hospital beds. Each time I sat and vigiled with someone, I learned something new. Each experience was different, and each person wanted and needed different things. No one who sits with the dying ever remains untouched. It is a holy experience.

I have tried to share in this book what I have learned about death and the sacred act of dying through hands-on information and also through stories.

Rachel Naomi Remen begins her book, *Kitchen Table Wisdom,* by saying, "Everybody is a story. When I was a child, people sat around kitchen tables and told their stories. We don't do that so much anymore. Sitting around the table telling stories is not just a way of passing time. It is the way the wisdom gets passed along. . . . It's the way life teaches us how to live."[1]

And I would add that it teaches us how to die.

1. Rachel Naomi Remen, *Kitchen Table Wisdom: Stories That Heal* (New York: Riverhead Books, 1996), p. xxv.

CHAPTER 2

Returning the Sacred
to the Act of Dying

I VIGILED ONCE with a young woman who was dying of cancer. The nurses said she wouldn't last the night. Her pastor had been in to see her just a few hours before, offered a prayer, and told her as she lay dying to remember her baptism in Christ.

"How am I supposed to remember my baptism?" she asked me. "I was all of six months old!"

She was right, of course. The event and symbol of her baptism had very little meaning for her.

I didn't have an immediate answer for this woman but instead asked her when was the last time someone had washed her hair. She groaned and replied, "I think it was about two years ago. No kidding, it feels that horrible."

I got water, a cup, a basin, some towels, and went to work. I took the cup, filled it with water, and poured it over her head. She gave a huge sigh.

"That feels so good," she said. "Keep doing it."

I kept up the stream of water, like a small waterfall.

The woman began crying. "My body feels so dirty and grimy here. I just want to be clean again. I want my body to feel fresh and clean and happy again."

I kept pouring the water, never saying a word.

Finally, when she was finished crying, I took a towel and gently rubbed her head.

"That was my baptism, wasn't it?"

I nodded. And then we sat together in silence—until she died.

> *To everything there is a season,*
> *A time to every purpose under heaven:*
> *A time to be born, a time to die.*
> —ECCLESIASTES 3:1-2

THE PROCESS OF dying is a difficult one, with many fears and anxieties, but it is also a very mysterious and wondrous process. It involves both the body and the soul in the greatest transition we are ever called to make. When I sit vigil with those who are at the edge of death, moments away from crossing over, I am constantly in awe of the process happening in front of me, one that each one of us must eventually go through.

It has not been easy working with the dying or researching and writing about rituals and spiritual practices used during the last moments of life. It was certainly not my choice to live my life always thinking about the dying process. But as most people who work with the dying can tell you, this work chooses you, not the other way around. Many people tend to be fearful and uncomfortable when death is mentioned in conversation, but in my experience those of us who live our lives this way are honored to do so, and are very humbled at the great mystery we must face each time another death occurs.

I receive calls from people in hospitals, hospices, and individual homes who want to make it possible to provide a spiritual death for their loved ones. These people often have no affiliation with a traditional religious faith or have only a marginal relationship with their clergy, and they feel more comfortable turning to someone neutral.

My experience is in theology, rather than in medicine or nursing. My academic background led to this very hands-on application of religious practices. I have always done rituals, sometimes with a group of women, sometimes in church settings, sometimes on my own. The academic and the spiritual began meeting in a very new arena for me, the arena of the dying. I had to take what I knew theologically and somehow translate it into very real, bottom-line situations. The dying do not want theories, they do not want academic exegesis. They need to know, right here, right now, who God is and what is going to happen to them when they die.

So I learned to take my theology, my beliefs, and even my own experiences—from school, from the monastic community I was a part of many years ago, from the congregations I attended and worked in—and to offer them as guidance and assistance. I found there were very few people in the community, religious or otherwise, willing to do that. I responded to a very real need—to attend to the spiritual needs of the dying. So that has become my work—sitting, talking, praying, helping with things those dying feel badly about, and creating rituals to help them let go. And then I vigil until they die.

A few years ago, an elderly mother had been ill for some time, and the process was taking its toll on all the family members. I visited the skilled nursing unit several times to be with them and to help with a number of rituals.

The eldest daughter asked me, "How can you do this time and again? I'm emotionally exhausted being here day after day." Her voice quivered and tears ran down her face.

I explained, "But you see, I come into a room without all the emotions and grief you face as your mother is dying. I can be neutral." My role is not to grieve but to help make the transition a spiritual one, deserving of careful and prayerful preparation.

There is such a tremendous need for spiritual guidance for those who are facing death, as a patient or with a loved one. Emotions and grief flood everyone involved. There are so many unknown factors. Many times doctors can predict what may happen physically, but no one can truthfully answer the big questions for us, questions like, What is dying like? Will it hurt? What is going to happen to me after I die? Is God going to be there waiting for me? Is God going to be angry at how I lived my life? These questions and fears clearly need to be addressed spiritually and not brushed aside.

Our society has tried to make death invisible, thinking that if we ignore it long enough it will go away. Often we as family and loved ones are so afraid of death that even mentioning the word to terminal patients is taboo. We think the dying are oblivious to what is happening to them.

Sadly, a dying person frequently feels afraid to bring it up him- or herself. When I enter a hospital room I often hear a sigh of relief. At last someone is there to help the family members come to terms with what is playing out before them. Death has too long been the elephant in the living room, while everyone awkwardly discusses the weather.

A Brief History of Dying

THE WAY WE die has changed dramatically throughout the centuries. In the Middle Ages, death was always a public event. The entire community gathered at the deathbed. Dying was a drama to be played out for all to see. Not only was it a time when the dying person publicly bequeathed all his worldly goods to his heirs, but it was also an opportunity for family disputes to be settled, often with loud voices and emotional bickering. Dozens of deathbed scenes from the literature of the time reflect the significance and intensity of this dramatic moment.

Once the family responsibilities were settled, however, the larger drama took place—the eternal drama. For Christian Europe, it was only at death that one was freed from the bonds of physical life and allowed access to eternal glory. Angels and the communion of saints stood at the gates of death, waiting to escort the soul to heaven. Of course, demons hovered nearby too, hoping to ensnare the soul at its most vulnerable moment. It was truly a moral and ecclesiastical drama being played out for the entire community to witness.

As modern medicine dawned and death became much more controlled, the dying person was no longer the center of attention. Instead, the focus was on the grief of those loved ones who were left behind. Grief was a noble calling, demonstrating devotion and piety. Queen Victoria was the supreme example of how one grieved. She mourned for her husband throughout her widowhood (forty years in all), laying out her dead husband's clothing and shaving water each and every day.

In the Victorian era, death was a part of family life and the home. Death took place in the family bedroom, and the body was laid out in the family parlor. However, instead of the entire community being present, only the immediate family witnessed the death. The mourners took center stage.

In the twentieth century death was removed from the home almost entirely and shifted to medical facilities. This change happened most dramatically after the Second World War. No one wanted to see death or have it near. When death was imminent, the family and especially the children were protected from the gruesome and unpleasant scene. As death was moved away from the home and the natural cycle of family life, it took on a whole new meaning. It became not only something fearful but also something invisible.

Currently, the sick and elderly are whisked away to hospitals and nursing homes. By relegating death to the medical and health care communities, we have taken it from the family structure and made it into a social taboo. Most physicians tend to see death as the enemy; those who give in to it are the defeated victims. The doctor's role is to "fix" a physical disorder, not facilitate the transition between life and death.

I once spoke with a family whose elderly mother was clearly dying. She had been in the hospital for several months, and because of insurance restrictions was subsequently transferred to a skilled nursing unit. The doctors were keeping the mother alive not only with a respirator but also a feeding tube. The family was told to start looking for long-term care for her.

"How did we get to this point?" the daughter asked me. "We brought Mother into the emergency room when she had her stroke and what happened? The doctors automatically took over by putting her on these machines. No one asked us about what she would have wanted. No one consulted us about their actions. And now after all this time, the doctors say that they can't do anything more for her, so we just have to wait it out until it's over. It could be months! She would never have wanted to end up like this."

"Hospitals push families aside, and, at best, treat them as guests. We are led to believe that death is a medical event best attended by the experts,"[1] says hospice worker Kathy Kalina in her book *Midwife for Souls*. Loved ones may have to make medical decisions regarding what treatments to continue, what course to follow if there is no living will, and when to actually stop medical treatments, but that seems to be the extent of

---

1. Kathy Kalina, *Midwife for Souls: Spiritual Care for the Dying* (Boston: Pauline Books and Media, 1993), p. 19.

family participation in how a person dies. Attention is focused on medical procedures and on logistics. Doctors are there to fix the diseased body, and when that fails, "arrangements" need to be made. Once the doctors or the hospital can no longer be active in the treatment, the family must find a place to take the dying person. The family must retreat in defeat.

Dying persons usually have very little say in what is going on around them. They become mostly objects to be dealt with. "What are we going to do now?" family members ask. "I certainly can't take him home with me; I have a family to take care of," or "We need to find a long-term nursing home that will deal with her." The cause of worry and fear is whisked away, far from sight.

And when death actually happens, the members of the family no longer wash and dress the body, preparing it for viewing in the home. Funeral homes now assume all the details, including making the person look "lifelike" and "natural." The dead are completely sanitized for our protection.

There are people who are attempting to handle aging and dying in a different way. They want to bring it back into the community, into the intimacy of home and family, acknowledging the spiritual dimensions of a natural life cycle. In my experience, however, the health care professionals who want to facilitate this change are running into a number of problems beyond their expertise, both religiously and culturally. As they turn to the religious communities for help, they find that few clergy are trained to sit with the dying and offer anything more than a few prayers or words of

> IF I HAD *my life to live over again, I would form the habit of nightly composing myself to thoughts of death. I would practice, as it were, the remembrance of death. There is not another practice which so intensifies life. Death, when it approaches, ought not to take one by surprise. It should be part of the full expectancy of life.*
>
> —MURIEL SPARK
> *Memento Mori*

encouragement. The cultural problems are just as great. As more and more culturally diverse people make their homes in Western society, they bring with them varied customs and traditions. These are often quite unfamiliar, and health care professionals are faced with unusual expectations that are often hard to meet.

Hospice as a Model

THE HOSPICE MOVEMENT, which found its way to the United States in the mid-1970s, is a viable alternative to the way death and dying are routinely handled. It was created to provide physical care, primarily palliative, at the end of life, while tending to the emotional and spiritual concerns of the dying person. Hospice care provides an opportunity for people to die either at home or in a residential site. Most people express desire for the comfort of familiar surroundings, away from an impersonal, antiseptic hospital setting.

I met with a family several times whose father was sent home from the hospital to die. His family had been very apprehensive when the doctor referred them to hospice.

"I was stunned at first," the son told me. "The word hospice to me meant a death sentence."

His wife nodded in agreement.

"At first we were disappointed that our doctor just handed us over; we never even spoke to him after we left the hospital. But then the hospice nurses came to visit us, and we were really impressed. They filled out all the forms to get us set up with a hospital bed, and oxygen, and a dozen other things we were going to need."

His wife continued, "The practical things were important, like organizing Dad's medications and things like that, but what I appreciated most of all was the emotional support for what we were going through. Social workers came to visit us and they even sent a chaplain. Our family actually sat down together to talk through what was happening. We could never have Dad at home like this without hospice. They are the best people in the world."

Hospice workers include physicians, nurses, social workers, and volunteers, as well as spiritual leaders. The philosophy of hospice seems new to our scientific era, yet it is really a return to an earlier, more natural view of death and dying. A number of books have recently emerged explaining the hospice philosophy and the impact it has made on those going through death in the family.[2] At a time when national healthcare is examining methods for caring for the terminally ill, hospice should be held up as a model of compassionate and humane care brought back into our homes and communities.

Sacred Dying: A New Paradigm for Death and Dying

ONE OF THE first steps in creating a new paradigm for death and dying is bringing it into our lives with greater ease and acceptance. This means confronting death face-to-face. We cannot "fix" death as modern medicine wants us to believe; we can only attempt to help our loved ones make the dying transition a more peaceful one.

Penelope Wilcock writes in *Spiritual Care of Dying and Bereaved People*:

> Our response to the helplessness of others is to take
> rescuing action, to be the cavalry coming over the hill
> (and it follows that our response to our own
> helplessness is shame). It requires little reflection to
> perceive that this approach breaks down in the spiritual
> care of dying people and their loved ones.
> Firstly, because we can no longer act to save them.

2. See especially Ira Byock's *Dying Well*, Jan Selliken Bernard and Miriam Schneider's *The True Work of Dying*, Deborah Duda's *Coming Home*, and Kathy Kalina's *Midwife for Souls*.

What is inevitable for all of us has arrived for them. They face their mortality, and we are helpless to prevent this. Secondly, because it is they, not we, who are the protagonists in this last act of life. The work of the dying is theirs, not ours. Ours is to travel alongside, as companions on their journey. Thirdly, because this act is an act not of power, but of weakness. It is the work not of building up, but of laying down, of achieving not mastery, but acceptance.[3]

As we confront death face-to-face, we must acknowledge that it is more than just a physical phenomenon; it is also a spiritual process. Unfortunately, when our society discarded death and dying, we also discarded wisdom about the process from our religious traditions. Few people today are aware of what their religious practices are at the time of death. Responses I typically hear from both the family and the person who is dying include: "I am Jewish, but I don't know the prayers that I am supposed to say." "Where is my faith now that I need it?" "Why doesn't the chaplain do more than just say a quick prayer?" "What does my religion teach about dying? About the afterlife?" It is time to reintroduce the traditions of our faiths into one of life's most important moments, the moment of leaving it.

Learning about Being with the Dying

As I WORK with people who are new to being present with the dying, I ask them to remember two things:

1. Stepping back from the physical and medical concerns of the patient, we must now focus on the spiritual.

3. Penelope Wilcock, *Spiritual Care of Dying and Bereaved People* (Harrisburg, PA: Morehouse Publishing, 1996), p. 4.

Dying is more than the physical body shutting down, although that is certainly the primary view in our society. The body will take charge on its own. The spiritual reality will not. Sacred dying means bringing the spiritual experience to the forefront. Deal with spiritual things, whatever they may be, first and foremost.

2. The sacred dying experience is for the person dying— all rituals and observances are for him or her.

This does not mean that the loved ones and their profound feelings of loss and sadness do not count or should not be a part of the rituals. It means, rather, that the grievers will have time later to mourn and honor their feelings of loss. Loved ones must try to respect the experience of dying, and even if they need to sacrifice their own feelings for the time being, they must try to focus 100 percent on the person who is dying.

The reality of the dying person is very different from that of the living. She is experiencing something we cannot fully understand or enter into. Many times the patient is unconscious, in a coma, or drifting in and out of heavy sleep. How do we communicate when someone cannot speak back to us?

If a person is conscious and able to talk, I always listen and take my cues from him. The desires of the dying, however nonsensical or puzzling they may be, are met. I always reassure the patient that I understand and will do whatever I can to make the request happen.

If the patient talks about the past, or about people long dead, I assume she is experiencing things we in the room are unaware of. I never discount that reality. I always try to acknowledge it and respect it.

If the person is unconscious, I speak as if he is able to hear and understand. Once again, I offer reassurance that all is well. I almost always tell patients that they are dying and that it will be all right to let go and try to let this happen peacefully.

If words from loved ones are forthcoming, it is again important to assume that the patient hears and understands what is being said.

The most important thing to remember is that the experience is about the dying person, not the survivors. Everything should be done to make this experience peaceful.

Recurring Issues as Your Loved One Is Dying

CERTAIN THEMES TEND to come up again and again for those who are at the point of death. Putting things in order, practically and emotionally, has been important in virtually every death at which I have been present, and religious traditions all support this through various rites. Another issue that almost always comes up is the afterlife. I never assume a particular doctrine, but rather try to understand the person's own religious upbringing and teachings and also her thoughts about it personally. Asking someone what she thinks the afterlife is like is a very good way to broach the subject of dying. Children, especially, have wonderful images of what the next life will be. It often helps the parents deal with this difficult situation to hear their child's vision of what is soon going to happen.

Dying is a profoundly emotional experience for everyone involved, and it tends to bring back memories and feelings about the entire life of the person. If he was an angry person throughout life, there may well be unresolved anger when people gather. Family dynamics of the past tend to be magnified in such stressful circumstances. If an opportunity is given to put things in order, then many family conflicts can be resolved, but most of the time the lifelong dynamics are carried through until death.

> AS DEATH APPROACHES *we do not need to turn away in fear. Instead we can choose to celebrate life and join hands with those we love.*
>
> —TED MENTEN,
> *Gentle Closings*

This is not to say that every issue in a person's life must be resolved before she dies. Quite the contrary. There are some things that simply must be put to rest rather than dragged out for one last rehash—the cues will come from the person dying. The things she needs to address usually rise to the surface, and all it takes is the quiet opportunity and perhaps a bit of encouragement and love to speak of them. It will become clear how to proceed if the focus is on the person and the internal work that she is doing to prepare herself for death.

Creating Sacredness

WHAT CAN PEOPLE do to help make dying a sacred event? How can we create a more sacred death for those who are traditionally religious? And what about those who are nontraditional or nonpracticing yet recognize the need for a spiritual experience at the time of death? This is the primary work in front of us. Frequently I go into a hospital room and battle with the staff for privacy and permission to perform simple religious rituals. Most healthcare workers will acknowledge and allow for religious attention to the person, but only if it does not interfere with their routine.

In addition, many professionals in most religious institutions, the clergy and pastoral laypeople, seldom know how to serve as a guide for the dying. There are classes and seminars in churches and synagogues about grief and mourning, yet few of those congregations offer classes entitled, "What happens when I die?"

I once asked a rabbi in a large congregation which prayers he used with the dying.

"You mean the Mourner's Kaddish?" he asked, referring to the prayer recited on behalf of the deceased.

"No," I replied. "I mean the prayers said when a person is actually dying."

"Oh," he replied. "I don't know. I've never seen anyone die."

He had been a congregational rabbi for almost twenty years. "I only get called when it's time to do the funeral," he explained. Clearly there is much to learn within our traditional religious communities.

When I sit vigil with people from a particular faith, I bring in as many rituals and symbols as possible, often just after visits from chaplains and clergy. I invoke ancient and wonderful rituals that have been perfected over the centuries. However, people often want more personal meaning from the rites. I address those needs too, creating nontraditional rituals as an addition to, or an elaboration on, the familiar rites. These are personalized and intimate, speaking to the very individual needs of the person dying.

On the other hand, I often work with people who are on the fringe of a religious community, having left the institutional church or temple. Many of them have what I call "Sunday school religion." When I ask what the family background is, I hear, "Well, I was born a _____, but dabbled in _____ when I was in college. I haven't really practiced much since then." Their beliefs and understanding of the faith are what they were taught as children. (And trust me, that is sometimes quite horrific!) Every situation is different.

When death comes, people who have not practiced much in adulthood often want to hear what is familiar to them from their childhood. So I offer them comforting words that are basic and well known. I speak of a God who is loving and caring. I find rituals and prayers within the religion that have some meaning to the person, and from there I expand once again into more personalized rituals. I have found that certain religious teachings and rites serve well as a foundation for something that has more meaning to the person in his individual life and experience.

As we create a new paradigm for death and dying, we must hold in esteem ancient and time-honored practices of the faith traditions. We also must have courage to create new personal rites that speak profoundly to the needs of our dying loved ones.

CHAPTER 3

Rituals for Embracing
the End of Life

I T HAD BEEN a long seven years. Carol had taken care of
her mother ever since her father died of Alzheimer's. Now
her mother was going through the very same thing, and it
was getting harder and harder to cope. First one and now the
other. Life was not easy. Carol lived about ten minutes from her
family home, the home where she grew up, and some days she
was with her mother more than she was with her own children.

Her mother was fading; the caregiver said that she was
refusing to eat. When I arrived at the house, Carol and I sat
down to talk things over.

"Mother's dementia is pretty bad. I'm not sure how lucid
she'll be for you. Sometimes she's aware of what's happening
around her, but most of the time she's in another world. She
talks about her childhood a lot. She thinks I'm her mother."

I reached out to take Carol's hand.

"I don't know how much longer either of us can last. I'm

pretty much at my wit's end. I love my mother dearly, but it's so hard to take care of her like this." She began crying.

"What do the doctors say?" I asked.

"Her Alzheimer's is becoming more pronounced. She also has a heart condition, but that could go on for another few years. They just don't know. She's stopped eating, you know. We try to get her to eat something, but she's so lethargic. If it goes on much longer, we'll have to put her in the hospital. I don't want that to happen. This is her home and she should be here. She should die here, in her own bed."

I let Carol cry quietly for a while before I asked to see her mother.

When I got into the bedroom, I saw a room that hadn't really changed from the 1950s, with the exception of the television in the corner and a modern clock radio. There were photographs on the wall that showed a smiling and loving family.

Margaret was in her bed. She was in her eighties, and she looked very tired and listless. I walked over, sat in the chair next to her, and introduced myself.

"My name is Megory," I told her. "I thought I would come for a visit."

"Did you bring me anything?" she asked. I looked around the room and spotted a small stuffed animal. It looked like something her grandchildren might have brought her.

"Yes," I replied. "I thought you might enjoy holding this while we talked."

I put it into her arms, and she gave me a little smile as she cradled it.

She and I talked a bit. I asked her about her life and the people she loved. Her dementia was pretty evident; she was back in her childhood, not remembering much else.

I had an idea.

"Margaret," I said. "I heard that it's your birthday pretty soon. We'd like to have a party for you. You need to tell me, though, what you'd like. Why don't you think for a moment and tell me what you really, really want for your birthday."

Margaret scrunched up her nose and thought hard.

"I want to go home," she finally said. "I'm tired of being here. I want to go home."

"All right," I replied. "I'll see if I can make plans for that. In the meantime, why don't we have a going home party for you? I know everyone here wants to say good-bye before you leave."

"Can we have a cake? Or maybe . . . ," she pointed to the ceiling and made swirls with her hand.

"Streamers?" I asked.

She grinned and nodded.

"I want to go home," she finally said. "I'm tired of being here. I want to go home."

"Okay," I said. "Let's do it tomorrow. You just relax and we'll get it all ready for you. Be sure and tell Carol if you think of anything else you'd like."

Back in the living room, I explained to Carol what my thinking was.

"She's confused about where she is and what's happening to her. All she knows is that she wants to find a place that feels like home. And maybe that means she needs a way to let go."

Carol nodded in agreement. "I think she's been doing that slowly for a couple of weeks now."

I continued. "Why don't you gather the family and we'll have a small party so everyone can say good-bye. We'll make it a happy party, though, so she feels good about leaving. We want her to feel safe about leaving."

Carol began making a list of things to do. "We can't make it too hectic; she gets confused when there are too many things going on at once. I think if we have a cake—and streamers—" she chuckled, "and a few little presents, that should be enough. Just having the family around will be enough stimulation for her."

I agreed. "Let's see what her mood is tomorrow when everyone is here, but I think she may enjoy people making a fuss over her.

Ask the family to bring things she has loved over the years, things that will make her feel secure. Maybe you can wrap them up and give them to her as presents. And ask everyone to think about how they want to say good-bye to her."

I agreed to come back the next evening and help with some rituals during the party.

The next evening when I arrived at the house, I was greeted by Carol and her husband and two children. There was also an elderly woman who identified herself as Margaret's closest friend, Joan. "I wanted to be here too," she told me. "We've been friends since we were young brides. I had to say good-bye to Margaret."

The family seemed ready, so we went into the bedroom together. There were streamers all across the room and a big sign that read, "Bon Voyage. We'll miss you." Margaret was sitting in her chair and beaming. She looked at all the people and exclaimed, "I'm ready!"

We brought in a cake and passed out plates. Someone had put on some music and the family was having a nice time chatting.

I saw Carol's youngest daughter, who was about seven or eight, over in the corner looking at some of the old pictures on the wall. I went over to her.

"Do you know who all those people are?" I asked.

She nodded and began identifying them for me. "That's my grandmother and grandfather, and there's my mom and my uncle a long time ago. They look different now. Can I ask you a question?"

"Sure," I replied.

"Are we saying good-bye to Grandmother for good? Is she going to die now?"

I knelt down so I could meet her eyes.

"I don't think she's going to die tonight, Holly," I began, "but it may be sometime very soon. She is awfully tired and wants to go home—her real home, with your grandfather and her own mother and father."

"In heaven?" Holly asked.

"Yes, in heaven," I replied. "Sometimes it's hard, though, to leave everyone you love in order to die. That's why we're here tonight, to make her feel okay about leaving."

"But I'll miss her," Holly said softly.

"Of course you will," I said. "Everyone will miss her terribly, but her body is wearing out; it's time for her to go. Wouldn't you rather see her happy about going rather than in a lot of pain?"

Holly nodded.

"Then tonight, let's wish her well. You can tell her how much you love her and she'll remember that in her heart. And you'll remember her in your heart too, won't you?"

She smiled. "Do you know what I brought Grandmother?"

"What?" I asked.

"My princess robe and crown. She gave them to me a long time ago for my birthday, and I thought it would make her happy to wear them tonight. She can be a princess for us!"

"That's perfect, Holly!" I exclaimed. "Why don't we gather everyone and begin with that?"

I asked for everyone's attention. "Holly has just told me that she has Margaret's first present tonight. Why don't we begin now?"

"Margaret," I said, looking at her, "we are all here tonight to wish you good-bye. I know you are ready to go home, and even though we will miss you, we wanted to have a celebration in your honor. Are you ready for your presents?"

Margaret was alert and eager to be the center of attention.

"Holly, why don't you tell your grandmother what you brought for her?"

"Okay," said Holly. "Grandmother, remember when you gave me these for my birthday? You told me that I was your very favorite princess. Well, I thought you could wear them tonight and be our favorite princess!"

She leaned over and put the sparkly tiara on her grandmother's head and then draped the pink robe around her shoulders. Margaret sat up straighter as the robe was adjusted behind her.

"I want to see. Where's my . . . thing?" she asked, holding out her hand.

Carol looked around her and said, "A mirror. I think she wants a mirror."

We found a hand mirror and brought it to her. Clearly, she liked what she saw.

One by one, the family brought gifts to her. There was a special teacup that Margaret fingered delicately. There was a photograph album of her childhood, with pictures of her mother and father as she remembered them. There was an afghan that seemed familiar to her and a piece of jewelry that she pinned to her robe.

I asked the family to begin telling Margaret good-bye. Again, one by one, they said their good-byes.

"We love you very much, Mother," said Carol's husband, Steve, "and we'll miss you, but I know you're eager to be on your way. Have a good journey and we'll see you again soon." And with that he bent over to kiss her.

Jason, Carol's and Steve's oldest son, was a bit shyer. "'Bye, Grandmother. I'll remember you."

Carol had a harder time. She knelt before her mother and hugged her with all her might.

"Good-bye, Mommy. I love you so much," she said crying. "I'm going to miss you but you know how much I love you, don't you?"

The other family members began crying quietly.

Holly suddenly broke through the circle with a piece of paper in her hands. "Look, Grandmother," she exclaimed. "I just made this for you. It's a ticket for heaven!"

We all looked at the magic marker ticket. "Ticket. One Way. Heaven. Good for angel wings too."

We all chuckled through our tears as Holly proudly gave it to her grandmother with a kiss.

"Thank you, little girl," Margaret said. "I'll keep it for when I get there."

I noticed that we were standing in a semicircle around the chair and I said without thinking about it, "Why don't we sing some songs?"

Margaret's friend, Joan, began to sing in a wobbly voice, "Good night Margaret, good night Margaret, good night Margaret, we're sad to see you go."

We all joined hands and began circling to our right, all the time singing to Margaret. She loved it, clapping her hands with glee. We sang over and over, until we saw her beginning to fade with fatigue. We then left the room quietly as her caregiver began getting her ready for bed.

In the living room, I asked the family how they felt.

"It was good," Carol said. "I think she knows we're all fine with letting her go now."

Steve commented that she seemed happy to have everyone with her.

Holly piped up, "Well, I think that she's happy to have her ticket now. That means she can go whenever she wants to."

Carol called hospice the next day and arrangements were made to have them come to the house to oversee things. Within a few days, Margaret went into a coma. Carol called the next week to tell me that her mother had died.

"That party was really the last thing she ever did," she told me. "I'm convinced that the rituals helped her realize that it was okay. We weren't going to hold her back. I think maybe by showing her, rather than just telling her, it got through."

They buried her with all the presents from that night, Carol told me. Even the ticket to heaven.

It matters greatly not only that we birth and die
but how we birth and die.
—RONALD L. GRIMES
Deeply into the Bone

RITUALS ARE A major part of our lives. Every time we light candles on a cake and sing "Happy Birthday" we are performing a ritual. Holidays often take on ritual characteristics, such as fireworks on the Fourth of July or turkey for Thanksgiving dinner. We also have cultural coming-of-age rituals. For instance, a huge milestone for teenagers is turning sixteen and getting the much sought-after driver's license. There are rituals that families practice over the years, adding to the history or tradition of their lineage.

What are rituals? What do they do? How do they work? According to theologian Tom Driver, "Rituals are primarily instruments designed to change a situation: They are more like washing machines than books. A book may be about washing, but the machine takes in dirty clothes and, if all goes well, transforms them into cleaner ones."[1]

Rituals transform one state of being into another. They carry us from childhood into adulthood, or from membership in our family of birth to the creation of a new family through marriage.

When many people hear the word ritual, especially in a religious context, they think of elaborate ceremonies or mysterious events that seem magical or elusive. Rituals can be very complicated, but they can also be very simple and personally meaningful. They can be part of a larger religious or social system, or they can be created solely for a specific need.

When I explain to people that I perform rituals for those who

1. Tom F. Driver, *Liberating Rites: Understanding the Transformative Power of Ritual*, formerly titled *The Magic of Ritual: Our Need for Liberating Rites That Transform Our Lives and Our Communities* (San Francisco: HarperSanFrancisco, 1991), p. 93.

are dying, I often see a look of fear in their eyes. Am I a voodoo priest? Will I bring out an animal to sacrifice? Will I light a fire in the middle of the hospital room and burn incense to strange deities? There are so many connotations we have, especially if we come from a tradition that shies away from formal ritual practices.

I explain that sometimes when we are in a situation that is very emotional or stressful, we don't quite know how to understand what is happening or how to handle our feelings. Rituals can help us see things in a clearer way. If we use the symbols to help illuminate what is going on around us, a difficult situation becomes easier to accept and move through. The symbols help us give names to those feelings, and the rituals help carry us beyond the situation to a higher understanding. They transform.

Rituals for Life Cycles

WHEN A PERSON is born, we have rituals to celebrate the arrival of a new life and a new member of the community. Faith traditions and cultures use rituals such as baptism, naming, or circumcision to welcome new life into the faith.

After the consecrated event of birth, the journey into death is the most sacred part of our life cycle. It not only marks the ending of a life and an era, but for many it also marks the transition into a new and fuller existence in the afterlife. In many Asian cultures, death means entering the land of the ancestors. For many Hindus, Buddhists, and other faiths that believe in reincarnation, it means shedding "old clothes" in order to take on a new life. For those who believe in heaven, death means being with God in a glorious place where there is eternal happiness.

We need to reclaim the special place of death in the cycle of our lives by marking its passage with new as well as time-tested rituals. Death should assume a place of significance instead of being a fearful taboo. Rituals can help us shift our understanding and restore acceptance of this most sacred transition.

The Psychology of Ritual

MOST OF US want to understand the true meaning of life and death, yet we don't know how or where to begin. Such a task seems overwhelming. This is where rituals can play a crucial role. Rituals have the ability to bring people an experience of something greater. They create a safe space and time in which we can touch the deeper issues of our existence. They have the power to bring to the surface and resolve very deep feelings and unnamed blocks that have been buried in our unconscious.

James Roose-Evans, an English theater director who is also an Anglican priest, works with ritual and liturgy. In his book, *Passages of the Soul*, he writes:

> *A ritual is a journey of the heart which should lead us into the inner realm of the psyche and, ultimately, into that of the soul, what Meister Eckhart referred to as "the ground of our being." Rituals, if performed with passion and devotion, will enhance our desire and strengthen our capacity to live. New rituals will evolve but the ancient rituals and liturgies are also capable of rediscovery as we learn to make them our own.*[2]

Rituals for the In-Between Place

WHEN I WALKED into the hospital room, I saw a young man who knew he was going to die soon. He was miserable. The nurses were good to him, he told me, but he was so upset and scared that it was making him even more sick than he already was.

"It's too much for me," he said, trying not to cry.

2. James Roose-Evans, *Passages of the Soul* (Rockport, MA: Element Books, Inc., 1994). p. 10.

He told me that he had friends in the area, but that his family was too far away to be with him.

"I guess they're waiting for my funeral," he said, with an edge of sarcasm to his voice.

The hospital chaplain would stop in for a visit every couple of days, but other than that, he was alone. When I suggested that we try some rituals to help address some of his needs, he was eager to jump right in.

"No one gave me a set of instructions on how to do this," he said with a grim chuckle. "So when does Dying 101 begin?"

What rituals are appropriate for the place between life and death? How do we help those who are dying? Is the person afraid? Does he want to talk about what is happening? Does there need to be a cleansing of space in the room? Of the physical body? Does there need to be an opportunity for prayer and meditation? Are people around him upset and anxious? Most of all, what is the experience of the person dying? What is blocking death from happening peacefully? All of these questions offer direction for what can be done with ritual.

Some of the most frequent rituals I perform include:

LETTING-GO RITUALS

When the dying person is in the in-between place and the family is afraid, there seems to be a tug-of-war going on. Rituals can help both loved ones and the person dying to let go.

RITUALS FOR UNRESOLVED ISSUES SUCH AS ANGER, REMORSE, OR SADNESS

Most people at the time of death have issues that are unresolved. Most of these issues are with family or loved ones. Many of them are with God. It is important to put things in order. The use of confession and reconciliation serves many needs.

PURIFICATION RITUALS

When a person enters the liminal place of the dying, there

is a desire to be pure and clean, physically, emotionally, and spiritually.

There are also rituals that serve to take the dying person from the state of living to the state of existence in the afterlife. They can carry the person, who is often too weak or afraid to venture alone, through the liminal state into the next life. Rituals have the power to do all these things.

Again, theologian Tom Driver says,

> *In such empowerment, the professional, whether medical or clerical, has an important role to play, a role perhaps more like that of a physical therapist than a surgeon or a drug therapy specialist. It is the work of showing the patient, who is really a learner, what she is able to do for herself. The patient needs to learn a practice of heightened attention to, and willing participation in, the mysterious process of pain and restoration, of death and life, that is going on within her, in this place at this time, in this way.*[3]

Finding a Ritual Specialist

WHEN CONFRONTED WITH a loved one who is dying, we find ourselves overwhelmed with the myriad of details that need to be addressed. If we add spiritual concerns on top of everything else, it may become too much. That is why a neutral outsider is often the best solution for creating a spiritual environment. Hospice worker Rodney Smith writes in his book, *Lessons from the Dying,*

> *Most of us do not know how to die. It is not something we have rehearsed or practiced. We have a mind full of*

---

3. Tom F. Driver, "What Professionals Need to Know About Ritual: A First Lesson" in *The Park Ridge Center Bulletin*, August/September 1998, p. 17.

ideas about what will happen but little if any actual experience with the process. We need to have someone who knows, guides, teaches, and reassures us, someone we can trust, someone who will stand naked with us, who will not be overwhelmed. The dying need much more than pat answers or good feelings. Their hearts call for someone who can open into the unknown, someone who will travel the road of fear with them. To find such a companion is a very rare and precious occurrence.[4]

I see my work as that of being a companion and midwife to the dying. It is a difficult calling. That is why loved ones will not have an easy time finding someone who will vigil with their dying. But hopefully, as more people become aware of the need for this work, there will be people willing to make themselves available.

If you are looking for a ritual specialist, there are several ways to begin the search. The chaplain's office at a hospital provides a clergy or lay chaplain, usually affiliated with a specific faith tradition, yet trained to be spiritually supportive to any religious background. Chaplains will offer prayers and an opportunity to talk through any concerns. The time they have is limited, though, and they will not usually stay with the patient until death occurs, although they may know of others who provide more intensive end-of-life spiritual help.

The nurses at the hospital may also know of ritual experts. Hospice workers have their own chaplains and are usually aware of people in the community who offer spiritual and ritual help.

I recently had an experience with someone close to me who was dying. I thought I would be able to assist not only with rituals but also in sorting through the difficulties the family was

4. Rodney Smith, *Lessons from the Dying* (Boston: Wisdom Publications, 1998), p. 100.

facing. That didn't happen. I was too close to the situation and too caught up in the emotional concerns of everyone in the family. I could not be objective enough to see what was needed for this person to die peacefully.

I realized then the benefit of an expert who is outside the situation. When I vigil with others unknown to me, I bring a neutrality and a strength for others to lean on. I am able to speak about the process without being emotionally caught up in the grief, and I am able to provide clarity for those who feel overwhelmed and afraid.

However, I have seen situations where friends of the family, those who had spiritual leanings, were able to come in and provide that same sense of objectivity with a bit more personal connection. Whether it is someone the loved ones know or someone from the outside, I find that it is better to have a person not in the immediate circle of loved ones to help with rituals at this very emotional and difficult time.

What Happens During a Death Vigil?

WHEN I WALK into a hospital room and meet a new family for the first time, I can usually perceive the situation almost immediately. I can see the family dynamics, and more important, I can begin addressing the needs of the dying person. If the family has difficulty in agreeing on what is to be done, I quickly bring them back to the matter at hand: their loved one's death. From there, it is just a question of how to use the time until the death.

FIRST, I ASK EACH PERSON IN THE ROOM TO PREPARE HIMSELF FOR THE TASK OF PRAYING AND VIGILING, TO BE CENTERED AND READY.

I ask everyone to take deep breaths, trying to focus on the rituals about to be performed. I suggest that people leave the outside world outside. They may want to wash their hands or other parts of their body. It is important that each person be as centered as possible.

Second, I create a sacred space.

I look at the space around me. How can I cordon it off to contain it? How can I create some privacy? I close doors and use blankets or sheets to separate the space from a neighboring space. I find markers, like chairs or tables, that will set the space apart. I create an intimate space that is neither too broad nor too confining.

Third, I create the intent.

I begin the ritual time with a statement of intent, a prayer, a song, or even just a time of collecting thoughts. If those gathered are religious, I ask for God's presence. If not, I begin with a simple statement: "We are gathered here to help our loved one as she dies." This doesn't have to be elaborate. The purpose is to bring everyone together and to express a common intent.

Fourth, I perform the ritual.

This is the main part of the work and activity. It can be anything at all, from a formal religious rite, like communion, to small personal things such as a simple washing. I read, use music, or chant. Some rituals address a particular need of the person dying or the loved ones. Other rituals purify and make ready. Some create a peaceful setting. It all depends on the needs of the present situation.

Fifth, I give thanks.

Once the ritual is done, it is good to give thanks, to God, to the loved ones present, or to the person dying.

Finally, I close the sacred time and sacred space.

This means in essence saying, "We're done." It can be accomplished by breaking the circle around the bed, by hugs, by moving outside the sacred space and removing the markers. It is important that the space be returned to its normal state. Most of the time, after the ritual is done, people want to sit in silence. I ask loved ones to reflect, pray, and just to "be" with the dying person. Silence can teach a person many things, and the silence that accompanies death is especially sacred.

Using Intuition to Decide on Rituals

THE WAY I choose a ritual is not always by the book. Rather, I rely primarily on my intuitive sense of what the dying person needs. Is it dealing with unfinished business? Does he want quiet and peaceful surroundings? Does he need to release anger toward God? If the innovative rituals are to speak to the individual and the present situation, they can't always be prescribed. It is much more a sense of seeing what is there, just under the surface, and trying to tap into it. Sometimes it takes more than one try. I have begun rituals that, five minutes into them, just weren't working, and I have had to shift to another area completely. That is why, as the loved ones look for a ritual expert, it is important to find someone who feels comfortable with being open to a variety of things, rather than having a prescribed set of rites.

HOLY MARY, MOTHER *of God, pray for us sinners, now and at the hour of our death.*

—A TRADITIONAL ROMAN CATHOLIC PRAYER

Learning the Religious and Cultural Background

WHEN I AM asked to perform rituals, the first thing I want to learn is the religious and cultural background of the family. This makes an enormous difference in how a person will react to ritual. If the person is a Southern Baptist, bringing in incense and beads is probably not a good idea. But if she is a Buddhist, incense and beads are definitely in order to create a prayerlike atmosphere for the family. If the person is a Hindu, having a public confession is not appropriate, since negative thoughts contaminate the sacred space of the deathbed room. But if the person is a practicing Roman Catholic, a priest should be called in immediately to hear his last confession and give absolution.

It is important for healthcare workers, chaplains, and anyone else caring for the dying, to recognize these variables. I remember working with a family that had enormous diversity within it. The woman dying had converted to Judaism when she married, and her immediate family, including her in-laws, were all Orthodox. Her mother and father, however, were evangelical Christians. When I arrived at the hospital, the room was brewing with shades of a religious war. Her father-in-law was reciting prayers in Hebrew, while her mother was desperately trying to get her daughter to "repent and return to Jesus." If that weren't difficult enough, there was a young person, a remote cousin I believe, sitting on the floor chanting something Buddhist. It was a comedy of errors.

It took some doing to sort out all the prayers and intentions, but we managed to briefly address everyone's particular agenda and then focus on the needs of the woman who was dying.

Although religious and cultural affiliations must be acknowledged, assumptions should never be made. There are many variations on religious practices in this country, and very few people practice religion "by the book." Despite that, it is important to

As Roshi Taji, *a contemporary Zen master, approached death, his senior disciples assembled at his bedside. One of them, remembering the Roshi, was fond of a certain kind of cake, had spent half a day searching the pastry shops of Tokyo for this confection which he now presented to Roshi Taji. With a wan smile the dying man accepted a piece of the cake and slowly began munching it. As he grew weaker, his disciples inquired whether he had any final words for them.*

"Yes," the Roshi replied. The disciples leaned closer to catch his words of wisdom.

"Please tell us!"

"My, but this cake is delicious," and with that he died.

—Source unknown

know what religions teach and what cultures practice so that traditional rituals can be available to a person if and when they are wanted.

What Do I Need for Rituals?

I BRING A variety of items to use for a ritual. Sometimes I use many of the items, other times very few. I like to have on hand:

- Music—a CD player and various discs
- Candles
- Oil—I use massage oil, usually very lightly scented, nothing too strong
- Religious objects—this includes anything from prayer shawls to crosses to prayer beads
- Water that has been blessed
- A communion set of bread, wine, cup, and plate—many Christians wish to use the symbols of bread and wine
- A large bowl or container
- Incense
- Miscellaneous items such as paper for writing or drawing, markers, scissors, and matches

When I am in a hospital or nursing home, I usually use other items around me, like sheets, blankets, pictures, photographs, and so on. If the patient is at home, I ask that loved ones gather personal items that have meaning. For burying or planting I often use soil, which can be brought in from outside.

Sitting in Silence

ALL THAT BEING said, when I am with a person who is dying, I don't spend the majority of the time in doing or performing.

Mostly I just sit and watch, listening and praying. When the rituals are done, and the dying person and the loved ones have said all that needs to be said, then that is the time for the vigil. I sit in silence, no matter how long it takes.

Sometimes people come and go during a silent vigil, and that is perfectly fine. I believe it is important to have someone present at the bedside at all times, unless it is perfectly clear that the patient wants to be alone.

Putting Mourning and Grief Aside

WHEN ATTENTION IS focused on the experience of a sacred death rather than on the survivors, it does not mean that the loved ones must put aside the grief that comes as they lose someone to death. Feeling sadness and even anger is part of the human experience. I find myself saying to the loved ones, more often than not, "Yes, of course you feel these things. Letting go is a very hard thing to do. You should tell him how you feel, that you are going to miss him terribly. But once that's said, let's find out what he needs to do and concentrate on that."

Many times, in the middle of a ritual, I turn to the loved ones and ask, "Are you all right? Do you need to take a deep breath? Go out for some air?" If they need some time out to get a handle on their emotions, I encourage them to leave the room for a bit. Then, when they return, they are stronger and more able to attend to the task at hand.

Sacred dying rituals are primarily and notably for the person dying. It takes great strength and courage to face death and to begin to move through it to the other side. And it takes great courage for the survivors to put aside their own fears and anxieties to help their loved ones die a peaceful death.

Letting Go

THERE IS A moment when the body is about to cease its natural functions, when it is important to accept that death is happening and to begin to let go, emotionally, physically, and spiritually. I have learned the signs when something is preventing this from happening. Perhaps the family or friends cannot accept that the loved one is dying. Perhaps there are some things the dying person has not reconciled—inside herself or with other people. Often there is fear of the physical act of dying.

Increasingly, as medical technology sustains life with life support or other artificial measures, it is not always easy to determine the point at which someone is ready spiritually or emotionally to die. When does one stop fighting to survive and go into death, not in defeat but in courage and strength? This is a hard question. I met with a woman named Marie several times before she died. As her death grew more imminent, she told me she was worried about her daughter being able to let go.

"I fought so long just to stay alive, through all the medical procedures and treatments. It seemed the thing to do at the time. But lately I've been getting ready to die. Those are two different things, you know."

I nodded in agreement. "We've been working on that, haven't we?" I asked her.

Marie smiled. "I'm not really frightened anymore. I think I'm doing all the necessary things to get ready."

But then a cloud drew over her face.

"My daughter is still back there fighting for me to live," she said. "How do I tell her it's time? I'm ready; she's not." Fighting to live, and having the courage to die, are important, and we need to know when one is no longer appropriate and it is time to begin striving for the other. It is when a person is able to let go, and the loved ones recognize that this process is happening, that death can come peacefully.

Waiting It Out Until the End

MOST PEOPLE DIE during the night, and it is important to realize that this time is very special. For many families who have been at the hospital or hospice day after day, the end may be so tiring for them that they cannot keep watch yet another night. The ritual expert can take over while others try to sleep.

As I vigil with the dying, I always agree to stay until death occurs. I believe it is important to truly "watch" until the end. Pastoral visits are often brief, with a few prayers and words of encouragement. The role of someone who vigils is quite different. Just as a midwife stays with the mother until the baby is born, I stay with the dying person until the last breath, and sometimes hours afterwards.

The journey into death is such an important one that I believe each person deserves as much support as possible. The loved ones who decide to stay and vigil with the dying person receive, I believe, as much grace and blessing as the dying. It is truly a remarkable experience.

CHAPTER 4

Traditions:
Incorporating Religious Rituals

ANIEL WAS WITH his father, Max, when the heart attack happened. They went to the hospital where the doctors said that it was serious and Max probably wouldn't last the night. "He is conscious, though, so you might want to call the family in."

Daniel went into the hospital room where his father lay attached to tubing and monitors. He was so still.

"Dad," Daniel said quietly. "Is there anything I can do?"

His father seemed to be saying something under his breath. As Daniel leaned in closer, he recognized it as the Shema, the basic Hebrew prayer he'd learned as a child.

"Dad, do you want me to call a rabbi?" Daniel asked.

The old man shook his head. "It's been too long," he replied.

When I arrived at the hospital floor, Daniel was standing next to the bed.

"Dad hasn't been inside a temple in years," he told me, "and

Kathy and I don't go. Kathy isn't even Jewish. But he's saying some prayers in Hebrew, and I think he wants some kind of religious help." I nodded.

It seemed as if Max wanted to die as a Jew. Faced with death, he wanted the reassurance of familiar prayers. We got permission to light a candle, placed it beside his bed, and began to offer comfort. I read from Psalm 139:

Search me, O God, and know my heart.
Try me and know my thoughts.
And see if there be any wicked way in me,
and lead me in the way everlasting.

Daniel wanted to do what he could for his father, but he was at a loss about Jewish traditions.

"We were cultural Jews growing up, but not particularly religious." he said, taking me outside into the hallway while Max dozed off.

"I had a bar mitzvah, but I pretty much stopped going to services after that. Kathy and I were married by a judge since we couldn't find a rabbi who would marry us."

"What about your father? Do you know if he was observant growing up?"

"I never really knew my grandparents; the family was pretty quiet when we asked about them. I do know they were from the old country, and I guess everyone was observant to some degree in those days. But as far back as I can remember, Dad didn't want to have much to do with religion."

"Maybe something happened," I said. "What about your mother? What's her story?"

"She died about two years ago. Cancer. It was pretty long and drawn out. Dad hasn't been the same since." He was silent.

We walked into the hospital room where Max was awake and looking weary. I sat down next to him.

"Max," I began. "I'm not a rabbi. We can get one if you want."

He shook his head vehemently.

"That's all right, it's not a problem," I replied. "We won't do anything you don't want to."

"Dad," said Daniel. "Remember that nice chaplain who came in to see Mom when she was in the hospital?"

"That was for your mother," Max said quietly. "Me, I don't want any rabbi."

He turned his head into his pillow and the tears began to flow.

I took his hand after a minute and said, "Max, it might help if you talk about this. Can you tell me why you're so angry with God?"

After a few moments of silence, Max spit out the words, "The camps, that's why. The camps. I don't want to talk about this. Everyone's gone. My mother, my father, everyone I knew. I lost everybody. I was only a kid when they got me out of Poland, but I ended up here and they ended up dead. God doesn't exist anymore. Not for me, he doesn't."

Daniel stood next to his father's bed, too stunned to speak.

"I never told you," Max said, avoiding Daniel's eye. "Your mother knew, but I wouldn't have her tell you kids. What's done is done."

Daniel wept silently.

"You must have been in extraordinary pain for all these years," I said to Max. "You kept it all to yourself, didn't you?"

He nodded yes.

"Pain is something we don't get over easily," I replied. "It stays inside us for a very long time. It sounds as if your pain has made you very angry."

"I was at a death last week," I said, abruptly changing the subject, "where a little boy died after a tragic accident. His parents were totally distraught. It was the most awful thing a parent can go through, I think, losing a child so tragically."

Max and Daniel were both looking at me a bit strangely.

I continued. "The parents blamed themselves for letting this happen. Nothing could have been done though. It was just an accident. No one could have saved him."

"Didn't they understand that?" asked Daniel.

"No, not in the middle of their grief. Maybe it will come in time, I don't know. Or maybe they will blame themselves as long as they live. Guilt can be a double-edged sword. It can call us back to do the right thing, or it can paralyze us. We think we're in control of the universe, only we aren't. Sometimes events happen and we can't do a single thing about them. We just have to live with the results. And make the most of it.

"Max," I said. "I don't know where God was when the ovens were burning in Auschwitz. A lot of people have asked that question. Did God turn away? Couldn't God stop it all? Why not? Why did it have to happen that way? But do you think that God didn't cry too?"

I felt my own tears streaming down my face.

"Being angry with God is hurting only you. Don't you think that God can take that anger? I am sure there has been a lot of anger thrown his way before you."

"I'm afraid that God is angry back at me," Max whispered. "All these years—I couldn't bear to think about it. I just stayed angry. I ignored him. If God wasn't there, then I didn't have to face what I was thinking."

"I know," I said gently. "You tried to have a good life. You gave a good home to your wife and your wonderful children. You were a good father and a good husband."

He nodded again. The tears began welling up in his eyes.

"But now things are coming to an end. It's time for the Angel of Death to come. Do you think God is waiting for you?"

He nodded his head.

"And do you want to die with that anger still inside you?"

"No."

"Then let's think of a way to get rid of it before the Angel comes."

I thought about the anger that was eating Max up, from the inside out. He needed a way to release it. I looked around the room; it was pretty sparse. I went out into the hallway and looked for something we could use. On a shelf in a corner were several old blankets. One in particular looked quite tattered and ready for the recycling bin. I asked the nurse if I could appropriate it, and she chuckled as she said, "It's been here forever; we were about to throw it away. Take it. Please."

Back in the room, I told them we would begin with some rituals. I asked Daniel to help me prepare some space around the hospital bed. We tidied up a bit and then closed the door to the room. I began with a moment of silence and then I spoke.

"Let us put our thoughts and energy into this moment with Max. He needs relief from all the pain he has been carrying around these many years."

I then took the old blanket and opened it up.

"This blanket is holding sixty years worth of anger and pain. It is all right here in my hands. I want us to see what it has done to Max."

Taking the top of it, I laid it out over Max like a shroud. It covered his face and it spread down over his feet.

"It has hung over you, Max, like a shroud. It has kept those you love from really seeing you. It has even kept you from seeing past it, hasn't it?

"What is it like underneath the blanket?" I asked him.

"I don't like it," replied Max, his voice rather muted from under the blanket. "I can't see and I am breathing the smell of it. It feels claustrophobic."

I pulled back the top to uncover his head.

"You have lived your whole life under that blanket of anger. I think it is time to tear it up."

"Tear it?" he asked.

"Why not?" I replied. "It's not doing you any good and it needs to be ripped apart."

Max surprised me by taking a corner and giving it a huge rip. There was more strength in that motion than I had thought he was capable of.

Daniel looked down at his father and said, "Dad, let it all come out."

I told Max, "Try to give a name to each tear you make. You don't have to tell us out loud what it is, but in your mind, try to put a name to your feelings."

He ripped another piece off the blanket. "Hitler," he said. "That was for Hitler."

I smiled. "I think you've got it now."

Rip after rip, he tore into that blanket, shredding it into dozens of strips. His hands shook, and his jaw was taut, but he continued one rip after another.

I could see the rage filling the room. All those years of holding it in. All those years of feeling guilty about his own survival. I saw all those feelings filling the room.

"This is for God," he finally said. "This is for turning away when you should have done something. This is for what you put me through. It wasn't right. It was mean and it was horrible." He spat out the words. That final tear was down the entire length of the blanket. It kept going and going. When he reached the end, he held the two pieces in his hands, looking at them.

"I'm sorry, God. I'm sorry," he cried. "I couldn't help it. You took away everything from me. I couldn't help being angry. I'm so sorry."

He brought the pieces of the blanket to his face and sobbed. Daniel stood at the bed, not knowing what to do. Max took his son's hand and brought it to his chest. "Son, will you forgive me?" he asked.

"Oh Papa. I'm so sorry you had to go through this," Daniel replied.

Soon the intensity of the rage began to quiet. All that was left was pure emotion. Daniel sat on the bed, holding his father's head while the sobs came forth. I can't say how long we all sat there. We remained until the emotions quieted and a sense of peacefulness washed over us all.

I reached over the bed and gathered the many strips of blanket. Laughingly I said, "Well, you sure did a good job on this blanket." Both men laughed.

"Why don't we do something with it?" I continued. "Here, let's tie these two strips together." I took two of the smaller pieces and knotted them together. I then handed a pile to Daniel and a smaller pile to Max. "Rope them together," I instructed.

We all worked happily, making knots. I finished my stack and took Daniel's and knotted the two together. Max then completed the rope by adding his. We held it up and saw that it made a very long rope.

"Can we use it for the escape?" chuckled Daniel. "I wonder if it will hold all the way down five stories." We looked toward the window.

"It's a lifeline," I said. "Or an umbilical cord."

Max took one end and brought it to his stomach. He smiled.

"Daniel," I said, "take the other end and wrap it over that metal rung." I pointed to the rung that held the neighboring curtain around the bed.

He walked over to the other side of the room, carrying the rope. He tossed the end over the metal rung and secured it. We now had a cord that crossed the room, swooping down gracefully and attaching itself to Max's bed. Daniel gave the cord a little push as he returned to his father's side. It moved back and forth like a swing.

"Let's all picture God on that other end. I think maybe he was there all along, holding his end."

Max silently nodded. He closed his eyes.

"My favorite words in the book of Isaiah are when God tells Israel 'I have held you by the hand and I have kept you.' It's true, Max. Feel it inside you now."

His whole body suddenly relaxed and he was able to know that experience for the first time. Daniel stayed very near. I left the room to give them some quiet time together.

As I wandered down the corridor of the hospital, I had an idea. I found the chaplain's office on the first floor and came across a stack of Jewish prayer shawls. Maybe this would help Max. I took one back to the room. I held the tallis out for both Max and Daniel to see.

"Why don't we wrap you in it?" I asked. It was a large blue and white tallis and it would cover most of his upper body.

I took one end and Daniel took the other. We tried the best we could to wrap Max completely in it.

"Think of this shawl as a way in which God loves you. It reminds you that you are Jewish and called into covenant with God. It reminds you that you have certain responsibilities because of that. But right now, it reminds you that God's love is all encompassing. It wraps around you and keeps you protected.

> "CAN YOU FEEL *how smooth this tallis is?" I asked. "Think now how lovely it is to feel God's love for you. It is all around you, holding you."*

"God has been watching out for you all these years, Max, you and everyone you love. Can you feel how smooth this tallis is?" I asked. "Think now how lovely it is to feel God's love for you. It is all around you, holding you."

Max became a different person as he took hold of the edge of the prayer shawl. He began reciting prayers under his breath. The Hebrew words came back to him.

"Let's help your father pray the *Vidui*, the final confession," I said as I handed Daniel a prayer book where the words were written out.

Daniel began to read for his father, "*O God and the God of my fathers. . . .*" After each sentence Daniel would stop so that Max could absorb the prayer and make it his own.

> *Forgive me for all the sins that I have committed in my lifetime . . . I am ashamed and abashed for all the wrong things I have done. Please accept my pain and suffering as an atonement and forgive my sins, for against You alone have I sinned.*

Often there were cries from Max, who offered to God his sorrows and confessions.

As the final amen was prayed, I held my breath and asked, "Do you want to say *Kaddish* now for your mother and father?"

Daniel turned sharply toward me and then looked questioningly at his father.

"Yes," said Max. "I want to do it now. Finally."

"All right, then let's pray it."

I began, "*Yisgadal v'yiskadash sh'ma raba. . . .*"

"Exalted and holy is God's name. . . ."

Max took over for me, finishing every word to the end.

By the end of the traditional Mourner's prayer, he was exhausted and drifted off to sleep. Daniel sat with him silently. There was a rattle in Max's breathing that told me it would not be long.

Soon his breathing stopped.

"The Lord has given and the Lord has taken away," I recited. "Blessed be the true Judge."

As Daniel pulled the white sheet up over his father's body, he said the prayer he learned as a child from his father, "*Shema Yisrael, Adonai Eloheinu, Adonai echad.*"

❧

> *If I should die before I wake,*
> *I pray the Lord my soul to take.*
> —A CHILD'S PRAYER

A PERSON'S RELIGIOUS background plays an enormous role in what happens at the time of death. Whether a lifelong and devoted Catholic, a marginal Jew, or somewhere in between, it doesn't matter. When a person is at the point of death, for better or for worse, faith and beliefs have an impact.

Each faith tradition has its beliefs and its symbols. Those symbols go deep into a person's psyche. That is why, when I sit vigil with a dying person, I always take into account her religious background. The symbols or beliefs often define the process of death itself and where God is for the person in the experience.

Even for those who have had no formal religious training, I have found that there is an undercurrent of religious beliefs. I often hear something like, "My parents were some kind of Protestants, but we never went to church. I don't believe in institutional religion." Yet when I begin asking questions, the individual has those Protestant Christian images of what happens when a person dies. Heaven. Hell. The Wages of Sin. God up there waiting to judge. If the person grew up in India as a Hindu, those symbols would be very different. I would hear him talking about letting go of the body in order to take on a new one in reincarnation. I would hear about karma and how that determines how he will return. There would be no talk of God's judgment in the afterlife.

The images we grow up with have a huge impact on how we die. Our Western culture has tended to adopt the Jewish/ Christian/Muslim belief that there is only one life and at the end of it we are judged and sent either to our reward or to our punishment. Of course, doctrinal beliefs differ in how we are judged and by what standards, but regardless, that is what our society tends to promote.

As we look at death and dying and how to bring the sacred into this experience, we must take into account religious beliefs and practices. That means first honoring the existing traditions, and perhaps then expanding to new ground.

Many of the rituals I help facilitate are part of formal religious rites and observances. In fact, almost all of them have their roots in traditional practices. The differences come from the people themselves and their experiences. Some are very active in a formal religious tradition and want to conduct rituals "by the book." Some have had a mixture of traditions in their history and are receptive to several different kinds of rituals. And there are those who want nothing to do with formal religious rites at all but want something much more personal to meet their spiritual needs.

Once I know the background and current status of the person dying, it is much easier to know how to meet the ritual needs. The rituals that come out of each individual death vary, as they should. The most important thing is honoring what the person believes and incorporating that into each experience. In all of these situations there are important things to consider.

For Those from a Formal Religious Tradition

MANY PEOPLE WERE brought up in a specific religious tradition, and they have observed the tenets and practices of the faith all their lives. This is true especially in ethnic communities where the ties to culture and religion seem to be stronger. Rituals at the time of death are pretty well defined in most cases. When death occurs within a family or community, people generally know what to do.

No two people or groups of people, however, practice a religious faith in the same way. There are many variations from culture to culture and even from family to family. Country of origin, background, and even individual preferences make up a vast array of practices within each religion.

I once worked with a Roman Catholic family who considered themselves to be very traditional. They were dedicated Polish Catholics who had a strong family history of practices and devotions. Yet, when they were visited by the hospital chaplain, who was a priest from Central America, they found that they almost didn't recognize his Catholicism. Their own particular brand of faith was quite flavored by their culture and family traditions. They thought they were good basic Roman Catholics just like everyone else, but what they learned was that they had a special way of doing things, not at all like everyone else.

Very few people practice a religion that is not flavored by culture and family history. For those who are rooted in a religious tradition, there are ways to approach death and dying that will take full advantage of already existing rituals and practices.

Identify and incorporate the symbols.

Religious symbols have great meaning. For instance, baptism with water is a fairly accepted symbol for most Christian churches, which believe it is essential for entrance into heaven. Water is also a symbol of purification and cleansing, so it is appropriate to use it in a ritual that will help the dying person prepare for death and for heaven.

A symbol for many Jews is the legacy of family or the deeds of one's life. At the deathbed, loved ones can respond to the dying person by focusing on these things. Another tangible symbol might be the prayer shawl and *tefillin,* the garments put on when one prays. They symbolize the covenant made between God and the Jewish people and God's presence in the lives of those who are faithful.

Bring the symbols that have meaning for the individual into the dying experience. This can be done in a very concrete way, with a prayer shawl, with prayer beads, with a statue of a Hindu deity, with an icon of a protective saint. Let the tangible items represent the dying person's faith and connection with the divine.

One woman I knew had grown up as a Presbyterian but had not really practiced for some time. When I suggested that she have a religious symbol with her in the hospital, she was silent.

"But I haven't been to church in so long," she replied. "And there certainly aren't any religious things in my house right now."

She was silent for a moment, and I could see her mind drifting back in time.

"I wonder if my Mom still has that porcelain statue," she finally said dreamily. "When I was a child, someone gave me a pretty little statue of Jesus holding a lamb. I used to love looking at it. It made me feel safe somehow, like Jesus was holding *me*. Do you think we could ask Mom to look for it?"

We did indeed call her mother right then, and she knew exactly where to find the statue. She shipped it that day, and the woman kept it at her side until she died. It was a connection with a childhood faith for the woman and I think it made her mother feel better, too, that she was able to be present with her dying daughter through something from their shared past once forgotten, yet now cherished.

Learn what prayers and rituals are rooted in your tradition.

Many people are not fully aware of the richness their tradition offers. Ask someone who has gone through death and dying rituals what they did during that time. Ask clergy or elders in the community. Ask people with connections to the "old country" to see what the traditions were in a less assimilated world. Look for books written on the subject. More and more people want to return to their cultural and religious roots these days.

A young student of mine grew up in Russia. Her family was Russian Orthodox but obviously unable to practice any of the traditions until just a few years ago. When her grandfather died, they wanted to have a traditional wake and funeral, but it took an enormous amount of effort to find out everything they were supposed to do. Some older family members remembered things from their childhood, and the local priest was able to supply some of the information, but the family had to be quite diligent in re-creating the funeral rituals. On the positive side, however, these traditions are beginning to surface again for the younger generation.

Take advantage of everything your religion has to offer, including the cultural traditions.

Many religious rituals during life-cycle events are cloaked in cultural and regional traditions. This gives flavor to the events, and it is an incredibly rich experience for everyone involved.

With more families being assimilated, it is important to resurrect some of the old ways. They speak volumes about beliefs and belonging. Does the cultural practice include the extended family being at the bedside of the person dying? Are prayers said? Scriptures read? Religious objects brought into the room? Ask what to do and why, and then participate fully. Even if it seems that only the older generation practices these things, learn from them and continue the line.

I knew a woman who was Japanese-American, at least fourth generation, and when her grandfather was dying, she and her parents decided to find out more about traditional Japanese rituals. They discovered that most death and dying customs were a combination of Buddhist rituals and prayers and localized folk traditions from Japan. During his lucid moments, her grandfather recalled his own grandfather's death over eighty years ago and some of the ceremonies that were performed. He especially remembered seeing his grandfather dressed in brightly colored silk robes as he lay in state. Wafts of smoke billowed from the sticks of incense nearby, and offerings of food and rice sat on the altar. Mourners walked past him solemnly, bowing in respect.

> LOOK UPON DEATH *as going home.*
>
> —CHINESE PROVERB

The family learned what they could about some of these traditions and were able to incorporate them into the last few days of the grandfather's life. Perhaps the most joyful moment for this woman, in the midst of all the pain and sorrow of the funeral service, was seeing her beloved grandfather dressed in beautiful silk robes she managed to find only days before he died.

For Those Who Want to
Expand Traditional Ritual Symbols

IT IS A sad reality these days that doctors don't make house calls and the local parish priest doesn't come running to the bedside at a moment's notice. Most of our clergy are overworked and cannot be where they really want and need to be—in this case helping the dying at the moment of death. Hospital visits tend to be brief and rituals are therefore abbreviated. People are left wondering what to do next and if that, indeed, is all there is. There are ways to take the existing rituals and make them into something personal and meaningful.

Find the symbols and make them personal.
It is possible to pick up where clergy or pastoral chaplains leave off. Did the lay pastor come for a visit to the hospital and offer a brief prayer? Did she bring communion? Use these symbols and adapt specific meaning in them for the individual.

One family I knew was from an evangelical church, and when the matriarch of the family was in the hospital dying, they wanted to find some way to let her know how much they all loved her. The pastor of the church came to visit, and while he was praying with the family, he laid his hands on her head and gave her his blessing. I suggested that the family continue that blessing the pastor had begun. They circled the hospital bed and, one by one, family members offered their blessings to their mother and grandmother. As the circle completed, one of her young granddaughters finished her blessing by saying, "Grandmother, I bless you on your journey to meet the Lord, but I want you to know how your presence in my life has blessed *me*. You've shown me what it means to have strength and courage in my life. You've given me an understanding of where I come from and who I am. And most of all, you've shown me what it means to be loved and to love in return. Those are my blessings from you."

Learn from other traditions.

We may be comfortable with what is familiar, but there is a vast array of wisdom and practices in other religions. This doesn't mean you have to convert to Buddhism in order to find meaning in quiet meditation. Explore other faiths and find out why they do what they do. See if it feels comfortable for the dying person.

One family whose elderly father was dying read that in Muslim tradition families gather around the bedside of the dying person, reciting prayers and portions of scripture. As the dying person nears death, they encourage him to recite the final prayer of faith, after which they keep total silence. This family very much liked the idea that those in the room should be prayerful and quiet. They asked everyone to participate in silent prayer until their father took his last breath. Even the nurses in the skilled nursing unit respected the silence, and they all agreed it was a very powerful experience for everyone involved.

Be careful about bringing in unfamiliar symbols.

Although it is often helpful to look at other traditions, it may be too much to try to integrate entire practices for someone unfamiliar with those rites. Erin was a young college student who was very concerned about her dying grandmother. She had recently read about a Tibetan Buddhist practice called the *phowa* (pō-wa). Tibetan monks spend their entire life learning about this intricate process in which the consciousness of the dying is received into the monk and then transferred into the dying person's next incarnation. Erin was a bit confused, and in her well-meaning attempt to help her very Baptist grandmother, she rounded up a few of her college friends and some drums and headed for her grandmother's hospital room. The young people sat in a circle and began drumming rhythmically. When I got there I discovered that they had confused the Tibetan *phowa* with a Native American pow-wow. The poor grandmother, her body reacting with each downbeat, didn't know what in the world was going on. I took the granddaughter aside and gently suggested that she might try sitting at the bedside and chanting softly to her grandmother instead.

For Those Who Want to Create Unique Spiritual Experiences

THIS IS CERTAINLY an age of spiritual seeking, and many people are finding their own paths and journeys. It is also the era of the baby boomer; we are the generation that created our own wedding ceremonies, brought on the return of natural childbirth, and saw the advent of birthing rooms in hospitals. It is a generation used to doing things differently and not quite so traditionally as previous generations. As boomers are coming face-to-face with death, standard ways of creating ceremony and ritual are certainly in for a change.

Just as it is possible to create your own ceremonies at the time of marriage and birth, it is equally possible to create rituals at the time of death. Each chapter in this book addresses ways loved ones can do that. The most important thing to remember is that dying is a sacred transition, and the rituals are there to help in the process. This time is for the person who is dying. If rituals are created with that in mind, and rooted in love and compassion, then there is no right way or wrong way to do things.

THE AFTERLIFE

I ALMOST ALWAYS hear that fearful question, "What is going to happen to me after I die?" As the body begins to shut down, people are, of course, afraid of what is happening to them physically. But even more so they are afraid of what is going to happen to them spiritually. What is waiting for them on the other side?

I have seen a whole range of afterlife beliefs, and I have been amazed at how much those beliefs play a role in how people physically die. Sometimes dying people have a strong faith that makes them feel quite confident about what will happen to them in the afterlife. They feel great comfort knowing that when they die, they will be reunited with loved ones. Or perhaps they look forward to heaven, a place where they will find rest from this hard life and where they will be with God. Perhaps they look forward to their soul finding another body to begin the process of life all over again.

Some people are less rooted in a particular religious belief and are often filled with fear and dread. They don't know what is going to happen to them, but they imagine all sorts of things, based mostly on what they've heard or seen.

The difficulty lies where the dying are terribly afraid of being punished for things they have done wrong. They begin panicking about dying, afraid of what lies ahead for them. One child I vigiled with was only ten or eleven years old. She was dying of cancer and after a long battle, she and her family were finally facing the inevitable. She was dreadfully afraid, however, and her parents weren't able to get at the root of her fear. When I asked her what she was most afraid of, I was stunned to learn that she was afraid of going to hell.

This child had very little religious upbringing, and certainly her family never even hinted that this was a possibility, so what was going on here? Why in the world did she think she was going to hell?

Television. Popular culture. They all taught her, directly and indirectly, that bad people go to hell. This innocent girl thought that she had done something very wrong to get cancer and that this illness was a sign she was being punished. And now, when death was in front of her, she was terrified of facing her eternal punishment.

I could not imagine how much pain and struggle she was going through. We talked a long time about God and about love and forgiveness. We even began speaking about what might await her in heaven. I think she understood, in the end, that her illness was not a punishment and that God loved her for being so courageous in bearing it all.

Differing Beliefs

ALL OF THE faith traditions have teachings about what happens to the soul in the afterlife. The possibility that the person ceases to exist after death is never even considered. All religions unequivocally believe in some sort of life or state of being after death.

Of course, most followers of a religious tradition rightly believe that their path is the true path and they must be held accountable to that. How they are held accountable varies with the teachings of the faith. Did they obey the commandments? Did they live out the practices the best they could? Did they obey the authorities? Were they worthy members? Did they live a righteous life? All these questions come into play at the end of one's life, and for the follower of a religion, they must ultimately be answered.

My academic work is in theology and I have taught university classes on afterlife beliefs, so I understand the broad spectrum of theological views. But when it comes down to individual people on their deathbeds, who are faced with very real concerns about what is going to happen to them, theological nuances don't matter. Ironically, various beliefs about the afterlife are not all that dramatically different. There are several main themes which occur.

Judgment

We are accountable for the life we lead. Buddhists may refer to mindful living and teach that if we don't achieve enlightenment in this life, we will be faced with the same issues in the next incarnation. Muslims may teach that our lifelong deeds are

I FEEL AND *know that death is not the ending, as we thought, but rather the real beginning—and that nothing ever is or can be lost, nor even die, nor soul, nor matter.*

—WALT WHITMAN
Democratic Vistas

presented to Allah at the last judgment and what is written in the Book of Life will determine if we go to heaven or to the depths of hell. It does not matter if our karma sends us back to try again, or if we stand before the judgment throne waiting our decree, some sort of judgment ultimately takes place. Our life, and what we did with it, matter.

It determines what will happen to us in the afterlife.

There is a difference, however, in how people perceive judgment. Most Eastern religions understand karmic judgment as the natural result of one's life choices and behavior. Reincarnation is just starting over, most often with the things people weren't able to master the first time. It's another chance to get things right, to become closer to the divine spark. Hindus or Buddhists, therefore, tend to be very calm and pragmatic about what awaits them. They often have a very profound peacefulness at the time of death.

On the other hand, Western religions tend to emphasize an omnipotent God who sits in judgment, meting out rewards or punishment. The image is so powerful and filled with dread that many people who practice Christianity, Judaism, or Islam approach death with significant fear and terror. If those beliefs, however, involve a God who is loving and forgiving, then the fear is not quite so prevalent.

Eastern or Western; it doesn't matter. Judgment comes in one form or another and we are sent on from there.

The Next Stage

So after we are judged, what is the next stage? There are different thoughts on this. Some religions teach that there is an in-between stage, a waiting place, either just before judgment or just after. For instance, Seventh-Day Adventists believe in "soul sleep," where the person goes into a deep sleep only to waken at the Last Day. Judgment of all souls takes place then.

Muslims believe something very similar. After a person dies, his condition is known as being "in the grave," a sort of holding place until the trumpet sounds on the Last Day. There is an initial judgment immediately after death, a small one, and the soul is aware of what is likely to ultimately happen. His body faces either toward heaven or toward hell, all in anticipation of the final outcome.

Some Christians believe that when we die, we go immediately to be with God. Others believe that judgment occurs at the end of time. Jesus becomes the advocate in front of God the Father, assuming responsibility for all sins.

Members of the Church of Jesus Christ of Latter-Day Saints, or Mormons, have a unique afterlife belief. They look forward to returning to the Spirit World, the place where all souls were born and where all souls return. It is a physical place in an unseen plane, existing all around us. Families are together in the Spirit World and continue to grow and learn about the Gospel. Because our souls were born in the Spirit World, it is a very familiar place. And because families are united in the Spirit World, it is comforting to know all will be greeted by our loved ones.

The Spirit World, however, is transitory. It exists only as long as the earth exists. At the Last Day, as in traditional Christianity, we will be judged before the Heavenly Father and sent for eternity to one of the three degrees of glory, or heavens.[1]

Heaven and Hell

Of course, we are all familiar with heaven and hell. Either/or. The Roman Catholic belief in purgatory is a way to get past the

---

1. Here is where LDS theology differs from traditional Christianity. Mormons believe that the highest degree of glory, or exaltation, is achieved for those who hold true to the tenets and ordinances of the faith. When souls are exalted, they become divine, creating a world, populating it, and ruling over it.

either/or concern, saying that souls in purgatory have a place and an opportunity to work out their problems and ultimately reach heaven.

Western images of heaven and hell have changed throughout time and traditions. Some believe in a very literal place; some are more theoretical. Our society tends to promote less-than-accurate heavenly images of pearly gates and angels and St. Peter at the gate. The images of hell tend to be Satan with the pitchfork standing in front of the fiery furnace.

THIS LIFE IS *the crossing of a sea, where we meet in the same narrow ship. In death we reach the shore and go to our different worlds.*

—RABINDRANATH TAGORE

Stray Birds

For most people, images are important. Indeed, Western scriptures are filled with images. We read in the Christian book of Revelation that the New Jerusalem is pure gold, clear as glass. God's glory shines as light. There is no need of sun or moon.

In the Qur'an, we read that heaven is an eternal garden with a river flowing through it; the righteous are clothed with silk robes and with wonderful jewels. They recline at the water's edge, drinking from it and eating the luscious fruits nearby from dishes and goblets of gold. Chaste young women are at their feet, waiting on them.

Hell, however, is a place where death never comes. It is filled with fire and boiling water. Similar images are true in Christianity. The book of Revelation describes hell as a "lake of fire and sulfur" where the wicked will be punished eternally.

Most people don't realize that layers of heavens and hells exist in many practices of Buddhism. The difference is that they are projections of one's own inner being and they are transitory. One goes through them rather than residing in them permanently. Pure Land Buddhists long for the Pure Land, or heaven, after death. But it, too, serves only as a transition until the person reaches ultimate enlightenment.

Union with the Divine

Many of the more mystical religious faiths stress the afterlife as an opportunity to evolve toward becoming one with the divine. This is especially true in Hinduism, but we see it in some other prominent faiths as well, such as Baha'i. Some nontraditional Christians, such as Christian Scientists, also believe in spiritual progression and ultimate union with the divine.

Face-to-Face with the Afterlife

When they are dying and the afterlife is imminent, just hours or even minutes away, people don't want to hear theology. They want their questions answered, their fears assuaged, and their hopes and expectations affirmed. The following are the words I tend to hear most:

"I'VE TRIED TO LIVE MY LIFE AS A GOOD PERSON."

Kay was born and raised Roman Catholic but stopped practicing right after she left parochial schools. She was now in her early sixties and her cancer was quite advanced.

"Somehow I can't believe all the things the nuns taught me about hell. I mean, does God really care if I eat meat on Fridays or not? One day it was a terrible sin and the next day they said it was okay.

"I guess I believe that it's the character of a person that makes a difference. I have tried to be a good person. I've loved my family and raised wonderful human beings. I've given my time and what I've had to those who were in need. I've tried to be a compassionate and caring person. Doesn't that count?"

"I KNOW MY FAMILY AND LOVED ONES WILL BE THERE TO GREET ME."

The Spirit World was very real to Joyce, a lifelong Mormon. She had her family with her as she lay dying, and they were all talking about the family members who were waiting for her.

"Mother, Daddy is getting ready to meet you," exclaimed Joyce's daughter, Robin, "and Grandma and Grandpa too. It's been so long since you've seen them. Won't it be a wonderful reunion?"

Joyce smiled as she thought about her mother and father.

"Yes, dear, it will be a wonderful reunion. I've missed them so much, but I'll be with them all soon. And when it's your time, I'll be waiting for you too. Don't worry about me now. I'm ready to go home."

"Jesus is waiting for me."

"I've been a good Christian all my life," Jessie told me. "I accepted Jesus as my Savior when I was eleven years old and I've never backslid. I know He's there waiting for me." Jessie was glowing as she described how excited she was to meet Jesus. "No more worries and no more pain. I'm ready to meet my Lord."

"I was brought up believing that if I ever left the faith, horrible things would happen to me."

Theresa grew up in a strict Seventh-Day Adventist home but left it as an adolescent, and her family was still praying for her to return. After a series of cancer treatments, she began facing her death, which was probably not too far off. When we spoke, she told me a bit of her background.

"Adventists believe strongly in heaven and hell," she said. "My family is convinced that I am going to suffer greatly for leaving the church. I'm not a bad person; I've tried to live a good life, but everyone keeps telling me to come back. I don't want to come back, but on the other hand, I'm beginning to feel scared. What if they're right?"

"I'm Jewish and we don't really believe in the afterlife. At least I don't think we do. No one ever talks about it."

Rose was in her nineties and she knew she was dying.

"What's going to happen to me? No one ever talks about what's going to happen when we die."

She and I discussed what the rabbis did talk about. They

often preached about leaving a good legacy—your children, your good works, your name.

"That I've done," she told me. "But now what?"

I suggested that she be assured that her children would remember those good things and so would God.

"All the prayers are about how loving God is and how he never forgets Israel," I told her. "Well, you are the people Israel, and God is not going to leave you now."

"I've done things I can't bear to face.
What's going to happen to me?"

Harold's life had been hard. He spent years on and off of drugs, which led him to a number of crimes. He never seemed to pull things together. When I met him, he was dying of AIDS. He appeared to be resigned to his fate, yet when we began to talk about dying, he fell apart.

"I just can't bear to face up to all the horrible things I did," he said, tears falling down his face. "What's going to happen to me?"

He grew up in a traditional Christian family, and he knew people were praying hard for his soul.

We talked for a long time about expressing sorrow and then letting things go, about confession and mercy. I found parables in the New Testament about people who had sinned and yet had experienced God's love.

Harold persisted, though, and kept coming back to images of hell and eternal damnation.

"I know God's gonna get me," he kept repeating. "The minute I die—wham! I'm done for."

It was like talking to a brick wall. Hell was all he saw.

"I know this body is giving out, but my soul will
return soon in another one."

Ramesh was having a hard death, filled with pain and drawn-out treatments. His children and grandchildren were present with him at the hospital, meditating and chanting Hindu prayers.

As we spoke, Ramesh was incredibly calm and composed. It was clear he was fighting the pain, but other than that, he was quite serene.

"This is only a body," he told me. "I have no more use for it. My soul is the most important thing now, and I must prepare it for the great journey. If I am at peace now with death, I will return with more ease. That is the most important thing."

"I'M PART OF THE CYCLE OF LIFE, DEATH, AND REBIRTH.
I KNOW I WILL CONTINUE ON."

Eileen practiced a new earth-centered religion. She was very aware of the cycles of life and death. Her prayers were for nature to take its course.

"I don't know exactly what will happen to me. My body will go into the ground and I will replenish it, of course. But my soul? Maybe it will return as another human being. Maybe it will come back as something else. Or maybe it just merges with others in the universe. All I know is that I won't end when I die. Nature continues on its course."

"I HAVE DEVOTED MY LIFE TO GOD
AND NOW I WILL FINALLY BE WITH HIM."

Ze'ev was a great soul, one of the holiest people I have ever known. His eyes shone as he spoke about his love for God, his gentle voice conveying words of wisdom and learning. He radiated love, humility, and compassion. I am grateful to say that he was one of the people I have loved most in this world.

Ze'ev was a rabbi and renowned scholar from Israel, widely respected for his work in Jewish family law. One of his later missions in life, however, was to seek out people in different faith communities, learning the many forms of the soul's journey. Buddhism especially intrigued him and he traveled often to Asia, speaking and meeting with Buddhist scholars and clergy.

After his last trip to Japan, Ze'ev returned home to

Jerusalem. Very suddenly and with no warning, he was found to have a brain tumor. Gratefully, his disease did not linger. Many of us never even knew he took ill.

Ze'ev died just before Rosh Hashanah, the holiest time of the Jewish year.

When I received the phone call from Israel, I, as so many others across the world, was devastated.

His wife, Mirjam, later spoke to me of the wonder of his death. "He died on Shabbat," she told me, "so we could not move him or prepare him for burial. We kept vigil with him the entire day. I sat and watched him as he lay there. His body was clean and pure and there was a gentle smile on his face, a profound sense of peacefulness."

As I wrestled with my personal grief, I felt great comfort when a friend revealed something to me. Jews believe that the Book of Life is opened every year for ten days beginning on Rosh Hashanah, the Jewish New Year. God then determines the length of our days. When He saw that Ze'ev was to die in the coming year, He was so saddened that He kept him on earth until the very last holy day of the year, the Sabbath before Rosh Hashanah. We had him until the very end, and then God took him for His own.

And as Mirjam said, "I saw him and I know beyond a doubt that he was with G-d."

A person dies according to beliefs, whether that is a belief in a God who loves or a God who punishes. I have seen it over and over again.

So what do I do when someone is rooted deeply in a faith that presents a terrifying image of the afterlife? Many people do believe in hell, and it is always a thin line to walk when confronted with these beliefs. Part of my work is to respect and support people in their religious beliefs, no matter what they are. It took me a long time to find a way that let me honor those beliefs yet comfort and help people who were dying. And once I knew the answer, at least for my own work and personal beliefs, it seemed simple. Even in the midst of terror or dread, I have been able to say, "Find the love." If a person can somehow hold on to even one fragment of love, then I believe he will manage to find his way into wholeness.

CHAPTER 5

Centering and Preparation:
Sacred Space/Sacred Participants

REBA LOOKED AS if she had not slept for days. Her hair was uncombed and her tight black curls were poking out from the combs she used to hold them back. She was in a sweatshirt and sweatpants, and her arms were filled with clothing, newspapers, and dirty dishes. The look in her eyes was apologetic, but she was too tired to give words to how embarrassed she felt.

"Come on in," she said. "Dad is in the room at the back of the house."

I knew that Reba had brought her father home from the hospital about a week before. He had not wanted to die at the hospital, so social services had arranged for hospice to take over. Reba was the only one who could take care of him, so she had arranged for him to be with her and her three young children. It was not a perfect solution, but it seemed the only option.

It has only been eight days, I thought, and look at her; she's a wreck. I looked around the house, and it reflected the same state of chaos. I hope he goes quickly. If Mr. Johnson lingers too long, it will be miserable for everyone.

Reba took me into the back room where her father lay sleeping. The room was as much of a mess as the rest of the house. There were dirty dishes, papers, clothing, towels, and medicine bottles everywhere. Reba again looked terribly embarrassed.

"It's all I can do to take care of him and the kids at the same time," she explained. "Maybe I should straighten up a bit."

I pulled her out of the room and sat her down in the living room.

"Reba," I said, "what do you want me to do here? Tell me the situation."

We talked for about twenty minutes, and all of her frustration and fears came pouring out. She was so caught up in the maintenance of caregiving that she really had no time to spend with her father and to come to terms with the fact that he was near death. There was always so much to do just to keep on top of his physical needs that anything else was impossible. I asked about her support system. She mentioned that some of the people from church had come by occasionally and offered to help.

"They brought me some food for the kids, and that helped. Some of the church sisters even took the older kids off my hands for the afternoon and dinnertime."

I asked her if she was active in church.

"Oh goodness, yes," she said. "We go to Bethel AME Church. We've been going there for years. My mama took us all there when I was little."

Had her father been active in the church too? What did he enjoy most about it?

Reba's eyes lit up.

"Oh my, well, he was in the choir for years and even played piano sometimes when the regular man was sick. He loved his music."

I took Reba's hand and looked in her eyes.

"Reba, my guess is that your father is feeling just as bad about this whole situation as you are. He feels awful about putting you out like this and causing such a fuss. Don't you think he's ready to cross over now? I have a feeling that the Lord is waiting for him, preparing his heart and his soul for heaven."

Tears filled her eyes.

"I think if he were to feel safe enough and supported enough, he would let Jesus come for him, don't you?"

She nodded.

"Then let's create something special for your father. Do you think you could call some of the people at the church, especially choir members? Could they come over and sing to him? Let's give him a choir of angels to take him to heaven, okay?"

Her eyes lit up. She jumped off the sofa and virtually ran to the telephone. Only two calls later she came back with a huge smile on her face.

"Shirley is arranging everything now. They'll all be here in an hour."

"Great," I said. "That will give us time to make things ready."

"Ready? How? What do I do?" she asked.

"First of all," I replied, "we have to do something about your father's room. The space around someone dying is very important. It can make him feel really supported and held, or it can create a feeling of messiness and chaos. Just think of the inside of your church. There is something special about it, isn't there? Something holy. It's space dedicated to God, right?"

"Right," she said. "But the preacher is always saying that we should worship God all the time and everywhere."

"Absolutely," I replied. "God is everywhere. But think for a moment about how special some places feel. Nature, for instance. When you are in a deep forest, can't you just feel the presence of God?"

She nodded.

"God *is* in all places, but it is important when we want God to be especially near to create a special place around us for that to happen. It is like cleaning up the house for company. You want the things around you to be inviting and welcoming."

"I see," Reba said. "It's like laying out a nice table for dinner. You're saying, 'I want you to know how special this is.'"

"Exactly," I replied. "And there are things we can do to make God's presence welcome too; it helps us as much as it welcomes God. It puts us in a good frame of mind."

Reba looked around the house. That fatigue came back into her eyes. "What do you think we can do?"

I smiled. "Let's go into your father's room. I think we can manage to get things in order there, don't you?"

"That's all? You don't mind about the rest of the house?"

"No, I think we can do just fine in the bedroom."

We walked back to the room and surveyed the mess.

"All right, the first thing we do is to straighten up. Let's get a bit of Godlike cleanliness here."

"THE SPACE AROUND someone dying is very important. It can make him feel really supported and held, or it can create a feeling of messiness and chaos."

Reba chuckled. "That's right. My mama would have done this *long* ago. She was one for cleaning. If anything was wrong, she cleaned. I guess it was her way of putting things right."

"Why don't you talk to your father while we clean and tell him what we're doing?"

She looked at me with a startled reaction. "He's been sleeping there for days now. He doesn't wake up much."

"I know, but I think he can hear us. He should know what's going on so he can get himself ready too."

"Well, all right, but I don't know about this." However, she did begin to talk to him. "Daddy, this here is Megory, and she is going to help us. She said you might be getting ready to meet the Lord any time now, so we thought we would help out. I know things have been a mess and kind of hectic, but that's going to get better. The sisters from church are coming by, and we are going to have a little service here. Just for you. They are going to sing for you, all your favorite hymns. Maybe we can have a little Scripture reading too. Isn't that nice? So right now, you'll have to excuse us while we get this room ready and looking presentable."

"Mr. Johnson, I hear that you were in the church choir for a long time," I said. "I'm really looking forward to hearing some of the hymns you love so much. I love music too, but I don't know many Gospel songs. Every once in a while I'll visit a Black church nearby just to hear the music. It takes over your whole being, doesn't it? It's a powerful way to praise God."

Reba stood up. "I always thought, even when I was a little girl, that when we sang in church, that was when God came to live inside me. I could feel him coming into me; I could feel the rhythm of the song, and I thought it was God's heartbeat inside me."

"Well, then let's help that heartbeat come to your father."

"I guess his is getting weaker, so God's heartbeat needs to be the stronger one."

I nodded, looking at the sleeping man in the bed.

We continued to chat away, cleaning up all the debris in the room. Eventually it looked fresh and ready.

"Okay Reba, let's think now about bringing in some things to help us focus on God. What do you think would be helpful?"

"What do you mean?"

"Well, we can use very traditional things to get us started. Candles are always very good. We want to take this space and make it holy."

"I have some candles on the kitchen table." She ran out to get them. I looked around for more ideas.

When Reba came back, she saw me searching for some clues.

"I have an idea," she exclaimed. "There's that little statue I have in Sammy's room of Jesus the Good Shepherd. We can bring it in here!"

"Wonderful idea!" I said. "How about a cross? Do you have one?"

"Oh, yes, there is a small one on Ruthie's dresser. She won't mind if we use it."

She came back carrying several more items. I took the cross from her arms and said, "Why don't we let your father hold this?"

Reba took it from me and gently placed it in her father's hands. "Daddy, you hang on to this while we have our service."

She placed the other objects around the room carefully. Each seemed to find a special place, where we all could see it.

The doorbell rang. It was her friends from the church. I suggested that she entertain them in the living room until everyone arrived.

I stayed with Mr. Johnson until the last woman arrived and then went out to greet them. We were all introduced, and I suggested that we go into the bedroom as if it were a church.

"Let's think of that space as something consecrated for a holy purpose. It is a holy purpose. Reba's father is about ready to meet his Lord. I think we should honor that."

There was a hush about the room.

"Why don't you begin with a quiet song out here and walk into the bedroom like you would walk into church?"

One woman began a hymn, almost whispering it, and the others joined in. They automatically lined up and began to formally process into the bedroom. Reba and I followed. A very different feeling had taken over the house.

When we were all inside, we circled around the bed, with several of the women lined up at the foot. I cleared my throat and began talking.

"Sisters in Christ, we are here to be with Ray Johnson as he prepares for a new life. Let us ask God's presence to be with us now in this room."

I lit some of the candles.

"Light is a sign of Christ's love. We light these candles and ask that his love fill this room and fill each of our hearts."

I picked up a small statue of Jesus carrying a lamb. "Here is our Lord, carrying us, his flock. We ask Christ to hold us now in his arms as we pray for the soul of Ray, who is ready to enter into God's presence."

I handed the statue to the woman standing next to me, and she closed her eyes, saying a silent prayer as she drew it to her breast.

I reached for a small bowl of water I had put out earlier and dipped my hands into it. I sprinkled the water around the room.

"This is the water that reminds us of the river Jordan. It cleans us and baptizes us. Make us clean, Lord, and help us remember our own baptism and proclamation that we are saved."

I looked over at the window. It was shut tight. I opened it, and a cool breeze made the curtains flutter. I could smell the flowers from outside the house.

"The Lord is in the wind. Let's welcome God's spirit here in this room."

The room seemed to quiver with energy. Some of the women were holding hands. One began humming quietly, and soon others joined in. Then they eased into a beautiful hymn. I have never experienced such a feeling of God's presence welling up inside me.

I began. "Let's focus our thoughts and prayers now on Ray. He's the reason we're all here.

"I WILL NEVER forget how we changed this room from a place of burden to a place of glory."

He's the reason we prepared this home. He's the reason we are asking God to fill this room with his holy presence and grace."

The singing continued softly as Reba began praying. I could feel everyone turning toward her father and concentrating on his needs. Reba sat down on the bed and held his hand as she prayed. I watched him during this time, seemingly unaware of what was happening around him, but his body was different. There was a softening about it, a gentle relaxing. His face seemed to take on more expression. There was no doubt in my mind that he was feeling and hearing everything that was happening in that room.

The women sang for over an hour. One of them had brought her Bible and intermittently read passages to Reba's father, but most of the time was spent in glorious music. It became the sound of the angels.

When the time for singing was over and the women were about to leave, they each came up to Ray and took his hand, saying a brief prayer. Reba sobbed quietly at the foot of his bed. I watched the candles flicker gently.

When she and I were alone with her father, Reba said shyly, "You know, I will never forget how we changed this room from a place of burden to a place of glory. I don't think I will ever see it the same again. I know God is here, watching over Daddy."

"Yes, that's true. You're still going to have to take care of him, though. He'll need his medicine; he'll need cleaning up."

"Oh, I can do that. I'll just do it differently from now on."

I stayed with her a few minutes, and then she told me that she was fine; I could go home. A few days later she called to say that her father had died during the night.

"The Lord never left that room," she said.

I would like, at the end, to be able to see the tree
outside the bedroom window,
to sit or lie on the flower-filled sun porch, . . .
to feel that the children and friends,
if they wanted to visit, could come to
the place of beauty that [we] had shaped.
—HERBERT AND KAY KRAMER
Conversations at Midnight

SACREDNESS MEANS SETTING apart. We enter into a space and time that has been designated for something special, something transcendent, and we help participate in that transcendence when we purposefully make the space around us something different. It then takes on a power of its own.

Sacred Space

THINK OF HOW special space is made in everyday life—a person cleans, brings in nice things, adds flowers and things of beauty. Sacred space is not all that different. The intent must be there, and the physical surroundings must be properly arranged.

The physical space surrounding the people who are in it is extremely important, not only for the person dying but also for the loved ones who are sitting vigil. When I walk into a room, I can tell immediately what the emotions are, what the level of caregiving is, and what the state of the dying person is, all by the physical surroundings. The room speaks many things. Is it antiseptic and cold? Is it institutional and devoid of anyone's personality? Is there something of the dying person's present? Who are the visitors? What is their emotional state? All these things make a difference as a person is dying.

It is not difficult to create sacred surroundings. We learn from various faith traditions how space is made sacred in their particular sanctuaries. First of all, there is movement from the outside to the inside. The outside represents the world, and the inside represents consecrated space; when you enter the sanctuary, the air takes on a very different feeling. In many Eastern sanctuaries—Buddhist, Muslim, Hindu—when someone enters a temple or mosque, shoes are removed as a sign of respect. At the door of some sanctuaries, there are basins of water that have been blessed for people to dedicate and purify themselves. Sometimes clothing is a symbol of respect for entering the holy. Many Jewish synagogues and temples and Islamic mosques ask that men cover their heads when they enter to pray.

Our behavior also tends to be different in general when we are in sacred spaces. Of course, because the intent in a religious house is usually meditation or prayer, it is natural to assume a quiet and respectful demeanor. But even those who come into the space to visit or explore tend to become quiet. The space itself commands it.

Sometimes spaces take on a prayerlike atmosphere without being specifically religious. When tourists visit the Lincoln Memorial in Washington, D.C., they become quiet and reflective as they ascend the steps leading to the great monument. As they enter the center where the large, white marble statue of Abraham Lincoln sits, conversation is conducted in whispers, people silently reflecting upon the famous words carved in stone or the imposing statue. This memorial is not a house of faith, but it does take on sacredness.

> THERE SEEMED TO
> *be a feeling in the house*
> *that something*
> *was there in the corners*
> *in the dark corners*
> *just beyond the light. . . .*
>
> —JIMMY CARTER
> *"When We Lit the Kerosene Lamps"*

Nature can also command a similar response. Just a short distance north of San Francisco there is a redwood forest called Muir Woods. It is an awesome place; the trees are giants, reaching toward the skies. Every time I walk through it the trees make me feel insignificant and humbled, but also as powerful as the universe itself. I am always struck by the deep hush as people wander through the forest. There are no sounds of human voices. There is no jocularity. The consecrated space of that forest encourages people to behave in a very different way: quiet and reflective.

Working with the Physical Space

There are some simple ways to take an already existing space and make it sacred. When a person is dying, she is usually in a bedroom or a health care setting, a hospital or nursing home. You cannot change that, so use it to your advantage. Use the bed as the center of a circle, making it a place of comfort and nurturing.

Think of a baby's nursery. The brand new room parents prepare for their baby is centered around the crib. The bed is warm and inviting, meant to take care of the child and to provide a safe space to sleep. The bed of the dying person needs to hold her safely in the same way. We all want our bed to be secure and protective for us. We want to trust our bed and to have it comfort us when we are tired. When our bed is uncomfortable, we don't sleep well; we feel it is the opposite of inviting and nurturing. Dying is often a painful experience. The body is not only shutting down but is also often fighting disease or violence. The bed needs to be a place of protection and warmth, at the center of the sacred space.

If a hospital bed is used, try to make it comfortable and clean. Bring in extra pillows, blankets that are soft, warm, and familiar. Think of the person's bed at home and try to re-create it.

Cleansing

Sacred space should be devoid of clutter and chaos. I find that when I go into a home or into a hospital room, if there is chaos in the room, it tends to seep over into how the people around are responding. Dying is not a time when people feel in control. The physical surroundings tend to reflect that feeling of helplessness. Straightening the surroundings can help make those involved feel better about the circumstances; cleaning up can also give a sense of purpose and helpfulness.

I have noticed that sometimes the patient has made her own order in the things around the bed. Be careful to protect that order; sometimes it is the only control the patient feels. Having the water glass on one side of the bed or putting a special photo exactly where she can see it when she wakes up is extremely important. *Be aware of what is clutter and what is there by design.*

Many times the air in the room is musty or stale. Opening the windows and letting in fresh air is extremely helpful. An air purifier or ionizer also helps balance the air. Rituals can be done or prayers said when opening the window. The symbol of air and wind—as the divine spirit—is part of many faith traditions and is easily invoked.

Sage is traditionally used for ritually cleansing a space. The dry leaves are burned and the smoke directed throughout the room. It can also be directed toward the people in the room. Native Americans often use a feather wand to distribute the smoke from the sage.

After I physically clean and open up the room, I find that I want to clean myself too. I'll wash again, making sure that once the physical job is over I am ready to begin a more spiritual work.

CONTAINING THE SPACE

After cleaning, tidying, and even scrubbing the room, it is important to create borders around the space. Many religious communities recognize the importance of defining whatever space is being used for rituals so that it can contain the work of the ritual. Containing the space allows for privacy and intimacy. If the dying is taking place in a hospital room, use blankets or curtains. Sometimes I put candles or lamps in the corners of the room to mark the space. Even chairs will serve that purpose.

If privacy is the issue, I close the door to the room and drape a blanket to create a curtain over the doorway. That blanket can also be used for hanging some special things, like photos or holy objects. If the dying person is at home or in a more private room, the blanket can still be used to muffle the noises from the outside.

Many people will want their own sacred objects to be with them in this space. For some, the objects are devotional, like icons, rosaries, crosses, prayer beads, or significant medallions. For others, the objects are something special from their lives. Prayer books or books of Scripture are often helpful to have in the sacred space. They are not necessarily always used in prayer and meditation; many times the person dying just likes to hold them close to his body. If there is anything that needs to be set up, like an altar, be sure it is in a place where it is visible to the person from the bed, well within the confines of the sacred space, but not in the flow of traffic. The purpose of the altar is for prayer, not for distraction.

Another way of marking sacred space is for people to encircle the bed physically, either holding hands or forming a circle around the person lying in the bed. This is a very powerful action. Not only does it direct other people's life force toward the person dying, but it also brings the sacredness of the physical space closer in and makes it more concentrated. In this way all the good thoughts and wishes, energy, and prayers are pointing toward the person dying. This encircling is intense for both the person dying and for the loved ones. It should be used primarily for times of directed prayer or ritual.

Sacred Participants

IN ADDITION TO creating sacred space, it is also important to create sacredness for the participants in the room. Being a sacred participant does not mean that only the righteous and "holy" can be a part of someone's sacred dying. Rather, it means that the loved ones, in all their ordinariness, can center and cleanse themselves as they prepare to spend time with the dying person.

The way I prepare myself before doing rituals with the dying is simple. I wash my hands and face before entering a room, and I take a few moments outside the door to breathe in and out while saying a prayer. I ask for the divine presence to be with me, giving me a sense of compassion and love. I imagine I am the dying person. What would I want? Acceptance and love, no matter what was happening.

This cleanses and focuses me inside and out for the work I am going to do. I want to be aware that something very natural yet very special is happening here, something beyond my own knowing. This is a time for the transcendent to take over.

When I work with family members or loved ones, I sometimes ask them to wash their hands before a ritual too. In all cases, before beginning a ritual I take a moment of silence to help focus each participant, asking everyone to remember the love they themselves want and need and to turn that toward the person who is dying.

Using the Senses

The senses present other opportunities to create sacred space. We can use sight and smell and sound to create surroundings that not only are conducive to comfort and ease in letting go but also provide a feeling of holiness. If we think of the senses as a guide for creating the space around a person, they can be used to create sacredness for the person's physical body.

Most people have a hard time with hospitals because of the overwhelming sensory experiences. We immediately notice the smell in a hospital. We notice the sounds of loudspeakers and people groaning in pain. We notice the antiseptic rooms. We see people in white coming from all directions. Think for a moment of those who were born and raised in Asian countries where white is the color of death and mourning. How would it feel to you, if you were coping with a grave illness, to be put in a health care setting where everyone was wearing funeral clothes? The sights and sounds around you are indeed extremely important.

Sounds

In Hinduism the loved ones lean in toward the person dying and softly chant mantras in his ear. Hearing the sacred sounds of the universe helps him find the source of the All Powerful and move toward it. In Tibetan Buddhism the loved ones read constantly to the dying person from *The Tibetan Book of the Dead* so that she may know and understand how to die. In Islam the Qur'an is read, and when the final moments arrive, there is complete silence. Silence is a very important sound.

In the West we have a hard time with silence. It often feels uncomfortable to us. But there is value in quiet. Sacred sounds for the dying are often a mixture of silence and of directed words and music. Both are important, and both are needed at the right time.

READING AND STORIES

Sometimes when I go into a room, I sense that the loved ones don't know how to use the time they have with the dying person. If he is asleep or unconscious, sitting and staring at the bed is not an enjoyable pastime. I often suggest several things. Sometimes I have someone read out loud. There are wonderful stories or books that are helpful to the patient as well as to the family. The stories don't even have to be particularly serious or religious. I have used *The Wind in the Willows* by Kenneth Grahame or C. S. Lewis's *Chronicles of Narnia* many times. In fact, reading from children's books gives people a sense of bedtime. I notice it makes people want to curl up and settle in with a pillow and blanket.

Of course, Scripture readings are important too, if the person dying has religious leanings. Even if the family is marginally religious, familiar psalms or stories from Scripture can be reassuring.

MUSIC

Music is an extremely powerful sound that affects us in many ways. Chapter 8 is about how music can be used with the dying for meditation and for healing. Here, though, as we address creating sacred sound for the dying, remember that music can soothe and inspire. It can also distract and irritate. It is important to know the distinction. Choose music that is soft and calming, music that can help the person let go of the pain and discomfort. Watch the patient's face and body for reactions to whatever music is being played.

Sound can also be used to retune the atmosphere of a room. In addition to music or chants, bells can be very effective for this. A Tibetan singing bowl is a powerful energy that creates a sacred space wherever it is played.

NATURE

When I vigil I always bring along a tape player and an assortment of CDs and tapes. I have several relaxation tapes of nature's sounds, like ocean waves or forest rustlings. I find that people respond most positively to them. They can take people from their present surroundings to the middle of a deep forest, or by the sea, where life is quiet and soothing.

There are also recordings of the sounds of the womb, often used for newborns so they hear familiar and comforting sounds. It is amazing how often people sink into a blissful state when I play those tapes. Perhaps death is linked to birth in ways we never thought or imagined.

SILENCE

Silence is a powerful experience. Most religious traditions have strong practices of keeping silence. It presents a setting that allows people to calm themselves and move into deep prayer and meditation. Long silences are necessary when sitting with the dying.

There is an art to knowing when someone needs to talk and when silence is best. Sounds are often difficult for most people who are ill—noises seem magnified and grating. A single telephone ring can startle someone from sleep and set off pain. Loud voices can also be extremely irritating.

Cultures differ in this regard as well. Many Asian communities value quiet in a way that seems difficult for westerners. Whereas westerners often feel the need to fill the silent void with words, the Japanese or Chinese may find that extremely rude and intrusive. Sitting still with the silence is an important lesson.

DIFFUSING OUTSIDE NOISES

In hospitals and nursing homes, "business as usual" is how things are run, regardless of the patient's condition. So it is important to muffle some of the sounds from the activities going on outside the room. This can be done by placing blankets across the door or by focusing on other sounds inside the room. Do not try to have your sounds compete with the outside sounds. Outshouting each other is not at all helpful. It is always appropriate to ask people on the outside to please keep quiet. I have done so many times and there has never been a problem.

Remember, too, that the sacred space you have created around the bed deserves special conversation. In almost every faith tradition, it is forbidden to speak of mundane things in the deathbed room. Judaism and Islam, for example, teach that those at the deathbed should turn their thoughts to repentence and divine mercy. Those present must be careful not to engage in any idle talk. This focus brings merit to the person dying.

In general, it is good to keep conversation to quiet reflections or to words of encouragement and love. It is nice to hear a daughter quietly tell her mother about the children and how well they are doing, assuring her that they will grow up to be good and loving people. I remember hearing a woman reminisce with her husband about when they first met and the struggles they went through to get married and raise a family. These are not mundane topics of conversation. They include the person dying, whether conscious or not. They are loving conversations about life, about family, and about things shared.

I have often walked into a room where discussions were being held about the person dying as if he were not in the room at all. I have heard conversations about dividing up estates. I have heard discussions about what a nuisance it is to sit in the hospital room all day long. None of those words belong in a dying person's room. Sacred space deserves sacred words.

Sight

When you go into a religious sanctuary, everything around you reflects the sacred. Sometimes it is in great art and stained glass windows. Sometimes it is in beautiful gold icons or mammoth crosses. It can be in brightly colored mosaics or hangings. Sometimes it is in images of the deities or in depictions of symbols or encounters between the divine and the human. It is in the grandeur or in the simplicity of the building itself. Images are important to remind us of who we are and who God is.

Holy Objects

When a person is dying, the sacred can easily be brought to her. Holy objects from home can be brought to the hospital. Instead of a flickering television set or a painting of clowns, why not put a sacred image in the line of vision? Bring in statues or pictures and place them around the room. Small icons or holy pictures can be held in the palm of the hand. Devotional objects, such as prayer beads, a rosary, or a prayer wheel, can be used for creating a sacred place. They reassure people. Even if the person dying is not physically capable of praying or meditating with these objects, just having the items present is often very soothing.

And, of course, mementos from home that are loved by the person dying may be considered just as sacred. For an elderly Jewish woman, I placed photographs of family members or loved ones next to Sabbath candlesticks, and she constantly reached out for both, wanting to hold them and bring them closer. She clearly felt love for her family and her faith, and she wanted symbols of both near her.

Altars

If you want to create an altar or sacred table and have never done so, ritual expert Eileen Walsh says:

> *A simple altar—or table—can be created anywhere with a little imagination and objects that you already have or can easily find. For the altar itself, one can use things like a turned-over milk crate, cardboard box, end table, small round table with screw-on legs (found in many*

*domestic departments in stores). In a crowded hospital
room you can even use something smaller like a shoe
box or stack of books.*

*Start by draping a piece of fabric over the altar. You
need not buy anything. Look around the house for
pieces of curtains, sheets, fabric. Scarves make excellent
draping material. Adding other small scraps of lace,
ribbon or fabric can provide a resting place or "pillow"
for a special object. Soft healing colors are suggested
either plain or with a simple design. You may want to
use colors that reflect the person's favorite colors or
ones that fit with a particular season of the year.*

*Choose objects for the altar that reflect the person,
a particular theme or that will be comforting to them.
Some ideas include icons, statues, a branch, pebbles, a
twig, a flower, leaves, a picture of an animal or a
stuffed animal, a scroll with a favorite prayer or poem,
photographs, a single rose, herbs that help create
relaxation such as lavender, rosemary or chamomile,
particular stones that have healing properties, quartz
crystals, amethyst, etc. Let your intuition guide you.
Whatever way you decide to create your altar is the
right way. Friends and family can add objects to the
altar as they see fit.*[1]

ARTICLES OF PRAYER

Religious articles of prayer are important for some people to
have nearby. You may want to have special clothing, beads, or
prayer rugs. Even if they cannot be used the way they were
intended, they symbolize a person's prayer experience and connection with the divine.

One woman had a particular shawl she used when she medi-
tated. It was a lovely cream-colored crocheted shawl that covered

1. Eileen Walsh, written especially for this book, July 1997.

her head and upper body. When this woman was in the last stages of ovarian cancer, she found that she wanted to wrap it around herself as much as possible. I think it gave her a feeling of protection and safety. When she slept, she folded it up and drew it close to her, embracing it to her chest like a pillow. She asked that she be buried in it, and her family honored that request.

CANDLES

Light and darkness are themes that come up again and again. In many faith traditions moving toward the light represents coming closer to the divine. Darkness can be frightening; it holds images of fear and of unknown powers. Many times a dying person will remember his childhood fear of the dark and struggle against it.

An elderly woman I worked with thought she was a child again and physically relived her fears of monsters in the dark. We brought in some candles and even a night light to help calm her. Her daughter wisely recognized the monsters in the dark as a metaphor for the actual fear of dying. We spent her last hours fighting those monsters, constantly pointing toward the light. At one point, we got a flashlight and danced the beam around the dark room. The mother loved watching the show. It calmed her down and also helped her to trust that the light would be there for her when she died.

Candles in a dark room do more than just provide light. I love sitting in a candlelit room, watching the shadows flicker. It makes me feel so peaceful and safe. I try to use candles whenever I can as I vigil. Sometimes, because of oxygen use, I have to find other alternatives, such as using oil lamps or shading artificial lights with cloths or scarves.

The dying see light so differently. I always try to soften overhead lighting as much as I can and rely on natural sunlight or on candles. I place lights all around the room, especially the corners. Each part of the room holds nooks and crannies that need illumination. Monsters, I have found, live in very peculiar places.

Smell

The use of smell in rituals for the dying is often difficult to manage. In the hospital setting we run into two situations. First is the smell of the actual place itself. And second is that when people are dying, their sensitivity to odors is acute—it can even bring on physical pain or nausea.

Certain scents evoke memories for people. With those who are dying, who are often lost in time anyway, smells can create many possibilities. I have seen elderly men and women return instantly to their childhood through an association with a certain smell. Once an eighty-five-year-old man, who was being cared for in his daughter's home, told us he found himself returning to the farm where he was raised, all because his teenaged grandson was mowing the lawn outside his window. He laughed and giggled as he romped in the fields in his mind's eye.

Scents are used constantly in religious sanctuaries. Walk into a Russian Orthodox church at any time of the week and you can smell the incense lingering from the previous Sunday. Candle wax is another smell associated with many churches.

Buddhist temples are also filled with incense, and many home altars have sticks of incense burning for hours on end. Sage and other herbs used in Native American and earth traditions have a distinctive association also.

It is important to be extremely cautious if you want to bring in any outside scents to a hospital or nursing home. They can be very helpful, but at the same time, the patient may have a negative reaction. As Penelope Wilcock writes in *Spiritual Care of the Dying and Bereaved People*:

> *In a place where people have wounds that will not heal, digestive problems, incontinence and diseased body tissue, there can be many smells to combat. The smell of disinfectant fighting the smell of urine does not lift the spirits. Scrupulous attention to cleanliness is a primary necessity. . . . Smell can be combated well*

by all the usual means of hygiene, air-fresheners. . . .
Also by more elegant additions; flowers,
aromatherapeutic oils heated by night lights (the
burning flame also helps absorb smells). Wherever
possible, eliminating the source of the smell is the
priority action. Introducing pleasant fragrance is good
for the soul; but powerful perfume disguising a bad
odour is not a happy combination.

The smell of a place is among its most powerfully
evocative characteristics, and will be strongly influential
in shaping the mood of the people who live and work
there. Our smell memory, almost indelible, is located in
the deepest and most primitive part of the brain, and
accordingly moves us at our deepest and most
primitive level.[2]

Some ways to incorporate scents into the sacred space are:

INCENSE

Psalm 141 in the Hebrew Bible says, "Let my prayer be counted as incense before thee" (verse 2). Virtually every religion uses incense as a way to make offerings to the divine. The sweet smoke rises to the heavens, just as prayer is thought to rise to God. It is a practice going back to antiquity. Sticks of incense with rising smoke sit before a Buddhist monk as he prays. Incense fills a temple as people congregate for special observances, and it graces many personal altars across the world.

Sticks of incense can be lit with little attention to them. Although they last only a short time, they fill a room with a scent that lingers. Incense bowls require crystals and some sort of charcoal to keep them burning. A bowl can sit on the altar

2. Penelope Wilcox, *Spiritual Care of Dying and Bereaved People* (Harrisburg, Pa.: Morehouse Publishing, 1996), p. 20.

or anywhere in the room. Desert sage and sweetgrass can also be burned as incense.

Scented Candles

If candle use is permitted, there are various scented ones that give off a mild fragrance. They are particularly helpful in overcoming some of the medicinal odors and can keep a room softly lit.

Flowers

Like scented candles, flowers can be helpful in counteracting medicinal or sickbed smells. They are also seen as offerings in some faith traditions, where they are placed on the altar and used for ritual purposes.

Sweet Spices

In the Jewish tradition, at the end of the Sabbath, a container of sweet spices is passed around the room to remind people of the sweetness and pungency of life. It usually contains fresh whole cinnamon, cloves, allspice, nutmeg, and other spices like ginger and mace. This container could be left in the sick room or used in rituals.

Aromatherapy

There are many new healing and relaxing therapies using scents called aromatherapy. The scents used for relaxation or letting go are chamomile, lavender, rose, and geranium. They can be used in oils for massage, or they can be burned like a votive light. A flame is put under a bowl of the essential oil, and a subtle aroma fills the room. There are also diffusers that, like humidifiers, automatically fill a room with the essence. Some diffusers can be placed over light bulbs.

Smells from Home and Childhood

There are many scents associated with home and family and even childhood. Of course, they vary from person to person, but some of the scents people respond most strongly to are baking (bread, cakes, cookies), simmering soups or stews, newly mown grass, or Christmas trees. If the patient is at home, these smells are much easier to arrange.

I have even seen a family arrange for evergreens to be brought into a room in the middle of summer. The father, who was dying, loved Christmas, and they wanted him to be able to celebrate it once more. He was unaware of all the preparations until the evergreens were brought in, and the scent triggered strong memories for him.

If the patient is in the hospital, it is a bit more difficult. Sometimes, though, freshly baked cookies brought to the room can still smell wonderful. Remember, the point is not for the cookies to be eaten, but to help the person dying have positive associations with the scents.

Scents of Loved Ones—Perfume, Clothing, Etc.

The scents related to a loved one bring many feelings as well as the potential for triggering memories and associations. Use articles of clothing with a trace of perfume or pillows or blankets with a small amount of scent. One teenager who had been in a car accident responded to the smell of the baby powder his mother used when he was an infant.

Conclusion

WHEN WE BEGIN a sacred event, we must be aware of ourselves and the space around the dying. We must prepare ourselves, through cleansing and through blessing, and then we must prepare our surroundings. Making sacred space is an important ritual in and of itself. Sometimes we forget that. It is easy to view cleansing and arranging simply as tasks.

Many times a pastoral visit will begin with a chaplain pulling the curtain around the hospital bed and placing a few religious items on the table before saying prayers. This makes the room functional for performing rites in privacy, but it hurries past an important element of the ritual—creating the sacred space.

As you walk into a room, look for ways you can bring in the divine presence. And then as you proceed, make each step intentional. Say a prayer as you close off the area around the bed. Sing as you clean and straighten. Talk to the dying person. If you light candles, ask a blessing. As you hang pictures, ask for the divine to watch over the room. If you form a circle around the dying person, state what you are doing and call upon the power of love and protection to hold the space for you. Each intention verbalized adds power and strength to the holy space.

CHAPTER 6

Letting Go of Burdens:
Rituals to Release the Emotions

KATY WAS ONLY eleven years old, and the last three of those years had been spent coping with cancer. There were surgeries and then chemotherapy and radiation. She didn't have much hair left, and just months earlier the doctors had amputated her left leg. Her friends at school and all her relatives were pulling for her. Even her thirteen-year-old brother, Philip, was on her side. But the cancer had taken its toll, and it was time to face the reality that Katy was going to die.

I arrived in the middle of the afternoon. Katy was in her hospital bed, surrounded by her mother and her father and her big brother. She was conscious but drifting in and out of sleep.

"I know something is on her mind," her mother confided to me, "but we can't seem to get it out of her. If we leave the room, could you talk to her and see if there is anything you can do?"

I sat beside Katy's bed, took her hand, and told her I was there to help her. She perked up, clearly wanting to talk. "Is this going to hurt?" she asked. "I mean any more than it already does?" I told her that the pain would probably get better, not worse.

"Well," she said hesitantly, "I mean, is it going to hurt when I die and God finds out what I've done?"

I was stunned. "What do you mean, Katy?"

"Isn't God angry at me? Isn't God going to do something bad to me when I die?"

I thought for a moment.

"Katy," I replied, "who do you love most in the world?"

"My mom," she said. "Well, my dad and Philip too, but best of all my mom."

"Okay, when you close your eyes and feel how much you love your mom and how much she loves you, it's pretty wonderful, isn't it?" She nodded. "Well, I think if you take that much love and multiply it a hundred times, you still can't come close to how much God loves you. And if you are loved that much, why do you think God would hurt you?"

Katy was quiet for a few moments, and then in a small whisper she said, "Because of all the bad things I did."

"Are those things making you hurt inside?" I asked.

She nodded and pointed to her stomach. "Right there. They feel awful."

"Tell me what they are, Katy, and maybe we can do something about getting them out. Can you name some of them for me?"

"I hit my brother once," she whispered, "but he was being mean to me. And once I got really angry at Daddy for making me come back to the hospital when I wanted to go to Jennifer's house. But . . ." There was silence. "But . . . the worst thing I did was to get cancer. It made everything bad. I think everyone is angry with me for getting cancer. I couldn't help it; I didn't do it on purpose. And I tried to get well, I really did. But now it's too late." She turned her head into the pillow and cried.

I went over and took a folded sheet from the shelf and spread it open.

I said to Katy, "You know that time you hit Philip? Well, this is the knot inside your stomach that it made."

I made a knot in the corner of the sheet.

"And here is when you had a fight with your dad."

I made another knot. And another, and another, as the list grew.

"And right in the middle is the biggest knot of all, the cancer knot. Now, do you want your insides to look like this?"

She smiled and said, "No."

"Well, what can we do about that?" She thought for a minute.

"I guess I can tell everyone that I'm sorry. That might help." I nodded.

"Yes," she said. "I think that will be a big help."

"All right, let's go call in the troops."

I walked out the door and located the rest of the family in the waiting area.

"Katy has some things she wants to tell you."

WE TALKED FOR a long time, about anger and hurt, about things not being fair, and about feeling so bad that it hurts right in the middle of your body.

Back in the room, Katy was clutching the white sheet filled with knots, her hands white and tense. Her family circled the bed.

"See all these knots?" I asked the others. "That is what Katy's insides feel like. She feels pretty bad about some things that she did and wants to tell you about them." Her parents looked surprised, but they waited for her to speak.

"Daddy," she whispered, "remember that time I was so awful when you had to bring me back to the hospital? I really wanted to go to Jennifer's, but you made me come here. I'm sorry, Daddy, I didn't mean to cry so much. You made *me* angry, and I wanted to make *you* angry. I'm sorry." Her father opened his mouth, but nothing came out.

"Philip, I was mean to you a lot. I took your favorite airplane once and hid it. I even tore up that picture you drew 'cause I was mad at you. I'm sorry, Philip," she said quietly. "I won't do it again." Philip brushed the tears away from his face.

"Mommy, I was bad so many times, and I made you angry. And when I got sick, I didn't mean to. I didn't get cancer on purpose. I'm sorry. There isn't much money left, and I can't get better. I made everyone really upset, and I didn't mean to."

Her mother gasped and took Katy in her arms. I went to the other side of the room while the family cried and held each other. The noises outside the hospital room seemed to grow dimmer while the loving energy inside the room seemed to swell. When everyone was cried out, I walked back to the bed.

"Why don't we undo some of these knots?" I said.

Everyone giggled nervously. With Philip on one end and Katy in the middle, we undid all those knots, big and little. Except the one in the middle.

"Let's take a minute here," I said, "and form a circle around Katy. Let's ask God to help with the big knot in the middle."

We turned our hearts and minds to the power of God. As I prayed for Katy to have peace in her body and peace in her soul, Katy was bold enough to offer her own prayer for her sorrow and regret. Her father asked God to help everyone with all the feelings they had, and Philip added a prayer that Katy would never forget them in heaven. Her mother asked that God take care of her little girl and love her as much as they all had loved her.

As we said "amen," I took the last big knot and undid it, saying, "See, God wants us all to know how much we are loved. We can be sure that God is waiting for Katy right now, with open arms."

"How do you feel, Katy?" I asked her.

"Good," she said. "Like I want to fly."

"Well, we can pretend you *are* flying." I took a corner of the sheet, gave it to each member of the family, and pulled back so the sheet was stretched out. I lifted it high over my head, and the others followed my lead. Katy laughed. We let it float back onto the bed, then pulled it high again. It ballooned up. We could almost feel Katy soaring high on that sheet, high into the air, and back down again. We laughed and laughed. And Katy flew each time, closer to heaven and closer to God's arms.

Sometime during that night, Katy died. There were many tears, but the reconciliation she experienced with her family and most of all, with God, led her peacefully through that journey.

If only we could be honest, both admit our fears,
touch one another . . .
Then, it might not be so hard to die—in a hospital—
with friends close by.
—ANONYMOUS
American Journal of Nursing

LETTING GO OF the burdens of anger, fear, sorrow, and guilt is an important preparation for death. Time after time I see people holding on to things done and things left undone. I see fear and guilt overwhelm the dying person to the point where she cannot let go and die a peaceful death. Most of the guilt has to do with relationships with loved ones. Most of the fear has to do with God.

With the help of rituals and various confessional opportunities or prayers, we may enable the dying person to experience freedom from the internal burdens. However, to let go of the emotional pain, he must also experience reconciliation with loved ones and with God.

There is joy and a kind of euphoria when physical encumbrances are released, and ritual can be of great help in that process. When Katy and her family came together in their tears, it was a wonderful experience to untie the knots in the sheet. That cemented the experience they had all just gone through. Most ritual is a response to what is already happening inside us. Ritual is a means of making our experiences tangible. For example, even though the words were spoken, the sheet gave them all a chance to participate in the release of the knotted feelings. And when the words had been said, it was Katy herself who inspired the idea of flying. Going into her hospital room, I had no idea we would do the ritual with the sheet. It came spontaneously in response to Katy's feelings and experience, and it provided the perfect way to help her soar.

Dealing with Anger

ACCORDING TO ELISABETH KÜBLER-ROSS,[1] anger is one of the five stages we go through when we are faced with death. Along with denial, bargaining, depression, and acceptance, anger is a recognizable force in the dying person's process.

There are many reasons a person is angry, and I have found that at the time of death it comes out in many different forms. Sometimes it is directed at the closest family members or the caregivers. It may be directed at the hospital or nurses and the way medical care is given. Sometimes it goes inward, and the dying person withdraws into silence and sadness. Other times it becomes the mask for fear.

I have seen people who hang on to their anger so tightly that they cannot die. It's as if the anger is the last hold on life. That can be helpful at times, such as when someone is fighting a

1. Elisabeth Kübler-Ross is the pioneer in death and dying research. Her primary book, *On Death and Dying,* written in 1969, has paved the way for subsequent research. See the Bibliography and Recommended Readings for a listing of her writings.

disease, but for the most part, when a person is close to death, anger gets in the way of a peaceful leave-taking.

When I work ritually with people at the end of their lives, I have learned that one cannot make the anger disappear magically. It is usually too late for that. I am not a psychologist or psychiatrist, and my role is not curing the psyche. Rituals don't analyze or cure. Rather, they can help identify the anger that is keeping the person from letting go peacefully and help move it aside or release it.

East Versus West

Western medicine and psychology say that unexpressed anger feeds other ills. It causes more harm inside us or destroys us. The solution, then, is to release it. But the release process itself is often extremely painful and difficult. It very often causes upheavals and additional tensions. Western religions teach that such pain and tension lead to forgiveness and reconciliation.

Eastern religions teach that such conflict is to be avoided at the time of death. It is harmful to the peace and tranquility that is necessary for the person to rightfully die.

Both understandings are valid. Sometimes anger needs to be addressed so that it will be released. Other times anger needs to be subdued so that peacefulness may be present. Perhaps all that needs to happen is just to put it aside. Rituals can be done in any of these circumstances. Choosing which route is the best, though, is often a difficult decision.

Releasing Anger

The anger inside a dying person usually has been there for many years. Now, when faced with death, she becomes all the more fearful and angry and focuses everything on the people around her. It is not easy to identify the actual source of the anger, but rituals have the potential for going to that source. They often act as a catchall for the entire cauldron of emotions.

Anger is a physical emotion, and rituals releasing anger are for the most part physical rituals. I try to think of a way to capture those visceral feelings and bring them outside the person. Sometimes it involves destroying objects, other times hitting or punching symbols of the object of anger.

BURNING SYMBOLS OF ANGER

Watching a symbol go up in smoke is a powerful experience. Fire is considered cleansing and can be felt intensely as you watch some symbol of yourself and your offering go up in flames.

I once worked with a family who bickered with each other and their dying father endlessly. There was always something—the food, the nurses, the noise, the way the sun came through the window. All of those things did, indeed, need adjusting. When the nurse brought in a chicken dinner for the man, who could barely swallow, that was clearly an issue to dispute. Bickering seemed the only way they knew to express the surfacing anger about other things.

I had the family gather in a circle around the bed and begin to name the things that made them upset. One by one, they named something while tearing off a sheet from a pad of paper, and we threw the strips into a large bowl. At first the complaints were superficial—the nurses, the hospital being too far away from home, and so on. As we kept going around the circle, passing around that pad of paper, the issues became deeper. They became more personal. Even the father in his bed became quite animated while tearing off strips.

The bowl was filled with paper, and when the last person could think of nothing to add, we lit the pyre. I asked the family to hold hands as we watched it burn. The youngest daughter began whispering under her breath, "Burn, burn, burn. . . ." Soon all of them chanted with her.

The nurses were still the same and the food service never did quite get it right, but the anger had somehow been diffused, and the family handled the difficulties in a completely different way.

The father drifted peacefully into sleep, and within the next few days he died.

TEARING

The physical act of tearing or ripping has emotional power.

One young man, William, was dying of AIDS. He had been in and out of the hospital for over a year and was extremely frustrated. He wanted to go home and die there, but there were things only the hospital could do for him, so he stayed. He hated it, though.

"The worst part," he answered me, "is that I'm not really a person here. I'm the AIDS case in Room 749. I can't do anything on my own to make things easier for myself. I mean, look at me, I even have to wear this stupid gown. I want my own bed and I want my own clothes."

I suggested that we do something about that. We called a friend and asked him to pick up some things from William's house. That afternoon, with William's favorite T-shirt and robe and blanket, we did a wonderful ritual. With permission, and charged to his hospital bill—it was more than worth the outrageous price—we ripped the hated hospital gown to shreds. All of William's anger and frustration came out in every single shred. We then washed him and dressed him in his own clothes and wrapped him in his own blanket. He said he felt like a man again, and it was wonderful. He strongly needed to control his own death and to feel as if he belonged to himself. He needed to tear apart the outward symbols preventing that.

THROWING AWAY

Sometimes all that is needed is to take offending objects and throw them away, to remove them completely. One elderly woman, who lived on her own, asked me to sit with her as she went through all her old photos and memorabilia. She created a stack of things that caused her pain and distress, and we made a lovely ritual of dismissing them from the rest of her things.

"They are out of my life now," she told me. "I don't want to remember them."

I took the pile out of the house and into the garbage. She gleefully told me that she had never felt better or freer.

ASKING SOMEONE ELSE TO HOLD THE BURDENS

Burdens can be hard to carry. Sometimes, though, they cannot be thrown completely away—they have to be dealt with down the line. But there is a way to release anger and hardships and hand them to someone else. Many times a loved one can be the person who will do the holding. Sometimes it can be God. In the Christian tradition, releasing burdens is an act of prayer and offering. In the letter to the Galatians, we read, "Bear one another's burdens" (6:2a), and in Matthew, Jesus says, "Come to me, all who labor and are heavy laden, and I will give you rest. Take my yoke upon you, and learn from me; for I am gentle and lowly in heart, and you will find rest for your souls. For my yoke is easy and my burden is light" (11:28–30).

In the Hebrew psalms, we are told to "Cast your burden on the Lord, and he will sustain you" (55:22a).

Rituals can be done to hand over anger or anxiety, from literally gathering symbols of the anger and handing them to a spouse or loved one to statements of prayer or intention. One man handed over a paper bag filled with his medical paraphernalia; he wanted to be rid of the anger he felt for the disease that was killing him. A teenager, angry that her family was pushing her to keep up in school despite her illness, packed up all her school books and papers and asked her best friend to hold them until she was able to deal with them again.

When someone prays for God to take on the burdens that are too much to carry, rituals can help that process too. Offerings can accompany prayer. If the family has an altar in the home or a place of private worship, symbols of the burdens can be left there.

When the spiritual community or clergy are present, there

are opportunities for a prayer of offering. It's important to understand that the person does not have to carry anxieties or anger alone.

"I hear you."

Angry words get louder when people do not listen. When a person is ill and dying, it seems as if no one understands what is happening. People are busy doing what is required for physical caretaking, but very often the inner needs of the person are ignored. Some respond to this by being impossibly demanding. Feeling in control and being heard are important issues for all of us. When external events are out of control, anger toward the situation increases. Find time to listen to what is behind the anger. Even if the dying person makes no sense, which is often the case, knowing that someone hears the words and the feelings behind the words, and is responding, makes all the difference.

Diffusing Anger

If the religious tradition teaches that anger should not be present in the place where a person dies, it is important to be able to diffuse it in some way or to supplant it with a stronger sense of peacefulness. This can be done in several ways, mostly through prayer and meditation. There are some rituals, though, that may help. Sometimes singing or chanting may create a peaceful atmosphere. Sometimes direct touch may help. I have often sat with a person, putting my hand on his chest near the heart, and tried to bring a sense of calm through touch. If the family or community is present, gathering in a circle around the bed and harnessing a peaceful energy may diffuse anger.

One woman I knew was a practicing Buddhist, and as her father was dying she was having difficulties responding to his outbursts of anger. He was incoherent and not aware of the words he was saying, but nonetheless it created a difficult and explosive atmosphere in the room. We decided to use the same methods she used when her infant was upset. She just sat and held his hand or his head and repeated soothing sounds to him. She used a mantra that was special to her, and even though the words had no meaning to her father, she knew the repetition of the soothing sounds would override that. It seemed to work; when he became agitated, the sound of her voice and the touch of her hands made him calmer.

The ambiance of the room also has a great effect. If the room is peaceful, and if it has an atmosphere of prayer and quiet, the person dying is more likely to take on that quiet. And if she gets upset or out of control, it is easier to calm her down if the room and the people in the room are peaceful.

Unfortunately, I have often seen hospital rooms where the family is upset with each other, hurling angry remarks back and forth, or sitting in stony silence, shooting angry looks at each other. And then they wonder why the patient is upset. Anger breeds anger. It is impossible to calm a patient's anger while those around her heighten the emotion.

When Anger Won't Go Away

There are times when a person is holding on to anger so tightly that nothing helps. Addressing the problem makes it worse and trying to diffuse it is impossible. There is really nothing to be done except acknowledge the situation and affirm that the person dying has a right to these feelings. It seems as if anger is the only thing left for him to hang on to, as if he is using it to prove that he is still alive, still able to feel at all. If he stays angry, perhaps he will not die. I remember being with one man who held on to the blanket on his bed so tightly that I could see the veins popping through his skin. I thought of a child desperately clinging to his security blanket and knew that instinct came from the same place inside. Reassuring him was really the only thing I could do. He held on with that rigid clasp until the very end.

Dealing with Fear

ANGER AT THE time of death is often actually fear with a loud voice. Death is frightening, and the closer a person gets, the more fear tends to surface. It is not always easy to translate the angry words or actions, but when I can't seem to make sense out of them, I assume that fear is the source.

Night is a time when fears need to be assuaged the most, and the moments and days before dying are clearly our nighttime. We all need the light in the dark to make us feel safe. We are all afraid of the monsters in the closet or what we can't see ahead of us. When we begin to die, strange things happen to our bodies and stranger things happen to our psyches and our souls. We begin to move toward the unknown land, and that is frightening.

THE FEAR OF *death is the fear of letting go. . . . Why would it be supposed that one's creative ability ceases at the moment consciousness leaves the physical? The instant that the Self releases from the human body, there is light, there is peace, there is freedom, there is home.*

—PAT RODEGAST AND
JUDITH STANTON
Emmanuel's Book

No one can tell us what is on the other side of death, but those of us here left to care for the dying can reassure the dying person and make her feel secure at this time. In all the sacred traditions there are many wonderful words from holy texts and scriptures that will help comfort the person dying. We read of God's mercy and love in the Qur'an or of God's presence in the Hebrew Bible or the assurance in the Christian Gospels that Jesus will not leave us.

The Hindu words from the Bhagavad Gita are beautiful and reassuring, and *The Tibetan Book of the Dead* helps a person cross over into death.

As human beings, we needed comfort and assurance of safety and love when we were children, and as adults we seem to think that this is no longer necessary. We never lost that real need, though, and when we are once again vulnerable and at life's major transition, we must learn to recognize how critical it is.

Unfinished Business

WHEN I WORK with dying people, there is virtually always unfinished business. When they realize they are dying, it is a natural response to want to put their affairs in order. Some people prefer to focus on the practical details of life—wills, bequests, family affairs. Other people want to put personal relationships in order. Both are important, and I would add a third—tending to one's relationship with the divine.

Unfortunately, most people do not approach these reckonings until the last moments, but by then they are ready to come to the process with honesty, without pretense or barriers. When the end is near, most people tend to want a bottom-line, no-nonsense handling of the situation. However, I have also seen families in complete denial of the impending death who refuse to participate in anything that sounds like concluding affairs. "No, Dad, you are going to pull through this. We don't want to hear about wills or insurance papers." And the family turns its back on the dying person's very real need to settle accounts.

I have also seen loved ones refuse to discuss anything to do with the past. They cannot handle the feelings and emotions buried in their family history. If the person dying wants to bring up concerns within the family, I've seen children or spouses literally walk away from the bed and out of the room.

There are many scenarios and differing needs when death enters the picture, but most faith traditions encourage those who are dying to put their affairs in order and to make amends and restitution for whatever has happened in their lifetimes. These faiths believe that unresolved relationships or practical matters affect not only the way a person dies but also his course in the afterlife.

Making Things Right

Living a moral and upright life is of course a major part of religious precepts. Codes of ethics, commandments, mindful living—all codify the teachings to the faithful, and most religions teach that there will be a particular type of judgment based on those precepts. When death is approaching, people who have been taught the precepts of their faith tend to feel a strong sense of reckoning about how they lived up to those precepts. Have I lived a righteous life? What about the things I did wrong? What about my failures? The things that caused harm? What about the things that are still not right? How will I be judged?

Many times, unfortunately, the motive is fear-based. If religious teachings have stressed strict judgment and tremendous repercussions for sins, then the dread of not living up to the mandates of the faith is uppermost in the dying person's mind. She may be terrified of what the afterlife is to bring and so will desperately try to make up for a lifetime of deeds during the last days or weeks before death. There are always last-minute repentances, with the hope that all will be restored in the final analysis. Mostly, though, there is a sincere desire to make things right where life has fallen short.

When people are dying, they seem to have an instinctual need to put things in order. Usually they begin with practical matters. What is the state of my will? Where are all the papers that people will need after I am gone? How do I want my funeral to be?

Yet once the practical things are out of the way, most people move to a deeper level. They begin to work out the knots in relationships. I witness apologizing and bringing up past hurts, secrets, or misunderstandings. There is a need to express love and offer reassurance, without the limitations life often imposes. If there are places where that love is blocked, the issues will usually surface, and then they can be addressed in talking, sharing, or ritual.

Reconciliation

ONCE THE OBSTACLES in relationships have been cleared away, the final step is reconciliation with the divine. The gospel of Matthew elaborates on this. "So if you are offering your gift at the altar, and there remember that your brother has something against you, leave your gift there before the altar and go; first be reconciled to your brother and then come and offer your gift" (5:23–24).

Reconciliation with God is the most difficult while at the same time the most uncomplicated. If everything else has been settled, then it falls into place. If there are things yet to be worked through with loved ones, it is more difficult. Faith traditions have different teachings about this. It is important to know how each religion approaches confession and reconciliation.

Roman Catholics and Eastern Orthodox Christians place a great deal of importance on confession to a priest before death. Any sins committed must be absolved in order to gain entrance into heaven.

Protestant Christians, however, do not require confession to another person. Instead, confession of the heart through prayer is preferred.

Jews have a final confessional prayer called the Vidui, which allows for specific mention of things done and not done. The prayer, and subsequent death, becomes in and of itself an act of atonement.

Islam has specific mandates for how to put things in order with one's family and community and thereby come to God with a clean page in the Book of Deeds. If the person dying is not able to make amends, the son must act on his behalf.[2]

Eastern religions, like Hinduism and Buddhism, do not believe in contaminating the dying process with negative words, so the act of confession and purification must be an internal one, ridding the self of all internal knots and defilements. Negative thoughts must be put aside.

---

2. Islam traditionally teaches that only the father and his son have the responsibilities described here.

All these things are difficult to do. They involve a certain awareness and willingness on the part of the person dying and the support and cooperation of the loved ones present. If that has not been the case in the family, reconciliation becomes a very demanding process. If words are to be spoken about things done and undone, then awareness and communication are the key. Sometimes rituals can help facilitate this process and take away the burden of how to accomplish reconciliation. A neutral person can often listen in ways the people closest to the dying cannot. A neutral person can often see blocks and begin to bring them out into the open.

When I go into a room where the family or loved ones are gathered and there is an impasse, I know that the first task is to begin to identify where the blocks are. Most often, the people themselves will identify them when we are alone, even though it may take some talking through to get to the bottom-line issues. Many times, though, they remain unidentified until the very end, when rituals are able to bring them forward.

In searching for rituals to help a family work through reconciliation, I have identified a series of steps or categories that may lead to recognition of the block. This is not a progression that must be followed—simply a guide based on the way I've seen people move through this process. A category may or may not apply, but there are rituals in each stage along the way that may help a person reach reconciliation and a place of peaceful detachment.

- Recognition
- Confession or untying the knots
- Last wishes
- Release
- Assurance
- Forgiveness
- Purification
- Restoration of community and reconciliation

Recognition

How hard it is for us to see the things closest to us! When we spend our entire lives trying to avoid certain memories or pain, it is not easy to confront them at the end. If family dynamics are strained, the tension of a medical crisis tends to exaggerate rather than smooth over difficulties. Ultimately, however, the family often comes to see that some things are much better left unsaid. Certain problems are not worth bringing up in order to make people feel better about the impending death. Knowing which way to go demands compassion and discernment.

> DEATH IS NO *threat to people who are not afraid to die.*
>
> —Lao Tzu
> *4th Century,* BCE

But if there is clearly a block that is keeping the person from dying, then it most likely needs to be examined. How do you find out what the problem is? When I meet with patients, they themselves usually point their finger toward the problem. If they cannot, then a family member may have a sense of what is happening.

Some steps you may want to take are:

TALK IT THROUGH.

If the dying person is able to communicate, give him the opportunity to reflect honestly upon past deeds.

SANCTIFY THE TIME FOR THIS PROCESS.

Tell the patient as well as the loved ones that the opportunity is now. Make this a holy time. If the patient is unable to communicate, there is still a way to sanctify the time. Loved ones can speak to the patient and assume she will hear and understand. Tell the patient you are making the opportunity for reflection and that it can be done in silence.

FIND SOMETHING THAT REPRESENTS AN OBSTACLE
AND MAKE IT THE SYMBOL.

If words are not adequate, then use a symbol. Sometimes words cannot convey what needs to be expressed. Find something in the room to symbolize the blocks, like tying knots in a sheet for Katy. Find paper and write down the guilty offenses. Put them in a bowl to offer and then destroy them. Perhaps petals from a flower can be plucked and put into the bowl and then burned or cast to the wind. There are many things that can symbolize the offenses without even naming them or bringing them to light.

Confession or Untying the Knots

If formal confession, speaking the words that are causing the pain and separation, is a part of a person's religious heritage, it is important to summon the appropriate clergy. If an informal confession is possible, then the person dying may or may not request a specific person to be present. If the person dying wants the interchange to be between loved ones, then that is all that is needed. If the religious tradition discourages bringing up negative thoughts or words, meditation may help in dislodging the block and securing peacefulness.

"When my older brother was dying," Ben related, "I was the only family member there. Near the end, he was in a lot of pain, but he needed to talk about all the hard feelings he'd had for our dad as we were growing up. It was pretty cathartic. Afterward, I pulled out an old, unhappy picture of the family from when we were kids, and we decided it was time to burn it. The two of us watched it go up into flames, and we knew that at last all the childhood hurt and pain were finally gone. We could be a family again, without the bad feelings between us."

HAVE A CLERGY OR REPRESENTATIVE HEAR A FORMAL CONFESSION.
Parish priests or hospital chaplains are normally available to hear confessions. They can be reached on an emergency basis if needed.

USE GUIDED IMAGERY.
If the dying person needs help in going to the source of emotional

pain and separation, using guided imagery may be useful. This enables the person to go inside, find the source of the pain, and begin to name it and expel it. It also helps calm anxieties and frustrations.

I vigiled with one woman who was unable to speak because of all the tubes in her throat. We sat quietly, and I guided her through an imagery, taking her to the place where all her fears and anxieties were. We found a "holding place" where she stored the guilt and memories of things she felt were wrong. She imagined that place to be cold and impenetrable, but through the imagery we were able to break through and find a way to diffuse the power it held over her. After the imagery, she felt much lighter and able to let go of her worries.

Use meditation.

Meditation, for those practicing Eastern traditions, is well known and understood. If the person dying is having difficulty with obstacles to inner peace and strength, having those in the room meditate with him can be extremely important. Setting the spiritual tone for a sacred time of meditation facilitates whatever work is left for a person to do.

Include the patient unable to communicate.

Many times the patient is unable to communicate his intentions or feelings. If the loved ones in the room understand that there is a reconciling process going on, regardless of words, they can participate even in the absence of conversation. Assume that the patient is aware and making amends. Never underestimate the power of the divine to facilitate a holy death. Use rituals and always include the patient—make the assumption that she is present and aware at some deep level. It is important that each person in the room knows this. Many times families do not think that comatose persons hear or understand anything. I believe that they do and always give them the time and opportunity to do whatever inner work is needed. I encourage loved ones to talk to the patient, to work through what they need to, and to accept that whatever the issues, peace is now possible.

Last Wishes

I have heard many times the last wishes of the dying. Sometimes they are practical matters, "I want my house to stay in the family," or wishes for the generations to follow, "Get married and have children; that's the most important thing there is in life." One woman's last wish was to dictate her obituary so that she would know exactly what was going to be said about her. Think of all these requests as the last of the unfinished business. It is important to assure the dying person that you will do everything you can to carry out the wishes, even if they seem trivial or impossible. The purpose is to give peace of mind and a knowledge that this life will draw to an end with dignity and confidence.

Release

Through ritual there are many ways to help a person find release. Steve was a successful businessman who'd had a massive heart attack before he was sixty. He felt that his high-pressured lifestyle had caused the heart attack, and he was angry with himself for losing sight of what was really important in his life. Shortly before his death, he sat with his wife and two sons going through his desk and papers, and he decided it was time to burn the reminders of his single-minded efforts. One of his sons made a bonfire outside and helped carry his father to it. Bit by bit, they each threw into the fire stacks of papers representing the life Steve had lived. As the fire dwindled, the talk shifted to memories of camping trips the family had taken and to other times they'd spent together as a family. Steve was comforted by knowing that he had really made time for his family and that they would carry those memories with them.

Rituals for the release that comes after the sorrow and pain have been addressed should be very personal. Take clues from the person who is dying; he will usually indicate what is needed. Think in terms of letting go, of symbolically freeing the soul.

Assurance

Often the perfect thing to do after a person has let go of burdens or guilt is to read to her. Because many of the people I work with are Christian or Jewish, passages from the Bible are most appropriate. There are so many wonderful sections of Scripture that speak comforting words, words of God's forgiveness and love. Some are familiar and some are often overlooked.

Forgiveness

It is often just as hard to forgive someone for a past hurt as it is to admit wrongdoing and ask for forgiveness. When a person is dying, wrongdoing can weigh heavily on the conscience. When someone wants to put things right, asking for and receiving forgiveness is extremely important.

I knew a woman who was dying of a very drawn-out disease, and as she was going through her treatment, she used the time to reflect on her life and her deeds.

"I'm not very proud of some of the things I did," she told me. "But I don't know what to do about it."

I suggested that she write to the people she had offended and ask for their forgiveness. When she told me that she didn't know how to reach some of them—"These things go way back," she said—I replied that we could deal with that when the time came.

She wrote letters for weeks. When I visited her next, she showed me the pile. "See that?" she said sadly. "That's a whole lot of terrible stuff I did to people."

I didn't say anything. I let her continue.

"Some of those letters I'm going to mail. I know exactly how to find the people I need to. But I think some of the letters are just fine where they are. Maybe I already know I'm forgiven. Just writing it out helped me realize that."

We posted about a dozen letters that afternoon, and within a week she had heard from every single person. Everyone forgave her, either in person or over the telephone, and she found peace through that experience.

Asking for forgiveness is not easy, but for those who are dying it is part of trying to put things in order. When we are approached by someone who asks for our forgiveness, it is critical to take it seriously and grant pardon. Brushing it off will not do. Honor how hard it was to ask and acknowledge that what was broken has now been restored. Rituals of wholeness, purification, or assurance are in order.

Purification

After someone lets go of the many concerns she has, there is often a feeling of lightness or cleansing. When Cheryl was in the last days of her breast cancer, her husband and teenage daughter were with her. They spent a long time talking, letting go of all the hurt and pain that had been a part of their lives together. Afterward, the daughter picked up a washcloth and began washing her mother's face. It was more than just wiping away tears and making her mother comfortable. Over and over again, the daughter repeated the phrase, "It's all right, Mummy, it's all right." The act of cleansing, and the assurance of her mantralike words, let Cheryl relax into a needed peacefulness.

Restoration of Community and Reconciliation

Once someone no longer feels estranged from loved ones, from God, or from the religious institution, using ritual to express that reunion can be a beautiful experience. Reconciliation is the experience that follows the release of inner pain. It allows the person to achieve a sense of purity and to regain the bonds of affection that had been clouded or lost.

After an elderly woman's tearful confession, her grown daughter held her mother's head in her lap and sang the songs she had heard as a child. There were lullabies—soft soothing children's melodies—now being returned to the original giver. That bond, through memories long put aside, was a beautiful way for mother and daughter to reconnect. Family stories can provide the same bond. Draw on times when love was present; draw on the emotions and tenderness of love.

Use rituals of religious faith.

Now is a perfect time to bring in the rituals of faith traditions. They represent community and tradition as well as a formal connection to the divine. For example, Christians can break the bread of the Eucharist. Jews can put on the prayer shawl and recite familiar prayers.

Honor family bonds.

Have loved ones reminisce about when the family experienced times of special togetherness. Talk of the love that was felt and that will continue. Objects of special meaning or significance can be brought in so that the person dying can hold them while people speak.

Celebrate the life of the person.

This is the moment to reflect on the life of the person dying and all the things he or she accomplished. Let everyone know of the good things that happened, all the struggles that were overcome, and all the joys that were shared. Go through the history of the person dying so that others can learn what this life has been.

Create loving circles.

If more than one or two loved ones are in the room, form a circle around the bed and reassure the person dying that he will always be held within the family and the community of faith. A quiet song or a prayer will help him feel the presence of love of family and community.

I did a ritual once that was a wonderful celebration. The family of the woman dying brought in photographs of each member of the family, as well as of all the homes she had lived in. They strung them on a banner and circled the hospital bed with it. Each child and grandchild spoke about a part of the woman's life and how significant it was. At the end, they tied the ends of the banner together, forming a circle, the circle of her life.

Conclusion

PEOPLE NEED AND want to die with a clear conscience, with a feeling that the burdens of this life are past, and with a knowledge that their wishes will be granted. It is important to give them an opportunity to do that in a sacred setting. Take your cue from the patient. Be respectful of what he needs most. Speak what he needs to hear. Provide an opportunity for the divine to heal and restore, and then reassure the loved one that you also love and forgive him and will do everything you can to carry on his legacy.

CHAPTER 7

Letting Go of the Body:
Rituals to Comfort and Release

M Y WOMEN'S GROUP was meeting in the hospital that month—one of our friends was dying of breast cancer. Sarah thought she was doing fine after the surgery and the series of radiation and chemotherapy treatments. But the cancer had come back into her lungs and lymph nodes. We were her support system, and we wanted to help out as much as possible. Our monthly gatherings had always included doing rituals, so we sat around her bed and asked her what rituals she felt she needed during this very difficult time.

"I know I'm dying," she told us. "I have been coming to terms with that for a long time. Well, especially since they told me the cancer was back. I guess I will need help with beginning to let go, but you know what I *really* want?" Her eyes began brimming with tears. "I *really* want my body to stop hurting. I hurt all over. It's not so much the pain anymore; it's the aches and the soreness. I feel grungy, from my hair, or what's left of it," she chuckled, rubbing her badly grown-in head of hair, "to my legs and feet. I just feel crummy."

I looked at Sarah's body. It did indeed look bruised and sallow. She had IV tubes in her arms, which were terribly bruised from all the needles. Her hospital bed was disarrayed and a bit soiled. I could tell she was not at all comfortable.

I turned to the other four women and they were thinking the same thing. Barb, who was standing to my right, said, "I wonder if the hospital will let us do some things to make you feel cleaner."

"I'm pretty good at massages," said Amy. "I did some training in it a number of years ago. I think we should give you a healing massage."

Sarah's face lit up. "That would feel *wonderful!*"

Caroline said, "I'll go check in at the nurse's station and make sure it's all right."

"And I'll start gathering some supplies," said Amy.

We all came back to the room, ready to begin. We had bowls of water, soap, shampoo, and towels. We had gotten some oil, too, to use for the massage. Caroline had thought to bring back some clean sheets and blankets to change the bed after we were done.

The group gathered around the bed holding hands and we had a moment of silence. This was the way we typically opened up our monthly meeting. Barb then spoke aloud our intent to be with Sarah in all her needs and that this time today would be for comforting her body so that her soul would feel more at ease.

We broke the circle and began the tasks ahead of us. I found Sarah's little tape player and put in some music she liked. Then we got the basins of water and cloths. Katherine pulled off the dirty sheets from the bed so that Sarah was free from them. There were four of us, so we could have done this quickly, but we decided to focus on washing one part of her body at a time.

"My hair first," said Sarah. "Please! It's been weeks!"

We all laughed. There is nothing worse than that unwashed-hair feeling. Katherine and Barb were the ones who managed the bedside shampoo. It was a bit awkward at first, but they made it work. While the lather was still on her head, Katherine spent extra time massaging Sarah's scalp and on down her neck. Sarah was ecstatic.

"That feels so good. Please don't ever stop!"

I smiled and thought about how wonderful it feels when I get my own hair shampooed and cut. The neck massage was something I looked forward to every time. Absolutely, there are things you want to last forever.

"Do you remember when you were little and your mother washed your hair in the sink?" asked Amy. "At least mine did. It was such an ordeal. I remember soap kept getting in my eyes, and bending over the sink was uncomfortable and awkward. I hated it. Then when I first went to a salon to get a shampoo, I thought, Now why didn't I know about this all along? I could do this forever! There is something so soothing about someone washing your hair." We all smiled.

When Sarah's hair was rinsed, Caroline and I took over toweling it dry. We went through a couple of towels, continuing the massage on her scalp and neck and shoulders. I could hear Sarah moaning to herself.

"Does it feel good?" I asked.

She didn't answer, but the look on her face was a clear give-away.

Katherine took a comb and began trying to arrange the scraggly hair. It seemed to stick out all over the place. The combing was a bit of a help though, and the hair was drying quickly.

"All right, now it's time for a bath," I said.

We got a couple of basins and washcloths so we could be at each side of Sarah. The curtain around her bed was already pulled, but we decided to close her door to insure privacy. Sarah remarked, "There is no such thing as privacy here in the hospital. I feel as if I am on display for the whole world."

"Well, let's just make this our own ritual," Barb said. "No one else is invited, not even in passing."

As we began washing Sarah's sore body, I began thinking about her request a couple of weeks earlier that our group prepare her body after she died. She wanted us to wash it and anoint it and then dress it for burial.

I asked her about it. "Is this what you want us to do to your body after you die?"

"Yes," she said. "But I think the intent will be different. Now you're all doing this for me to make me feel better. I'm still here in my body and it hurts. I need to feel clean and soothed. Later, after I die, I think it will be more of a purification. You'll be taking care of me in a different kind of way."

"I'm still here in my body and it hurts. I need to feel clean and soothed."

Katherine, who is Jewish, told us about going to the mikveh, the ritual pool.

"It's for purification, for cleansing. You immerse yourself in this huge pool of rainwater. I went there before I got married, and even though I was nervous, I felt so good afterward. I know women who go each month after their period too. There is something quite lovely about feeling that clean."

"It makes me feel ready for anything," said Sarah quietly. "This cancer has been so painful, especially the last few weeks. Everything hurts. I have been so focused on all the points in my body where it hurts that I always seem to be fighting back the pain. That is all I do—brace against the pain. This helps me let go of that. I can feel myself just sinking into the bed, relieved to let go."

I thought back to times when I myself had been in extreme pain. I knew exactly what she was talking about.

After we toweled Sarah dry, Amy got out her oil. Before she began massaging, though, I suggested that we anoint various parts of her body.

I took some oil, said a blessing over it, and placed it on her forehead, saying, "Sarah, may this oil heal your mind from all worries and fears."

Caroline then took the oil and anointed her hands. "May this oil heal you so you can use your hands again in blessing and in good work."

Katherine took the oil from Caroline and anointed her feet. "Sarah, may this oil heal you so you can walk down your path, whether it be in life or in death." Her voice wavered.

Barb took the oil and poured a little on Sarah's chest, where her breasts had been removed. The incisions were still red.

"Sarah, may this oil heal your brokenness and your pain. And may it give you strength in your heart."

We all were crying at that point.

Amy continued pouring oil on the rest of her body. "I usually put oil just on my hands when I give a massage, but I think you need to feel the oil on you as I do this. It's there to heal you. Just let it seep in for a bit."

She began massaging Sarah's tired and aching body, soothing the flesh as well as the muscles. I watched as she relaxed under Amy's soft hands. We were all silent.

The massage lasted a long time. None of us wanted it to end. For a little while, a couple of us massaged Sarah's feet while the others worked on her hands. She was able to turn over so Amy could work on her back. The sense of touch was strong. We could give her our own strength through the massage, and she could let go of some of the need to fight the pain. I could actually feel her muscles begin to soften.

When we finished, we changed her sheets and her gown.

Everything was clean and fresh.

Sarah was crying when we were ready to leave. "Thank you so much. This has helped me more than anything else."

The five of us were able to come back once more a couple of weeks later and do the same cleansing, but that time it was much more ritualized. We knew that she did not have many more days left to live, so the washing and the anointing and the massage were focused much more on preparing her for death. She asked us to pray with her as we cleansed her. Each act felt sacred. Each act was a preparation.

The third time we washed and anointed her was the most somber and sacred occasion of all. That time Sarah was no longer in her body. We only had the shell. Her death had been quiet and peaceful, and afterward we approached her body with familiarity. We had done this before, and we knew what Sarah wanted. It felt right, and we knew she was with us in spirit.

❧

Remember when you taught me how to swim?
Let go, you said,
The lake will hold you up.
I long to say, Father let go
and death will hold you up.
—Linda Pastan
"Go Gentle"

WHEN A FAMILY member, friend, or companion is faced with the approaching death of a loved one, the focus is primarily on the medical treatment for that person. However, this medical emphasis usually means that the person has been subjected to extensive physical management for a period of time. Whether it is surgery, treatment for cancer, machinery hooked up to the body, or even invasive testing, all these things are painful offenses to the body.

When the time finally comes for a person to face death, it is also important to know when to ease away from medical solutions and move toward the kind of care that enables the person to die peacefully and with grace. Most of the faith traditions teach that the process of dying is when the body ceases to function in order for the soul to be released to a greater existence. Dying is the physical phenomenon of a spiritual experience.

Because people die in different ways, they experience these phenomena in a variety of manners. But neither health care specialists nor religious communities address questions of how to help someone through the physical experience of leaving the body behind so that the soul can move forward. There are many unanswered questions. How can we help the person detach from his body? How can we best facilitate overcoming the pain and tiredness of the physical in order to move into the spiritual realm? How can we honor the physical body, which has been the host of the person for a lifetime, and yet at the same time prepare to discard it?

Different traditions have different views and legends on how the soul separates from the body. Islam, for instance, teaches that the Angel of Death visits each house daily, and when the time is right, he removes the soul from the body. For those who are righteous, it is painless, "as easy as a piece of hair being removed from dough."[1] For the wicked, however, there are great horrors accompanying the death.

In Tibetan Buddhism, the phases a person goes through are well laid out in *The Tibetan Book of the Dead*. The soul goes through several *bardos,* or in-between stages, before reentering the world. Most Eastern thought, as opposed to Western religions, is much more insightful on this fluid transition from life to death.

Virtually every religious tradition, with the exception of Christianity, has specific instructions and rituals for the physical care of a person's body immediately after death. Most of the customs

---

1. From "Death and Dying: An Islamic Perspective," by Ahmad H. Sakr, in Joan Parry and Angela Ryan, *A Cross Cultural Look at Death, Dying and Religion* (Stamford: Wadsworth Publishing, 1995), p. 58.

involve respectful washing and purification, sometimes anointing, and the wrapping and clothing of the body to ready it for the funeral. The body is physically purified for this death-to-afterlife transition.

It is ironic that very few faiths have rituals for making the body ready *before* the actual death occurs. There are, of course, some small traditions. Islam encourages the person dying to face Mecca. Judaism teaches that the comfort of the person is to be considered above all. Some forms of Christianity practice anointing, the use of holy oil on the body. But the practice has been reduced from applying the oil to virtually every afflicted part of the body to a brief touch to the forehead, sometimes the hands, and even less often, the feet.

In my work I have discovered that there is a great need for attention to the physical in a way that allows the inevitable to happen peacefully. Over and over, I have seen the confusion that occurs when the body begins to die. Many things seem to be occurring all at once, and there is often no one to help the dying person or the loved ones understand what is happening to the body while letting go of the soul.

The Soul Separates from the Body

IN CHAPTER 5, which addresses sanctifying the space, attention was paid to the details in the surroundings. Just as important are details about the body. If we view the physical space as something that holds the person and can either work for or against sacred dying, the same can be said for the physical body. When medical treatment has disrupted everything internally, it is important to bring order to that chaos.

How can ritual help honor the body, which has been diminished, in order to help purify it for death? Sometimes ritual can help by soothing, sometimes by relieving pain. Sometimes we need to create the same process as when we put order into the physical space by cleaning it and making it fresh. If the body is prepared, the person will be more likely to let go of it in a peaceful way.

The Use of Touch in Rituals

Imagine being poked and prodded, having tubes attached to you, and being moved from one place to another. Surgery leaves a person with wounds, treatment for cancer leaves poisonous chemicals inside the system. Various tubes are inserted, and needles seem to be a daily event. When a health care worker touches someone who has been ill for any length of time, the touch is usually not about healing or comfort; it is usually about more pain. Even a simple act like taking blood pressure can be painful if the arm is filled with bruises and tubes. The body is worn out from all the abuse.

If a person has AIDS, the issue of touch is even more dramatic. AIDS is such a hands-off disease. Health care workers wear masks and gloves to approach the patient. Friends and family keep their distance out of fear. During the last days and weeks of life, the person's body withers away, often covered with external lesions and sores. Touch is the last thing outsiders want to do, but it is often the most needed and wanted sensation.

Even without AIDS, touching is not always the easiest thing to do, especially if the family's culture or upbringing makes them uncomfortable around it. Rituals can help that awkwardness. If there is a structure or format that allows and even encourages the use of physical touch for comfort and relief, it becomes acceptable. Again, as in every situation, the cues need to come from the person dying. If touch is too painful or if it is emotionally or culturally uncomfortable, then honor that preference. If the person dying has begun detaching and wants less emphasis on her body, it is not appropriate to force rituals that may not be needed.

There are some things that remain appropriate no matter how detached from the body the person has become. These are:

- Keeping the physical body clean and purified
- Keeping the person comfortable and at ease
- Offering some kind of physical contact for assurance or as a sign of love and affection

CLEANSING

Being clean on the outside is important for feeling clean and ready on the inside. After long periods of illness in the hospital or at home, most people feel grimy and unclean, from the hair down to the feet. Bathing and feeling clean give the person a whole new sense of energy and outlook. I have met many people just hours away from dying who want to "shed" the outside garments. There seems to be something symbolic about wiping away the dirt and grime of illness and wanting to take on a clean new form. If the old self can be washed and made to feel pure, then it becomes easier to learn how to let go and take on the new clothes in the afterlife.

I once vigiled with a teenage girl who was dying. We washed her hair and then moved down to her arms and legs. That gave me an opportunity to ask her what she thought her "new" self would be like. I remember her giggling and replying, "Well, I sure hope I don't have red hair again!" We laughed and laughed. She told me all the teasing names she had been called and how much she hated it.

"I hated it, but I didn't hate it," she told me. "My red hair made me different, but it made me special at the same time. No, I guess I wouldn't mind so much if I got red hair again."

That conversation opened up speculations about what would happen to her next and what she would be like after she died. I remember her saying that she couldn't imagine not existing after her body stopped breathing. She felt so sure of life after death, much to the surprise of her agnostic parents, that it seemed to give comfort to her family.

"I'm not sure about reincarnation," she told me, "but I do know that I'll be back in some way or another. Even if it is just to haunt my creepy little brother."

Her grin was wonderful.

She looked at her body in a very detached way as we washed it. "I'm really sorry it got so sick," she said. "I wonder why. It did okay up until last year. Then everything kind of fell apart. I'm glad I don't have to worry about it anymore. It's time to send it on its way."

Sometimes the dying look at the body as if in a dream. There is no connection at all between their consciousness and their limbs. I once saw a man look at his arm while we were massaging it and asking, "Who does that arm belong to?" Detachment comes in different forms and at different times for everyone.

HAS THE BODY a soul? No. The soul has a body. And well does that soul know when this body has served its purpose, and well does that soul do to lay it aside in high austerity, taking it off like a stained garment.

—LUCIEN PRICE
Litany for All Souls

Water is the primary symbol of cleansing and purification, and I use it in almost every ritual I do. It is filled with religious symbolism, and it is certainly central in every faith tradition. Judaism, Buddhism, Christianity, and all other traditions use water in symbols of renewal and rebirth.

Some ideas for incorporating cleansing rituals follow.

WASHING THE FEET

The feet have many nerves in them that correlate to other parts of the body. I have sat with a dish of water and a cloth and washed and massaged someone's feet for almost an hour. The feet represent our journey; they take us where we need to go. I sometimes do a guided imagery while washing the feet, helping a person visualize the journey ahead.

WASHING THE HANDS

Similar dynamics pertain in rituals for the hands as for the feet. The hands reach out in blessing, both in receiving and in giving.

They also represent the work a person has done in her life. I often tell stories about life and legacies and try to relate it to the patient.

Washing the Hair

Eastern religions teach that the soul leaves the body through the top of the head. Because energy rises during death, the head and scalp play an important role in releasing the soul's energy. Whether that is the belief of the person dying or not, focusing on the head and hair can be very comforting as well as helpful. People often talk about the things they have dreamed or seen in visions while having their hair washed.

Cleansing the Face

The face is similar to the hair in bringing to the surface dreams and visions. There are times I use a wet cloth to wipe the face or to stroke the forehead. This seems to bring up memories of childhood and times of illness when a parent would wash their face.

Cleansing the Entire Body

Sponge baths are often performed in hospitals and many times patients will request one during rituals. This should be performed by family members or loved ones if possible, for purposes of modesty. Bathing is an intimate experience. This is a good opportunity to use visualizations that stress putting away the old body, while anticipating a new self waiting in the afterlife. I also use images of wiping away pain and hurt and, when appropriate, washing away sins.

Bringing in New Sheets and Blankets

It is important to have the bed fresh and clean after ritually washing a person. Sometimes when I'm putting on sheets, I use images from the Bible like "He makes me lie down in green pastures. . . ." I try to convey the image of a place that is refreshing and clean, one that will support and hold all the weary feelings.

BRINGING IN NEW PILLOWS

I once heard a new pillow described as "soft as angel wings." The elderly woman smiled and said she was being carried away to heaven on her pillows. They are there for comfort and ease, and it is important to help the dying person feel that comfort and gentleness.

MASSAGE

Sue is both a chaplain and a massage therapist. She works at a local hospital, often with those who are dying. She tells the story of walking down the hall one day and seeing a woman in a room by herself. It was as if the woman was relegated to the smallest, most out-of-the-way place in the hospital. She was unconscious and clearly dying, with no one attending to her. Sue felt herself being drawn in. She went over to the woman and stood beside her, wondering who she was and why she was alone. Then she reached out and took the woman's hand in hers.

"I began to pray for her," she told me. "I had no idea who this woman was, but my intuition told me it was important that I begin praying with her. Without knowing why, I first prayed for all the people who had loved her. And then for all those she had loved. It was a prayer of thanksgiving and of joy.

"Then, as I stood with her, I found myself praying that she be able to forgive all those who had hurt her. The pain that had built up over all those years was still inside this woman. She needed to forgive her tormentors and release that pain. As I felt her body getting softer, I then prayed for forgiveness for her. I saw all the people in her life that she had hurt in some way and prayed for them to be given a chance to forgive her and love her again. She needed to feel the joy of being forgiven and set free.

"As I stood there holding her hand and offering my prayers, I knew she needed to be touched. I began by just lightly massaging her arms and then legs, asking for a blessing on her as she let go of her physical body. Then I found myself very gently stroking her whole form. It wasn't a massage so much as a caress, a gentle movement up and down her entire body. I could feel the electricity running through her body as well as my own.

"Then it stopped. Just like that. 'It is finished,' I thought. She had died.

"I was able to separate my hands from her body. All the electricity had gone. I never found out anything about her. And I don't know exactly why I was the one to be with her, but I do know that in order to die, she needed to be forgiven and to forgive, to be blessed, and to be touched."

Massage is an intense experience not only for those who are ill and about to die but also for the person on the giving end. Touch carries power through the tangible and also the intangible. I use massage constantly when I vigil with the dying, most of the time in conjunction with and immediately after washing. A foot massage or a hand massage can last for a long time and bring relief and pleasure. Here again I read to people or tell stories when giving a massage, stories about long journeys or places we have been, stories about lives well lived. Many times the person will begin to open up, to talk and share some of her fears and anxieties.

To ALLOW ANOTHER *person to touch me is an act of openness, of acceptance on my part of what that person wishes to communicate or to give me in love.*

—GODFREY DIEKMANN
"The Laying on of Hands in Healing"

One massage therapist said that in her experience, when she visits hospitals and begins to massage, the dying person usually relaxes and becomes much freer in talking about the experience he is having. There is something about the intimacy of touch that opens an area of trust and confidence. It helps people relax so they can begin to let go. Many times when people are very close to death, in that in-between state, I have found that they often have visions or other profound experiences. By relaxing the body, the mind and soul are free to go through the natural process of dying.

One massage therapist recommends strongly that the loved ones or caregiver be careful not to assume and invade the patient's privacy. Wait to be invited to touch and comfort. Many dying people do not want to be touched. The level of physical pain often precludes any desire for more invasion. If there is a desire, though, use a very light touch, slow, gentle, and soothing. While washing is a gentle cleansing, a wiping away of all the dirt and pain of the past, massages tend to be about soothing and going deeply into someone's body and history. Massage moves into the muscles and the tendons, which hold all the memory of pain and worries accumulated throughout the years, and helps a person release those fears and worries. I find that most people move into a strongly meditative or highly relaxed state when they are being massaged. When attention is being focused on helping the body relax, it becomes easier for the person to go beyond the pain and discomfort.

ANOINTING

I frequently use lightly scented oil in rituals with the dying. Besides its historical and ritual heritage, it offers a powerful hands-on experience for the person dying. It involves intimacy and touch. The oil soaks into the often dry skin and into the muscles; it conveys deepness and penetration. It connects one person to the other; the oil is felt by both.

Many Christian chaplains who make pastoral calls will anoint with small amounts of oil on the head and sometimes the hands. I take it further and anoint the wounds and bruises and sometimes the whole body. Or I anoint the back and shoulders and certainly the forehead and temples. Most often, the anointing I do proceeds to a more extensive massage.

When I use oil, sometimes scented, sometimes not, I go

slowly and deliberately. The purpose is to help the person feel the sacred in her body and to experience purification and blessing for the journey ahead.

The Use of Taste in Rituals

In Hinduism, vials of water from the sacred river Ganges are often kept in family homes. A few drops are placed on the tongue of the dying person not only to quench thirst but also to remind him of what is holy. In Christianity, tasting the "bread of heaven" in the sacrament of communion is used as a final rite in many denominations. The Gospels also recount the story of Jesus at his own death. He was thirsty and was offered only vinegar to drink by a bystander.

Thirst is a part of illness and a part of death, even though during the last hours swallowing is often extremely difficult. Rituals can be used to help a person use taste to create sacred moments. Taste can be nourishment not only for the body but also for the soul. Taste can be relief for thirst. Taste can be a symbol of something sweet, anticipating the transition ahead.

- Pieces of ice or drops of water help to relieve physical discomfort. The water can be from sacred rivers like the Ganges or the Jordan, or specifically blessed water, symbolizing entry into the sacred realm.

- Existing rites such as Christian communion can be given as holy food and drink.

- Significant food or drink can be used to symbolize family love accompanying the person.

- A taste of honey on the tongue reminds the person dying that life has been sweet, but the journey to the afterlife is even sweeter.

Remembering that taste and the ability to swallow are often difficult, approach these rituals carefully. A tiny drop or two is all that is needed for the symbolism to be realized.

Visualizations

Visualization or guided imagery is a process many people use with the dying. It is not difficult and it helps calm people when they are experiencing fear and anxiety. It also helps them realize that there is a safer and more peaceful place within their reach.

The purpose of a visualization is first of all to help someone achieve a calm, meditative state. Then it provides an image within to come back to again and again when fear builds up. The image may be of a place that is pain-free or safe from fear. It may be of a journey to a wonderful place, or it may simply be a letting-go experience. The imagery depends on what the dying person needs most at the time.

There are many books that teach techniques, and it may be helpful to read one of those before attempting guided visualizations for the first time.

Here are some things to remember if you are guiding the visualizations:

- Speak very softly and very slowly. I use a quiet, singsong voice.

- The purpose of a visualization is to bring the person into a meditative state, so the first thing to focus on is helping her to breathe slowly, deeply, and in a quiet rhythm.

- When you give someone images to see in the mind, imagine them yourself and allow time to experience them fully.

- Assure the person that the imagery will remain with her, whenever it is needed.

- Bring the person back from the imagery slowly, giving her time to readjust.

Conclusion

THE BODY HAS been an integral part of a person's life. As it ceases to function, there are ways of letting it go that honor the body while knowing it will return to dust and ashes. The paradox of honoring something that is being destroyed can be expressed ritually through cleansing and purifying. Helping someone get past the pain and discomfort of illness in order to detach from the physical is a powerful spiritual process. It cannot be dealt with medically.

The person dying knows his body well and can give a clear indication of its most pressing concerns. Physical difficulties can be put aside, and even the most distressing signs of the body shutting down can be handled with respect and compassion.

CHAPTER 8

Music: Healing and Transcendence

THE KIM FAMILY had emigrated from Korea over ten years before, and they were settling well into American culture. Their two children were in school, and they had established their own business in the city. Their community of friends was still Korean-speaking, however, and they relied on the children to help them when it came to matters that had to be conducted in English.

Mrs. Kim's mother, whom all the family called *Halmony* (grandmother), was staying with them that year, helping out with the house and children. But she had been taken ill, and it looked as if she would not be able to return to Korea.

At the hospital, her family was gathered around her, as were many members of the Kims' Korean Presbyterian church. The pastor had come and said some prayers, and the elders were standing in the corner talking to Mr. Kim. There was some concern because Halmony was a Buddhist.

When I arrived, I spoke to Yoomi, the eldest granddaughter. She explained to me the dilemma. "Our pastor doesn't think it's right to call in a Buddhist priest, but my mother doesn't know how else to calm Halmony down."

I looked over at the bed. Her grandmother was indeed rather agitated and looking around the room. I could understand why. There was quite a bit of commotion with all these people.

"Yoomi, was your grandmother a devout Buddhist?" I asked.

Yoomi thought for a moment. "She had a little altar in her room where she lit some incense every now and then. I guess she was saying some of her prayers."

"Did she ever go to the Presbyterian church with your family?" I asked.

"A couple of times, but not very often," Yoomi replied. "She mostly went there because of her friends, the other *halmonies.*"

I looked over at the woman in the bed. She seemed to be less concerned with what kind of prayers were needed than with wanting some peace and quiet.

I told Yoomi she could suggest to her mother that some things from the altar at home be brought to the hospital later that evening. And perhaps the pastor could read to her from some of the Psalms.

And then I had an idea. "Why don't you ask some of the family members to sit and talk to her about Korea? I'm sure she is missing her home and her family there. Maybe your mother could talk to her about some of the things she remembers when she was a child in Korea."

Mrs. Kim overheard our conversation and nodded in agreement.

"I think my mother is missing Korea very much," she said.

Mrs. Kim took the lead and went over to her mother's bed. She began speaking to her in Korean, and even though I couldn't understand a word she was saying, I could see the results. Mrs. Kim had settled into a singsong way of speaking. It was very lulling.

I looked at Yoomi questioningly.

She told me, "My mother is talking about the countryside where our family home is, how beautiful it is, how green the hills are. She is saying, 'I remember the spring flowers on those hills.'"

I smiled.

"It must be hard," I remarked to Yoomi, "to be so far away from everything she knows and loves."

Just then Halmony muttered some words.

Yoomi translated for me, "She said that she will not die until she can be in her home again."

Halmony began to wail.

The family members in the room were clearly distraught.

THE MUSIC HAD taken her where she wanted to be, to the green hills of her home.

Mrs. Kim took her mother's hand and began singing to her in Korean. The noise in the room immediately stopped. There was only the sound of a lovely tune.

"I've heard that song before," I remarked. "What is it?"

Yoomi replied, "It's called 'Ah-rhee-rang.' It's a Korean folk song, a song we sing every time there's a special celebration."

I sat and listened to Mrs. Kim sing—it was so beautiful. Slowly, all the family members began congregating around the bed. One by one, they joined in the gentle song.

Ah-rhee-rang, ar-rhee-rang
Ah-ra-rhee-yo.
Ar-rhee-rang ko-keh-reul
nehm-u kan-dah
nah-reul buh-rhee-koh
kah-shee-neun neem-eun
Sheen nee-doh mot-gasu
bar-byung nan-dah.
"Ah-rhee-rang—the beautiful hill. . . .
If you leave me, you will be hurt. . . ."

There were tears in people's eyes as they sang about leaving the green hills of Korea. Verse after verse, the room filled with the sound of the sweet and simple melody.

I watched Yoomi's grandmother lying on the bed, eyes closed, tears falling down her face. She was back in Korea. The music had taken her where she wanted to be, to the green hills of her home.

Only by the form, the pattern,
Can words or music reach
The stillness. . . .
—T. S. ELIOT
Four Quartets

"MUSIC IS A holy place," says Don Campbell in *The Mozart Effect*, "a cathedral so majestic that we can sense the magnificence of the universe. . . . Music can drum out evil spirits, sing the praises of the Virgin Mary, invoke the Buddha of Universal Salvation, enchant leaders and nations, captivate and soothe, resurrect and transform."[1]

This chapter is not a technical analysis of the healing power of music nor is it about how certain strains within the structure of music can aid someone in a physical way. It is not about the formal discipline of musicology nor of music therapy. There are many books and studies that give information and training for those wanting to learn the pragmatic side of the use of music and healing.

1. Don Campbell, *The Mozart Effect: Tapping the Power of Music to Heal the Body, Strengthen the Mind, and Unlock the Creative Spirit* (New York: Avon Books, 1997), p. 1.

Instead, this chapter is about people's experiences of the power that music has and the different ways it affects people who are dying. I have seen music act as a tremendous calming influence. When a dying person is upset, afraid, or even hysterical, I have used certain kinds of music to help him over that fear, and almost instantly he becomes calmer. Music can transform an entire room from frenzy into peacefulness. Music also has the ability to decrease pain and distress. And music can carry a person from this life into the next.

Music and Memories

MUSIC CAN TRANSPORT us back in time, to another era, to another place. Think of all the songs you know that instantly take you back to the time when you were a teenager, when you were in the throes of a love affair, or when you were most happy. Music triggers memories on a very deep, visceral level.

When a person is dying, she often has a very fluid perception of time, wandering in and out of all the eras of her life. Music can help focus on specific times, places, or events.

Many times loved ones will notice that someone who is dying lives in the past. He is experiencing events that took place years ago. Perhaps he imagines that he is a young boy again, or newly married or, most commonly, a small child. It is important to acknowledge that perception because it is very real for the person. He is somewhere else. The family can best serve his needs by going to that world rather than trying to force the person to come "back" to this time and place.

Childhood for most people was a time when others made decisions. It was a happy time, when the world was an open and exciting place. Others looked after you and loved you. When a person goes back to his childhood, it is often to seek a happier time, a time of beginnings and not of endings. The music of childhood is usually about happiness, comfort, security, and love. Think of children's songs, think of soothing lullabies, think of simplicity.

A dying person may want to be in another place or with other people. Music can help take him there. The point is, first, to meet the dying person where he is, and then to provide a connection to feelings of happiness, assurance, "home," or spiritual ease.

Music here is not about the classics or even good taste; it is about what is in our consciousness and in our memories. I usually try to elicit popular songs, children's songs, religious hymns, or any songs that stir memories. These songs touch the heart, and the family members or loved ones usually know best which music to offer.

Here are some examples:

LULLABIES OR CHILDREN'S SONGS

Many times the songs from our childhood bring us the most joy. They also remind us of times with those who cared for us, being tucked into bed, assured that we were safe and sound. Lullabies evoke nighttime. They evoke letting go and drifting off to sleep. If roles are reversed and now the child is parenting the parent, it is helpful to use that image of parent/child in choosing music.

I have seen many elderly people who have had little recognition of family suddenly perk up and see visions of their mother in front of them. One man kept reaching out his hand to whoever was in the room, crying, "Sing to me, Mummy, sing to me." He wasn't at peace until he heard a song he remembered from his childhood. He wanted his mother and the way only she could comfort him.

CHRISTMAS CAROLS

I remember one family who gathered around the bed of the dying grandmother. There must have been a dozen people in the room milling about. I overheard one of the daughters mention how sad it was that grandmother wouldn't live until Christmas.

"She loved Christmas so much," said the daughter. "There were carols on the record player all month long. I can't walk into Nana's house without hearing Christmas carols."

I suggested that the family gather around the bed and sing carols to Nana.

"It doesn't matter that it's September. It's what she loved."

I must admit that I was in tears when the family ended the caroling, singing *Silent Night*.

"Sleep in heavenly peace," they sang, "sleep in heavenly peace."

ETHNIC OR PATRIOTIC SONGS

Songs from the old country and from particular ethnic traditions stir up emotions inside us. Many elderly people in our families or communities have ties to other places and other times. One family didn't have a clue how to help their dying aunt until a longtime family friend came in to visit. The two of them had grown up together in Russia. The friend sat at the bedside, wiping the tears from her face, until she asked her much loved friend a casual question, "Do you remember that old woman back in the village who was the midwife? What was her name? Do you remember?"

The dying woman smiled as she thought back to their childhood and the memory of the old crone shlepping her worn-out bag up and down the streets.

"What was that song she used to sing?" asked the friend.

They both remembered at once and began singing a simple tune in Russian. It was a sweet tune, and it took both old and wrinkled women back to a different time and a different place.

RELIGIOUS HYMNS

A person's faith is very personal and intimate; it often spans an entire life. Music is a part of every religion, whether it be sacred hymns or informal melodies. From the great repertoire of Christian hymns to the Jewish niggun to Buddhist chants, music forms a vital part of the spiritual experience.

When music is used with the dying, it isn't always necessary to go to formal hymnals or prayer books for ideas. The point is to use familiar and much loved music, like a favorite seder song from Passover or even a brief melodic phrase from religious ceremonies.

I sat at the bed of a young boy who had been involved in a horrible automobile accident that severely damaged his spine; he must have been about seven or eight. As he was coming out of surgery and lying motionless in his bed, his parents anxiously looked for signs that he was regaining consciousness. Could he move his fingers? Would he blink his eyes? As they watched every breath he took, he surprised everyone by beginning to sing, in the faintest of whispers,

Jesus loves me, this I know.
For the Bible tells me so.
Little ones to Him belong.
They are weak, but He is strong.

FAMILY FAVORITES

Every family has familiar music that evokes memories of events or of special bonds. Sometimes they become part of family legends; sometimes they just sit quietly in loved ones' memories.

One elderly couple, dealing with the wife's illness, found themselves singing songs to each other from when they were courting. They met during World War II and were parted almost immediately after falling in love. He went off to fight in Europe and she stayed home, writing him every day. Their romance was carried on with the war in the background. The music of that era was wrought with emotions and inspiration. "I'll be seeing you in all the old familiar places. . . ." The music they brought back into their current situation had the same inspiration. It brought back the same emotions of being parted yet having a love that would survive it all.

Music as Meditation and Prayer

VIRTUALLY EVERY FAITH tradition abounds in liturgical, ready-made prayers set to music, such as chants, scriptural psalms or hymns, and entire liturgical texts, such as the Mass. I use them at the deathbed, both formally and informally. Sometimes, when clergy or chaplains visit, there will be a short service with music. Other times, family members will use selections of music from services by themselves. There are no rules for what to do or what to use; there is no set of instructions.

A Jewish friend of mine said that several friends of a dying person gathered at the bed and just sang various nigguns. A niggun is a melody without any words. They sat at the bedside for hours, humming and singing softly to the person dying. One person would begin a new niggun and the others followed suit.

Another friend said that when his father was dying, he brought in a recording of the Mormon Tabernacle Choir. The family members were devout Mormons, and the choir singing hymns was meaningful to everyone present. "What better way to leave this world," he said, "than to be accompanied by the greatest choir on earth singing God's praises?"

Most Eastern religions use chant as an integral part of devotions and consider it essential at the bedside of the dying.

It does not take a trained musician to use sacred music for meditation and prayer at the deathbed. Anyone can:

- Create a small family prayer service where music is the main component.

- Use recordings of sacred music to bring loved ones together in a reverential manner.

- Bring in musicians or people from congregations to create a musical and prayerful experience.

Music to Calm

Music is used all the time to help people focus their energies and create a feeling of calm and peace. Recorded meditative music is available in most places. The difference between sacred music and meditative music is that sacred music includes actual prayers and liturgical words set to music, for instance, the Lord's Prayer, the Twenty-Third Psalm, the text of the Mass. Meditative music, on the other hand, is reflective music. Its purpose is to lead someone to a meditative state; the music becomes secondary so that the act of meditation can be primary. This music is usually instrumental and quite peaceful and relaxing.

When I use meditative music, I try to create a quiet atmosphere in order to calm people and allow them to meditate. Many people prefer silence for meditation, but when the situation is difficult, and when people are not used to the effects of meditation, music can be an important tool. It gives the patient an opportunity to take time apart, calm the body and mind, control the pain, and focus on breathing and restoring peacefulness.

It is easy to find recordings to create this time apart each day, even if the person is unconscious or asleep. The benefits, for the patient as well as the loved ones, go beyond the logical. I have never known a situation where sitting quietly with meditative music has not been greatly appreciated.

Secular Music to Evoke Prayer

All sorts of secular, or specifically nonreligious, music can have for us prayerlike qualities. They take us to a place where we experience God and a sense of the whole creation. I have special favorites in my music collection that help me pray, and I often take them with me to hospital rooms when I vigil with the dying. They are usually classical pieces, sometimes choral works, sometimes simple, uncomplicated works.

Each person or family has favorite pieces of music that already have special meaning. Everyone's taste is different, so there is not one list of "appropriate" music, but in choosing music to take to the sick bed, be aware that a German opera might be a bit intense. Try to strive for quieter and more peaceful compositions.

One of my most often listened to CDs is Yo-Yo Ma's *Unaccompanied Suites for Cello* by J. S. Bach. That single instrument is so beautiful and so haunting; it pulls me deeper into prayer every time I listen. The movement I love most is the Sarabande of the Fifth Suite. I use it all the time when I sit with the dying, and many people have told me how much it means to them. It brings people to a very special place, one close to God.

I recently saw a film of Yo-Yo playing the Bach suites, and during the fifth one, he made a very interesting comment.

> *Dance then, wherever you may be,*
> *I am the Lord of the Dance said he,*
> *And I'll lead you all wherever you may be,*
> *And I'll lead you all in the Dance said he.*
>
> —"The Lord of the Dance"
> *a folk song*

"The Sarabande of this suite," he said, "is the very last piece I played for my father before he passed away. This suite, for me, is a prayer. . . ."[2]

Music does not have to be liturgical in order to be prayerful. It has only to touch us in a way that makes us want to be close to creation and to the universe.

The Healing Power of Music

MUSIC HEALS. IT affects us physically as well as emotionally and psychologically. There are many research studies that examine the hows and whys. Many music therapists build on that research to effect specific forms of healing. There are many ways music can "heal" at the deathbed. It can seep into the unconscious and calm

---

2. From "Yo-Yo Ma: Inspired by Bach, Suite No. 5, Struggle for Hope," Sony Classical Video.

fears and anxieties, it can help control pain, it can regulate breathing, it can soothe, and it can create sacred surroundings.

Therapists look for the pathology and find ways to cure. In the case of the dying, music is not a cure; it is rather a way to help the individual get past fears in order to let go of the physical. It seeks to restore a natural process.

Live Music

Live music is an incredibly powerful experience. There is something about the combination of the instruments or voices in the room, the sound as it resonates throughout the space and into our bodies, and the energy of the person actually playing or singing that adds an indescribable dimension to the experience. Music takes a moment in time and transforms it into something extraordinary.

If an outside person is coming in to work musically with the person dying, it is important to use the opportunity as something extremely special and set apart. This means clearing the time and the space around the person and focusing as much as possible on the experience. The ritual of music is intense and has enormous power, and it should be honored as such.

Recorded Music

Most of us do not have the opportunity to use music therapists or thanatologists and have to rely on recorded music. This can be just as helpful and just as meaningful. There are, in fact, instances where people have had powerful experiences of healing just from listening to a CD.

No one knows what music will speak to each person individually. Loved ones can only take their cues from the person dying, but as a rule, try to find music that is familiar, soft, and comforting. There are many recordings on the general market that are specifically used for meditation and relaxation. Some are for background, for mood and atmosphere, and others are for focused listening.

Background Music

Background music is a tool that helps calm a room, and it can be used in different ways. I often put on some music, ask the family or loved ones to be silent for awhile, and then I resume conversation or move into a specific ritual. The music "holds" the atmosphere of quiet and calm.

Active Listening

If it is appropriate, I use the music to act for me. This involves active listening and responding to the music. Many times I ask those in the room to breathe more slowly, synchronized with the rhythm of the music. If the dying person is fearful or agitated, I often lay my hand on his chest and say softly, "in, out, in, out" along with the music. Many times I do that silently and watch for our breaths to coordinate together and with the music. It is not difficult at all for each person present to relax and let the music take over. Other times I recite a phrase or mantra to the rhythm of the music. One phrase I use a lot is simple, "It's all right . . . it's all right."

Intent of the Music and the Musician

On a day when I was visiting a cancer patient at the hospital, a group of teenagers came through with their guitars wanting to sing some songs to the patients. The guitars they used were acoustic, and they were skilled enough to make the music enjoyable, but for some reason most of the people there found the music somewhat uncomfortable after a short while. Once they left, one of the nurses commented that the kids were sweet to do this, but they didn't have much patience when they were asked to adapt the songs or the loudness of the music to some of the patients.

"They wanted to play what *they* thought would sound good," the nurse explained, "not what the patients could manage to listen to."

It is very hard to describe a feeling that comes when music is not right for the person or the situation. On the outward level, the *kind* of music is easy to distinguish. Clearly, something like rap music or loud jazz is not going to be helpful to those people who want quiet meditative sounds surrounding them.

There is another element to consider, other than the nature of the music itself, and that is the intent of the musician. I believe that because music—as well as other art forms—is so susceptible to any kind of influence, the intent of the one offering the music makes an enormous difference. Of course, skill and technique play a large role when a musician performs, but I have no doubt whatsoever that it is the love and extraordinary soul of those musicians that is the critical factor in healing and music. I have seen it too many times. On the other hand, someone who has no singing voice whatsoever can sing to a loved one, and it will be the music of angels.

Transcendence: "Beth's Story"

I ARRIVED AT the hospital to meet a young and clearly distressed mother. Her four-year-old daughter had leukemia, and it was unmistakable that she was on the verge of dying. Susan, the mother, told me a bit about Beth as we stood in the hallway. She had been sick during the entire year. There were treatments for the leukemia and lots of hospital stays. I gathered that in their family there was just the two of them. Susan mentioned that before the leukemia, Beth was a wonderfully happy preschooler. She was vibrant and outgoing. She was talented in many things, especially music. She had begun playing the violin in a Suzuki class and was beginning ballet.

I was taken into the room and there, totally enveloped in the large bed, was Beth. She was so tiny. Her head was shaved, but there was still a bit of blonde peach fuzz poking up in odd directions. She had tubes coming out of every place imaginable. I looked at that tiny child in the bed and could somehow imagine her dancing about the room in a happier time. She opened her bright blue eyes and smiled at me.

I spent the next hour being practical and helping Susan. We made the space in the hospital room a bit more cozy, and we spent time in prayer. Beth was asleep for most of this.

When things were quiet, and Susan needed some time alone, I went over to the tapes of music I had with me. I usually brought tapes that are peaceful and meditative, but for some unknown reason I had grabbed an additional tape that afternoon. I looked at it now, wondering why in the world I had reached for that particular one. It was a live broadcast of "La Serenissima," a cello concerto performed by Carter Brey, a very special friend of mine, now principal cellist of the New York Philharmonic, and composed by Daniel Brewbaker, to whom Carter had introduced me and who was also becoming a good friend. I loved that piece of music, not only because it was so beautiful but also because it was so personal. But would a cello concerto be the right music to play as a four-year-old was dying? It seemed unlikely.

I turned the tape over and over in my hands. I could just as well have reached for another tape of piano and harp, "mood music," but I put Daniel's concerto in the player, and just as Susan came back into the room, I pressed "play."

The moment the music began, Beth responded. She responded with her whole body. I could see her arms and legs moving, her head straining to hear it better. I took the player closer to her bed. She was riveted to the music. She was not only hearing, but I could tell that she was also straining to see something.

"Beth," I asked her, "what is it? What do you see?"

"Oh, it's wonderful," she replied. "They're dancing everywhere. There are children and babies, and they are dancing. Can't you see them? They are dancing on the water." Her face was lit up with joy, and I could actually see with her the movements of the dancing children.

She looked up to a corner of the room, her eyes darting back and forth.

"Tell us what the music is showing you, Beth," I said to her. She was seeing it so vividly, and I was sure that she wanted to tell her mother and me all about it. We were going to see this wonderful vision through Beth's eyes.

She listened intently for another moment or two. The cello was playing lightly and joyfully. "That's not a violin," she said. "It sounds like it, but it isn't."

"No," I said. "It's a cello. It's bigger, so the sound is much deeper." She continued to listen intently to Carter playing. Her brows were furrowed. She then opened her eyes and looked right at me, holding tightly on to my hand. "Our friend is making that music. I can see him. He is playing the big violin on the floor, and the music is for the children dancing by the water."

I looked right into the place where she was staring, and then for a brief moment I was able to see Carter too. He was there, in the midst of a wonderful city of water, filled with children dancing.

"Is that him?" Beth asked me. I looked at her, my own eyes wide with amazement, and nodded.

"Yes, that's Carter. That's Carter and his cello. He's in the place where there's water."

I looked toward the player, wondering how she knew that this piece of music was written about Venice, the City of Water.

We continued to listen, and now and again I actually saw Carter's image. I know I wasn't imagining it. Carter was somehow there, playing for Beth. A moment later she asked me, "Does he have little girls? Are they dancing with him?"

"Yes," I said slowly. "He has one little girl. Her name is Ottavia, and she is about your age." I looked at Beth. "She has pretty yellow hair like you do and she loves to listen to music."

Beth smiled and said, "I like her. I want to be her friend."

The music played on.

Susan sat in the corner, watching, eyes wide, and not saying a word.

Beth listened more. "Tell me about the music man, the one with the cello," she asked me.

"He's a very special person, Beth," I replied. "He makes the sky all beautiful when he plays his music." She nodded solemnly.

But then she began telling me, "And he is a good daddy to his little girl. And they go to the place where the water is with their mommy. And they find the music there, and they all love each other very much."

I thought of Carter and his family spending summers in Italy.

Beth was quiet for a moment and then she said, "Look at all the angels around him, dancing with his music! The angels are dancing all around him and holding him up! Do you see them? Oh, they love it so much!"

We sat and watched the angels for a few minutes. The music played on.

Susan, still sitting in her corner quietly, began crying.

Then Beth sat up in her bed and looked frantically around the room, asking, "Where's Daniel? Where's Daniel?"

I looked at Susan, who clearly didn't know who Daniel was. I asked Beth who she meant, and as she fell back on her pillow, she said, "The other music man. The one who sees the music."

I tried to see what she was seeing, and even though it was less clear this time, I knew it was Daniel, the composer. We kept listening to the music, and she said over and over, "Look at the dancers dancing with the stars and with all the children. It's like the *Nutcracker*!"

As the pace of the music increased, so did the dancers'. And so did Beth's. Her body was trying to dance to the music, and even though it physically could not, there in her mind's eye she was dancing with each of the angels.

I saw the angels too, in brief flashes. They were swirling about in joy. The notes of the music carried them on and on.

Beth was getting tired, though. By the fourth movement I could see things change. It is a very rich but sad movement. When I first heard it broadcast on the radio, months before, I cried and cried. It had pulled on every emotion inside of me. Beth felt it now; I could tell. She began weeping quietly.

"I'm sorry," she cried. "Tell the music man I'm sorry I can't dance any more to his music. I'm just so tired."

"Shhh," I said. "Shhh. It's a quiet dance this time. Just close your eyes, Beth, and try to dance to it in your mind's eye. Try dancing quietly inside your mind."

She lay there a long time listening and trying to dance inside that place where the music was taking her.

Sometimes I thought she was asleep, but every now and then she would murmur something about the dancers and about Daniel. "Tell him to find the dancers in the clouds," she said. "They are in the clouds, not in the streets, or in the rooms or anywhere else. He has to find the right angels to dance, and they are all in the clouds."

I closed my eyes and tried to see what she was seeing. Daniel was looking up and down and all over for the right dancers for his music, but he couldn't find them. And when I looked up to the clouds, I knew exactly what Beth was looking at—there were his angel dancers waiting to hear his music and begin dancing. They were all dressed in beautiful white gowns, more beautiful than any ballet dancers I had ever seen.

I opened my eyes and looked at Beth. She was fading in her body, but inside she was struggling to follow the music. "You see them, don't you?" I said yes. She smiled at me, closed her eyes, and fell deeper into unconsciousness.

The last movement of the piece was playing and it was getting more and more intense. My heart was pounding as I watched her follow each note. She was trying so hard to listen to its meaning for her. This movement was not about dancing; it was about reaching out to Beth and asking her to do something special. There seemed to be a gathering of forces. I felt the growing energy and power inside the room itself. As the tempo of the music increased, so did the energy, and so did my awareness that something extraordinary was happening. Susan and I would glance at each other every few moments, not daring to say a word.

Beth continued to be connected to the music in a way that was for her alone. Her body moved and her eyes followed visions in front of her. She said nothing. The music reached a crescendo.

I wanted to hold her hand, but I knew that I couldn't.

As the very end of the piece came—and I knew it was coming—she let out an enormous gasp and cried out, "The music is taking me!"

As the last note was played, her breath stopped.

She died. The music carried her home.

The story of Beth is one that will always be a part of me. I was able, because of her extraordinary experience, to be a part of something transcendent. Sometimes, and in some situations, human beings can have experiences that take them beyond ordinary capabilities. Human beings can glimpse a piece of other realities not normally seen. There is no prescription for enabling transcendence to happen at the deathbed. There is no set of guidelines for how to make it happen. It happens when it happens.

We read of saints and mystics having transcendent experiences. I think that, because Beth was such a young child and so close to death, she was able to see things and hear things that many people might not normally pay attention to. The music not only provided her with a doorway into that world, but it also gave her the very room itself in which to experience the transcendent.

Maybe it was because I knew Carter and Daniel and, in a sense, brought them with me into that room. Perhaps it was because they brought something extraordinary to the music itself. I am sure that while Daniel[3] sat at his computer composing that music and when Carter sat on stage performing it in front of an orchestra and audience, neither of them knew that one small child, escorted by swirling angels, would be carried by their music as she died.

It was one of those unexplainable things that happen.

And music's role? Only to be there and carry the person forward. Music has that ability, which I think not many other

3. For more information on the music of Daniel Brewbaker, please contact: Brewbaker Music, 400 West 43rd Street, #37Q, New York, NY 10036.

expressions have. Perhaps it is because it is transcendent in and of itself.

Those loved ones who witness this transcendence can be a part of it, albeit from the sidelines, or they can dismiss it. There are no rituals; there is only the opportunity to be present when it happens.

Beth's story is a simple one. Her story involves music and the musicians who created and played the music. It is a very personal story for me, but it also points toward the power, both in form and in essence, of the music and how it offers to carry us to a new life.

CHAPTER 9

When Loved Ones Are Not Present

AREN GOT THE call when she walked in the door late one night. Her twin brother had been involved in a car accident hundreds of miles away. The hospital was on the line, explaining that he was in pretty bad shape. The doctors said that there was nothing anyone could do that night; they were about to take Mark into surgery. The next day they hoped to have more information on how he was. Karen looked at her watch. It was already after ten; there was no way she could fly up to Seattle that night.

Karen was numb. She took a deep breath and sat quietly for some time. There was going to be a lot of arranging to do, and she wanted to feel a bit of calm before the chaos took over. She tried to pray.

"Why is it that we only pray when things are at their worst?" she wondered. "All I ever seem to do is say, 'Please God, fix this.'"

Suddenly she felt a flash of darkness in the pit of her

stomach, and she knew something had happened, something not good at all. She looked around her living room frantically.

"What is it?" she said to the empty room. "What's going on?" Then there was stillness. Nothing.

Karen waited a few moments, listening to the silence of the room. She felt a cold chill going up and down her body. "It's Mark," she thought, "I know it's Mark."

She saw a picture of her brother in her mind's eye. As twins they had always been strongly connected to each other. She remembered growing up and all the things they had shared. The coldness got worse.

She got up and started pacing back and forth, not knowing what to do.

Before she could think the whole thing through, the phone rang again. It was the hospital, the same doctor as before.

"I'm sorry," he said, sounding weary. "We barely got him into the operating room. His injuries were too severe. He didn't make it. The other guy will make it though—the one who ran into him, the drunk driver. He'll live. I'm sorry about your brother. Here, let me put the state patrol officer on, and he'll tell you what happened."

Karen sat and listened to the details of her brother's accident. Typical drunk driver running the median. Could she come up and fill out the forms and identify her brother?

The words went past her; she was too numb to pay attention. All she heard was that Mark didn't make it. He was dead.

Karen knew that she would have to take charge of things, and the first thing she knew she had to do was call her mother back east and tell her the news. Her mother was getting older and this would be very difficult.

"Mom," she said tentatively. "I just got a call from Seattle. Mark was in a car accident. They took him to the hospital and they tried to operate, but he didn't make it. He died a few minutes ago."

"Oh, no," cried her mother. "Oh, no."

Karen was silent for a moment. "I guess I'll have to go to Seattle in the morning," she said. "There are some things they want me to do."

Her mother was crying.

"Mom," she asked quietly, "should I go ahead and have him cremated up there? That's what he wanted, you know."

"That doesn't seem very nice." Her mother was obviously upset. "You're supposed to have funerals when people die."

"Maybe we can have a nice memorial service in a few weeks. Wouldn't that be all right?"

Her mother was quiet and then replied, "Yes, I suppose that would be better. We can have a memorial service out here for the family and his friends."

"Okay," Karen replied. "We can deal with the ceremony later. Right now, I'll just focus on what the hospital wants me to do." She hung up the phone.

As she climbed wearily into bed, Karen felt her brother's presence in the room with her. Again, there was a cold chill that ran up and down her body.

"What is this?" she thought. "Why does this keep happening?"

The next morning, Karen flew to Seattle. At the hospital, she met the doctor in charge of her brother's surgery. He was apologetic that the surgery hadn't been successful. But he quickly changed the subject, directing her to the coroner's office and urging her to speak to the police.

Having to identify her brother's body was awful. After huge amounts of paperwork, she was led into the morgue. The doctor pulled back the sheet from the head. It was Mark. She felt sick to her stomach.

The doctor led her to a small room where he told her she could sit quietly for a few moments and be alone with her thoughts. One minute Mark was here, everything normal, everything the way it always was, and the next minute he was gone. Just like that. A stupid drunk driver had changed their lives.

Once again, that cold feeling went through her body. She

looked around, trying to find something or someone to help identify it for her. There was no one. She felt the tears running down her face. Numbly, Karen made the arrangements for the cremation. The ashes would be shipped back to her home in a few days.

A few weeks later, Karen and I sat talking about the whole experience.

"The thing is, Megory, I still feel this strange coldness every day or so. Everything is upside down since Mark died. I can't eat or sleep; I can't seem to focus on my work. I wish I could just get on with things, but there is no way to do that."

"You are in a state of mourning," I replied. "You have to give yourself some time."

"I know that, but this is different from the grief I feel when I cry. It's as though something is hanging over my head."

All the next day I turned her words over in my mind. Mark had been killed tragically. His death was unexpected and violent. I wondered if that was the answer—Mark hadn't had time to make the transition between life and death. Plus, he was young, barely forty. Within minutes he had been brutally pulled from a happy and productive life to death. I thought of the Asians I knew who believed that the soul was very close at hand after a tragic death, trying, not always successfully, to move on to the next life. I knew that Karen and her family probably didn't believe in reincarnation, but maybe there was something to consider about Mark's soul being "stuck."

I called Karen and asked her if she would like to do some rituals that might help "settle" things.

"Maybe Mark was taken so suddenly," I explained, "that he didn't have a chance to have the peaceful death that everyone deserves. Perhaps because it was so violent he is having a hard time breaking away from his physical body."

She thought for a moment. "I haven't really done anything for him, you know. I haven't even prayed for him because it seemed pointless somehow."

"Well, if he is having a hard time moving on, we can do

some letting-go rituals and see if they help. My guess is that they will."

I asked Karen if she wanted to do this alone or invite some friends; she opted for just the two of us.

"I think this is about Mark and me. We were so close, especially as twins, that I'm sure he's staying with me for a reason."

We agreed to meet the next evening.

Sitting in Karen's living room, we lit candles and incense. We had gathered several things in front of us: a bowl of salt water and a bowl filled with earth, photos of Mark, yarn, and sage. Karen also brought in the small box of Mark's ashes, which she was keeping until the family could decide what to do with them.

"We're not going to try to conjure up some ghost, are we?" Karen asked nervously.

I laughed. "No. Not at all. Maybe we can think of this in another way. When babies are born, they are attached to their mothers by the umbilical cord. It feeds them and keeps them attached to their mother when they are in the womb. But after they are born, they don't need the cord anymore. It will cause harm if it isn't cut.

"I think that after we die there is another kind of letting go. The invisible umbilical cord that keeps us attached to this life is no longer needed. In most cases that cord is cut automatically when we die. Sometimes, though, when death is very sudden or violent, the cord remains intact, and we continue to feel the person's presence around us in a very strong way. I think those cold chills you have been having mean that Mark is letting you know that he needs help in moving on."

"I am aware of Mark's spirit," said Karen. "It isn't a nice, warm memory, though. When I walk into a room, I get that chill, and I feel as if he is just around the corner. It doesn't feel good."

> "I THINK THAT *after we die there is another kind of letting go. The invisible umbilical cord that keeps us attached to this life is no longer needed."*

"That tells me these chills aren't about you or your being able to mourn. I think they are about Mark. So we can try some rituals that will help cut the cord and see how that feels for you."

We began with a moment of silence. The candles flickered around us. Karen had put one large photograph of her brother on a small rug in the middle of the floor.

"He was so young," I thought, "and it was so senseless. This isn't the way it should have happened." His death was not only sad, but it also felt wrong. It felt like it was a mistake.

I began with a prayer, asking the Spirit to guide us so we might know what was needed to be done. I then began talking about Mark, about how good he was and how much he was loved.

"Mark was taken from his life much too soon and much too violently. We ask for peace with that experience now."

I took several strands of yarn and asked Karen to braid them for me. She made a braid a couple of feet long. I took the braided yarn and held it up.

"This is the cord that has tied Mark to life all these years. It has held him and kept him alive here on this earth, but now he has been taken from us. The cord still hasn't been completely cut. We need to bless Mark and give him permission to continue his journey apart from his body."

Karen took the yarn and held it to her. Tears rolled down her face.

"Mark," she said, "I know that something is keeping you here. We've always been so close, almost as if we had one cord between us. Well, now it is time for you to cut free. You have to go ahead of me. I know we will be with each other again, but you can't stay here anymore. I'll try to live my life for both of us. I'll do my best here and you have to do your best there."

Then she picked up the scissors and cut the cord in half. One half began unraveling.

"Let's send him out into the four corners of the universe," I said.

Taking the bowl of salt water, I scooped up some in my hands and flicked it out into the room. Karen did the same and flicked some in the direction of the photographs and mementos of her brother.

"There," she said. "The salt water blesses you, Mark. What do you think we should do next, Megory?"

"Let's burn some sage and send the smoke into the air," I replied. We lit the dried sage and when the billows of smoke rose into the air, Karen took the yarn and fanned the scented smoke out into the room.

"Mark, you are like the smoke now, and you can rise into the clouds and go on your way. I wish I could see the world from the sky like you can."

We watched as the smoke filled the room and then gently wafted out the open windows.

I looked at Karen, wondering what she wanted to do next. Clearly she was the one taking the initiative here. She smiled as she looked at the large bowl and charcoal we had brought along. She began to light a fire.

"Fire is considered sacred in India, you know," I said.

When the fire was burning steadily, Karen put in a couple of strands of yarn. "You don't need this anymore," she told Mark. And then she took some letters. "And I don't need these anymore either," she said. As we watched them burn, she continued, "I know that this part of Mark's life is over. I can remember him, but I don't have to hold on to him. This feels good." We sat and watched the fire until it died away to just a few embers.

The last thing we had was a bowl of earth. "I know what I want to do," Karen exclaimed. She hopped up and ran into the kitchen.

"I have some seeds I've been wanting to plant. I'll plant them here, now. We can keep his memory here in this dirt."

She dug into the earth and placed some seeds around the bowl. As she covered them over, she said, "Mark, we'll keep your memory alive in this way, through growing things and through beautiful flowers. It will be good for both of us this way."

I smiled at her as she patted down the brown dirt and then brushed her hands together. I took some of the salt water and dampened the earth. "Blessings, Mark, on your memory and on the cycle of birth and death."

Karen took her brother's picture and held it to her. "I think I'll ask Mom if she wants to find a garden back east that we can make into a memorial for Mark. I know she'd love to take care of it and that may help her remember Mark in a good way."

"That's a good idea, Karen. Do you feel as if he can move on now?"

She looked around the room. "Yes," she replied. "I think he can be set free."

She looked down at the photo and whispered, "We love you, but it's time for you to go. Good-bye, Mark. Good-bye."

And ever has it been that love knows not its own depth
until the hour of separation.
—KAHLIL GIBRAN

WHEN THE DEATH of a loved one occurs, we are usually not able to be present physically. We may be miles away, involved in our own lives. Even if we are just around the corner, we cannot be present twenty-four hours a day when our loved one is dying. I know of people who missed their loved one's death by a matter of minutes.

We cannot change history.

If a horrible tragedy occurs and we are not present, we have a myriad of feelings—that we should have known and prevented it, or that we should have said something differently the last time we spoke to that person, or that we wish we could have been there to ease the pain and shock of death.

There is often a tremendous guilt that accompanies this. "It was my fault. I should have been there." "Why didn't I leave the house an hour sooner?" "Why didn't I know he was going to die this morning?"

No one can read the future, and no one can change the past.

Rituals cannot change circumstances, but they can certainly help when a tragic or unforeseen death has occurred. For the survivors, rituals can assist in the mourning process, and there are many books available to help us cope with grief and mourning. Here, rather than focusing on the mourner, the emphasis is on the person who has just died and how to help the natural course of releasing the spirit.

Religious thought is concerned with the soul. Each of the faith traditions has a theology of the state of the soul after death, and most acknowledge that there is a fluid nature to a person's soul immediately after she dies. It is in the religions of the East that we see this clearest. In the West, it is much more subtle, but we see it in both the theology and the practical application of the doctrine.

The religions of the East are highly cognizant of special rituals that are needed, especially after an unnatural or untimely death, when it is possible for the soul to be trapped unhappily between this world and the afterlife.

Chronos into *Kairos*

IN THE SACRED act of dying, time is better understood as *kairos*, God's time, than as *chronos*, our own chronological view of time. Rituals transcend both time and distance.

Families and loved ones who have not been able to be present when death occurs often feel at a loss about what to do. Sometimes the restraint is distance, and they were not able to be at the hospital or nursing home in time. Or the patient was in surgery and died on the operating table. Regardless, I tell people that their absence is not as crucial as they think it is.

Whatever the circumstances of death, there are several things to remember. One is that neither actual time nor distance matters. It is possible to be with the loved one in prayer, in thought, and through ritual, at any point and still make a difference. This does not mean that you can change what happened or could have done anything to change it had you been there. But it does mean that, if death does indeed occur, the transition can be made easier and more peaceful through prayer and ritual.

The second thing is to try to put the shock and grief aside for a short period of time, if it is at all possible, and think about what is most needed for the person who has just died. What help does he need in making the transition to the afterlife? How can we, the living, help make that transition more peaceful and calm?

Third, knowing that the soul of the person is still close by, how can loved ones honor and bless it while lovingly cutting the cords to this physical life?

Prayer

HOW DO WE pray when a situation hangs in the balance between life or death? Most faith traditions teach that one must always choose life.

There have been many prayers recited in emergencies, often by people not used to praying. "Oh, God, keep me alive and I will do anything you want me to," or "I know I haven't prayed much in my life, but please spare my husband's life." When we are in crisis, our thoughts easily turn toward the divine.

I have often been asked to help pray in life and death situations, especially when loved ones cannot. It is hard to know how to ask for divine help. I cannot possibly know what should be done. I cannot even pray, "God, make this person live." What I can do is pray that whatever is in the divine plan should happen with grace and with ease.

I am concerned that when many people pray for healing, they mean that they want the body to be made well; they want life. If life is not granted, they feel that God has failed them. But healing does not always mean curing, and death does not always mean failure. To be healed is to be granted wholeness, and sometimes wholeness means entering into the fuller life after death. I do not see death as defeat, and when I pray for healing, I must accept that sometimes death is the best healer.

> THE HOUR OF *departure has arrived, and we go our ways—I to die, and you to live. Which is better only God knows. Perhaps God in his kindness is taking my part and securing me the opportunity of ending my life not only in season but also in the way that is easiest.*
>
> —SOCRATES, 399 B.C.E.

I have learned that if I approach a difficult situation with what the Buddhists call "mindfulness," then I can be assured that things will play out in the best possible way. I do not want to get in the way, nor do I want to mold things to my own wishes. I only want to be present in the situation. The rest is up to God.

When We Cannot Be Present

When our loved one is out of our reach, we can do the following things.

- If the person is across the country, or across the world, find ways to connect the two of you. Use prayer or ritual objects, find a photograph or perhaps a memento to realize the depth of love between you.

- Bring peace and calm to the situation. If there is confusion and panic, center yourself and try to create a sacred space that allows people to become calm, even at a distance. The emotions and surrounding space provide a framework for the person who has just died. If there is chaos, she will have a harder time separating from the physical plane and the concerns of life to move toward the afterlife. If peace and quiet can be established, it will be much better for everyone, living and dead.

• If the death has occurred without your being there, take time to sit and reflect on the person who has just died and to be with her. If you are nearby, you might want to sit with the body. If that is not possible, find a symbol that represents the loved one—a photograph or a memento. Speak from the heart and put things in order between you and the loved one. Know that she is very near and that her presence is very real. Talk out your feelings and make amends. Express your love and sorrow. Treat this time the same way you would if the person had not yet died.

• Don't be afraid to talk to your loved one. There is a closeness immediately after death that is significant. It doesn't last forever, so take advantage of it while you can. You can sit and talk to the physical body, or you can use something symbolic, like a favorite piece of clothing or object. Perhaps you can go to a special place she loved. Even though the body has died, the soul is very close at hand. Take a few moments after hearing of the death to honor the person. Say your last words.

• Bless the body and the life of the person who has just died. This can be done whether you are near the physical body or far away. See Chapter 12, "After Death: Until the Funeral," for specific rituals on cleansing and purifying the body. Even brief prayers that acknowledge the sacredness of the person's life and physical body will help.

- Visualize cutting the cord to this physical life for the person. If the life has been ended abruptly or unexpectedly, there has been no time to prepare for death. Help the person make peace with what has happened to her by cutting the cord to life. Help release the soul by allowing the person to find her way to the afterlife.

Tragedies and Circumstances Beyond Our Control

When the Death Has Already Happened

Many times family members have been sitting for hours or even days with the loved one during illness and pending death. Then just as they take a break for the night to stretch and get some air or some coffee, the patient dies. This is not at all unusual. Often the person dying will wait until he is alone in order to die. He has a reason. It's not to punish or to impose guilt, but rather the dying person desires privacy and solitude. This withdrawal offers the occasion to focus on the other world rather than to be pulled back into the realm of the living. Remember, if this happens, it's the way the person dying wanted it. Hospice worker Kathy Kalina writes:

Some people love a crowd, and will not die until every last relative is gathered in the room. Other people are very private and will wait for everyone to drift off to sleep before they go. One man, whose wife never left his side, waited for her to go to the bathroom and then slipped away. . . .

If someone is not present at the time of death, it

doesn't mean that they've failed or that they're loved less than the ones who are there. For whatever reason, the patient believed that seeing the death would be too hard for that person. Or, perhaps the bond was so strong that their presence would have made leaving harder."[1]

Martin, a friend whose father died several years ago, is still struggling with the memory of missing his father's death by only minutes. He was in town but didn't make it to the hospital in time, arriving just minutes after his father was pronounced dead. To this day he feels as if he failed in some way.

When a colleague's grandmother died, she got the call at home and arrived at the nursing home about an hour later. The nursing home had left her grandmother undisturbed in the room, so the woman was able to take time and sit privately with her.

> IF EVEN DYING *is to be made a social function, then, please, grant me the favor of sneaking out on tiptoe without disturbing the party.*
>
> —DAG HAMMARSKJÖLD
> *Markings*

"I talked to her as if she were alive," she told me. "I could still feel her spirit in the room and I knew she'd been waiting for me. I thought back to some of our visits and apologized to her for being so hurried and distracted during them. It felt good for me to tell her these things, and I knew she could hear me.

"Afterward, I collected her possessions from the room to take home with me. There were some of the things I had given her over the years, a brooch, some notepaper, photographs of my kids. I found myself thinking back to all the times we had together.

"'Remember the Christmas I gave you that brooch, Grandmother?' I said to her. 'That was the year we had the big snowstorm, and you made us hot chocolate as we all came tramping in from the cold.'

---

1. *Midwife for Souls*, p. 63.

"When everything was ready, I sat beside her bed and told her that I was glad she had such a long and happy life.

"'I know you want to be with Grandfather now and all those who are waiting for you. We'll be fine here, and I'll make sure all your grandchildren and great-grandchildren remember you and your life.'

"I gave her a kiss, gathered her things, and then left the room."

Even though she hadn't been there when her grandmother actually died, the time with her afterward was very special. She knew her grandmother heard every word of that conversation.

Distance

When the phone rings and we hear that a family member or friend has died, we are stunned. The world seems to spin and suddenly the room is different. We are far from where the death occurred and suddenly we are faced with decisions about traveling and funeral arrangements. We have to deal with our shock over the actual death and at the same time we have to make practical plans. The death of our loved one often gets lost in the midst of logistics.

I often recommend that people take some time right away to do several things.

- First, take some quiet time to connect with the spirit of the person who has just died. Find a photograph or something he gave you or something that reminds you of him. That way you can capture his spirit and have a chance to be with him.

- Speak of his death. Say you are sorry you couldn't help him when he was dying, but you want to help if you can now. Express sorrow over having to be separated.

- Find as much love within yourself as possible in order to send it to the person.

- Recall the person's life and how much it meant to you. Try to spend time just experiencing those memories before the stress of travel and family dynamics takes over.

- Do something symbolic for the person who has just died. If he loved to garden, sit in the garden and get your hands in the dirt. Plant something; dig up something. The symbolic gesture will be meaningful for both of you.

- Try your best for the moment to look beyond yourself and your grief and stunned reaction. Focus your thoughts on the person who has just died, on sending love to his soul. Create an atmosphere of intimacy with the spirit of the person who has died and is still present near you.

Surgery

Many times I have sat with the friends and families of loved ones in hospital waiting rooms to hear the results of surgery. It is a time of horrible suspension. There is nothing to do but wait while life and death are in the hands of the men and women down the hall. Sometimes the surgery is successful; sometimes it is not. There is no way of telling beforehand if the loved one is going to die. The doctors may say it is a risky surgery and the reality is that one has to prepare for the worst.

When the future of a medical situation is unknown, I often advise the people I work with to prepare for death and yet hope that life be extended. I often think of the prayer of confession in Judaism, called the Vidui.

It says, in part, "I acknowledge to You, Adonai, my God and the God of my ancestors, that my life is in Your hands. May it be Your will to heal me. But if You have decreed that I shall not recover from this illness, I accept the decree from Your hand."

It says we always must ask for and hope for healing, but when death is inevitable, we should accept it with grace.

I worked with a family who were Roman Catholics from Mexico. Their mother, the matriarch of the family, was scheduled for some very extensive surgery, further complicated by her advanced age. The doctors did not give very good odds, but the family insisted that everything be done.

The extended family gathered in her hospital room before the surgery, all very optimistic and encouraging to Mrs. Alvarez. I watched the old woman as her family told her she would be up and about in no time. She was very calm and peaceful as she lay in her bed. Her English was limited, about as limited as my Spanish—but I went over to her and sat with her. Without communicating in words, I knew that she expected she would die. Although I had been asked to help with healing rituals, I began thinking we should do some rituals to prepare her for death.

The big question was how to make the family see that their mother was getting ready to die. First I asked if they had called the priest.

The eldest son replied, "No, we didn't want to bother him."

"There must be a chaplain here at the hospital who is not busy," I replied. "Why don't we ask him to bring your mother the sacrament and maybe even some oil for anointing?"

Immediately that caused alarm.

"The last rites?" they asked.

I sat them down and tried to explain, "Your mother is going through something very difficult right now. She is going on a journey. The surgery itself is very taxing. She needs strength to endure it. If the doctors are able to fix her heart, then she will need strength to heal. If her heart is too weak, then she will also need God's strength."

I paused. "Why don't we ask the priest to give her the strength the sacraments have to offer?"

The family agreed, and the priest came to the room and spent time with Mrs. Alvarez.

Later, when I was talking with one of the daughters, she asked me if I thought her mother was going to die. It is so hard in situations like that to know what to say. You want to give the family hope, but on the other hand, if there is any preparation that needs to be done, it's important not to lose that opportunity.

I chose my words carefully. "I don't know what God has in store for your mother. If I were in that bed and if there were any chance that I would not survive the surgery, I would want to go into the operating room with everything in order, feeling peaceful about everything and everyone I was leaving behind."

The daughter thought a moment. "I don't want her to think we are sending her off to her death."

"Of course not," I exclaimed. "But don't you want her to go knowing how much you love her and that you will be waiting for her? You can put this in God's hands but still be ready in case she does die."

She nodded and wandered over to where her sisters were talking. After several moments of discreet family discussion, she asked me to help with some rituals. "Not to say she is going to die, but just in case, we want her to know how much we love her."

I asked the family to begin focusing on their mother to give her strength for her journey ahead. There were so many people in the room that I asked some of them to gather around her bed and others to make a wider circle around the room. One daughter had a Bible, and I asked that she read from it as the rest of her family gently placed their hands on their mother and prayed for God's grace. The feeling of power surged as all those people began to focus on one thing only, their mother. I asked each person to step from the circle and go to Mrs. Alvarez and tell her how much she meant to him or her.

"Tell her why you love her so much," I said.

One by one, they went to her and spoke from the heart, some in whispers into her ear, some speaking boldly so all could hear. It was a very powerful experience for each member of that family and most of all for Mrs. Alvarez.

The elderly woman survived the surgery, but only for a few days. She never regained consciousness, so the last thing she knew was how much her family loved her.

Dr. Rachel Naomi Remen, cofounder and medical director of the Commonwealth Cancer Help Program, is the author of the book *Kitchen Table Wisdom: Stories That Heal.* She writes about the use of rituals with someone going into surgery:

> *For more than twenty years I have offered a very simple yet powerful ritual to people before their radiation, chemotherapy, or surgery. I suggest they meet together with some of their closest friends and family the day before their procedure. It does not matter how large or small the group is, but it is important that it be made up of those who are connected to them through a bond of the heart.*
>
> *Before this meeting I suggest they find an ordinary stone, a piece of the earth, big enough to fit in the palm of their hand, and bring it to the meeting with them. The ritual begins by having everyone sit in a circle. In any order they wish to speak, each person tells the story of a time when they too faced a crisis. People may talk about the death of important persons, the loss of jobs or of relationships, or even about their own illnesses. The person who is speaking holds the stone the patient has brought. When they finish telling their story of survival, they take a moment to reflect on the personal quality that they feel helped them come through that difficult time. People will say such things as, "What brought me through was determination," "What brought me through was faith," "What brought me through was humor." When they have named the quality of their strength, they speak directly to the person preparing for surgery or treatment, saying, "I put determination*

*into this stone for you," or, "I put faith into this stone
for you."*

*Often what people say is surprising. Sometimes they
tell of crises that occurred when they were young or in
wartime that others, even family members, may not
have known before, or they attribute their survival to
qualities that are not ordinarily seen as strengths. It is
usually a moving and intimate meeting and often all the
people who participate say that they feel strengthened
and inspired by it. After everyone has spoken the stone
is given back to the patient, who takes it with them to
the hospital, to keep nearby and hold in their hand
when things get hard.*[2]

Medical Emergencies

If you walk into any emergency room, you will see critical situations where life and death are on the line. Medical professionals are trained to assess the threatening situations and to fix
them as quickly as possible. The highest priority is to combat
and forestall death. If someone has a heart attack, doctors rush
in to save the person, often attaching lifesaving machines to
help him live. The bystanders can only watch from a distance
as their loved one is at the center of great commotion.

I met a woman at a conference whose husband had had a
heart attack some months before while they were having dinner.
She immediately called 911, and as soon as the ambulance
arrived, she was pushed into the background. Suddenly her husband was in the care and control of medical people. They rushed
him to the hospital where he died a short time later. When I met
her, the woman was still grieving, but she was very expressive
about how pushed aside she felt. Throughout the process, all she
felt she could do at the time was sit and wait.

"What would you have done differently?" I asked.

---

2. *Kitchen Table Wisdom*, pp. 151–52.

She replied, "After hearing what you said about distance and time not making such a difference, I would have done things very differently. First of all, I would have tried praying rather than panicking. All I did in that waiting room was sit and panic. It was awful. I knew he was going to die, and my thoughts and fears made it all worse. No one came to tell me what was going on. I could have been invisible for all they cared.

"I sat there for hours, holding his watch in my hands, turning it over and over. Rather than playing with it nervously, I could have used the watch to focus my energy.

"Looking back, I would have called everyone and had them come to be with me so we could pray. I didn't have to have the panic around me; we could have created a calm and peaceful atmosphere. I know Kevin didn't have that where he was, so I could have created it for him from where I was.

"And instead of worrying and trying to imagine the worst, I would have tried to find a way to tell him how much I loved him and wanted him to be all right. After thirty years of marriage, I know we could have communicated without being physically present with each other. I had that watch, and it was the perfect object to hold in prayer and to symbolize how much he meant to me."

I asked her if she thought it would have made a difference in his death.

"I don't know if he would have lived if I had done those things. It doesn't do any good to think about that now. But you know what, Megory? It would have helped me to know he died in a different way. I never had a chance to tell him how much I loved him. That was wrong. I know he knows that, but to be able to say it out loud to him—well, I feel so bad that I couldn't do it."

Tragedies

Tragic deaths occur every day. When we see stories on the news, we think "how horrible." Most of the time, tragedies do not come directly into our own life, but sometimes they do happen to us. Our lives change in an instant because something horrible happens to us or to someone we love.

The questions we ask during tragedies are good questions and right questions because they come from the very core of our heart and soul. "Why is God doing this?" or as in Psalm 22, "Why has God abandoned me?" Even at his own death, Jesus called out, "My God, my God, why have you forsaken me?" Many times it is just, "Why me?"

There are philosophers, theologians, and clergy who have attempted to answer these ageless human questions. I find that I keep coming back to the mystery of it all. "I just don't know" is the most honest response I can usually offer. When someone is going through tragedy, attempts at answers are not always what the heart needs to hear. I have found myself many times getting angry at the stock answer, "It must be God's will."

Madeleine L'Engle, in writing about her husband Hugh's death from cancer, said:

> *Consequences: cancer is a result of consequences. It is not sent as a punishment. I do not have to make the repulsive theological error of feeling that I have to see cancer as God's will for my husband. I do not want anything to do with that kind of God. Cancer is not God's will. The death of a child is not God's will. The deaths from automobile accidents during this long holiday weekend are not God's will. I would rather have no God at all than that kind of punitive God. Tragedies are consequences of human actions, and the only God worth believing in does not cause the tragedies but lovingly comes into the anguish with us.*[3]

3. Madeleine L'Engle, *Two-Part Invention: The Story of a Marriage* (New York: Farrar, Straus & Giroux, 1988), p. 172.

For the person who has died, the worst part is over. Again, it is the soul's transition that is of concern. Once I do a ritual of release, I try to find some way to help the mourners come to terms with their shock and grief. Over time, it is important to recognize that the loved one has gone and that there is a difference between remembering her in love and holding on in anger and grief. Sometimes it takes doing a letting-go ritual many times for the mourners to finally transform their feelings into acceptance. Sogyal Rinpoche says in *The Tibetan Book of Living and Dying,* "Some families resist letting their loved one go, thinking that to do so is a betrayal, and a sign that they don't love them enough."[4] But that is not the case. The love that was there for the person who died can be transformed wonderfully into something positive in the face of tragedy and sorrow.

Conclusion

DISTANCE AND TIME do not mean that the loved ones cannot be fully present ritually when someone has died. The soul often stays close by after death, and our feelings and actions can have impact on its transition to the afterlife. There are rituals that can help lead the soul peacefully, regardless of how death occurred. And there are ways we can be with the person who has died in a meaningful and loving way for our final good-byes.

4. Sogyal Rinpoche, *The Tibetan Book of Living and Dying* (San Francisco: HarperSanFrancisco, 1993), p. 184.

CHAPTER 10

Dying Alone

P AUL WAS ALONE in the city. He couldn't have been more
than a teenager, eighteen or nineteen at the most, and
he had AIDS. Annie, a social worker friend of mine,
called me about him, knowing his situation and hoping I might
be able to help. He had gotten lost in the social services system,
and she was concerned that he had no one to be with him when
he died. He didn't want to be taken to the hospital, so he was
left on his own.

I was a bit nervous as I walked into his small and dingy
rented room in the middle of a seedy part of town. I saw a child
alone in his bed, and my heart went out to him. He had long,
stringy, dirty blond hair that was matted to his pillow, and his
body was reduced to bones protruding through his flesh. My
first thought was that he needed his mother.

Annie had told me Paul's story. He'd run away from home
several years before and ended up in San Francisco with other

gay runaways. His family was quite religious and had been extremely upset when he'd come out to them as homosexual. Their strict religious convictions left them with a huge dilemma. Would they adhere to their church teachings at the expense of their own son? Or would they try to accept their son and his homosexuality at the expense of their church and community? I had known many cases where it came down to this choice, and regardless of the decision at the end, no one was the winner. Here I was again, seeing an abandoned child left to die alone and in pain.

Paul was barely conscious as I sat down on the side of his bed. "My name is Megory," I told him. "Your social worker thought it would be all right if I came to sit with you for awhile. She didn't want you to be alone."

Paul began to cry. There were no words to his sobs, just the need for release. I held him and let him cry. When he had tired himself out, he drifted back to sleep. I looked around the room and saw wall-to-wall mess: papers, dishes, clothing, and medicine strewn all over the floor. I began clearing the space around the bed, freshening up his room and opening the window to let in some air. It felt chaotic, looked chaotic, and even smelled chaotic. This could not be comforting for him at all. When he woke up, I had a basin of water and a fresh cloth, ready to tidy him up. It seemed to revive him, and he talked to me as I gave him the sponge bath.

He spoke about his family and "back home."

"I quit school and left," he said. "It was too dictatorial. Everything we did had to be the church. Church this and church that. I hated it."

"You didn't fit in," I said. He nodded slowly.

"I couldn't be what they wanted me to be, so I left. I came here because I thought everyone here would have to accept me. If you're gay, you come here."

"Did you find what you needed?" I asked.

"Well," he paused, "I don't know. I found other kids like me, but they were all pretty screwed up too. No one knew what to do. So we hung out and had fun. No one told us what to do, no one yelled at us."

"And no one took care of you either, did they?"

"No," he whispered.

"When did you get sick?"

"It got really bad last year. I guess I didn't think that AIDS would happen to me; we just wanted to have fun, that's all. When I first got sick, I didn't know what to do. I went to the clinic and they helped out there. Social Services came and they sent Annie to help me. She's pretty nice."

"She tried calling your parents, didn't she? Did you ask her to?"

He nodded. "I wanted to go home."

"What did they say?"

"I guess the church leaders told them to say no. They wouldn't talk to me or let me come home. They said I was already dead." The tears started pouring down his face.

"I'm so sorry, Paul. That's not right. It's a bad situation on both sides, but they shouldn't have told your family not to bring you back home. You must miss your folks very much."

He nodded again.

"You're a long way from home, but maybe we can help bring home here for you. Do you want to try?"

"Yes," he said, a new light in his eyes.

I tried to think of ways to bring a bit of home and a bit of the love he needed to this sad and empty room. I looked around for some clue.

"What was your bedroom like at home? How was it arranged?"

He thought for a moment and then answered, "Well, it was a bit smaller than this, with the bed over in that corner and the nightstand next to it."

"You think we can rearrange it to look like your room?"

He gave me a huge grin. "I bet we could, if all this other stuff is trashed."

"That's easy enough. What do you think closets are for?" I laughed as I began scooping up piles of clothes and trash and putting them away.

"Now hold on. I am going to move this bed into the corner. I'll try not to jiggle you too much." With that I slowly moved the bed into the corner of the room. Paul closed his eyes and held on to the sides of the bed. When he opened his eyes, he immediately began giving me directions on what to do next.

"You're a long way from home, but maybe we can help bring home here for you. Do you want to try?"

"Okay, now the nightstand, and then move the dresser over against that wall there."

"Yes, sir!" I chuckled, thinking, "This is going to work."

When we finished the arranging, I sat on the bed and looked around. "Not bad," I told him.

Paul replied, "Yeah, not bad. If only we had stuff for the walls."

"Do you have any pictures of your family here?" I asked.

"In the drawer over there. I brought some with me when I ran away."

I went to the drawer and found not only several pictures of his family but also a baseball mitt and, of all things, a lightly scented woman's scarf. I put the scarf on the dresser top and brought the photos and the mitt back to the bed. I asked him to tell me about the pictures.

"Oh, well, that's just my mom and dad, my sister and me. It's in front of our house."

"And this one?" I asked.

"That's me and my best friend Jeff."

"And this is your baseball mitt."

Paul grinned. "Yeah, I even got to use it a few times here. I was on the team back home. My dad bought this for me on my fourteenth birthday."

He sat quietly for a moment and then started crying again. I encouraged him to hold the mitt, and he rocked back and forth, cradling it.

I stroked his forehead and said softly, "Paul, your mother and father really love you and wish they could be here with you. They wish they could hold you and make everything better. Why don't you close your eyes and picture them in your mind right now? Picture your house and your bedroom. Do you see them now?"

Paul nodded, eyes tightly closed.

"Can you smell something wonderful coming from the kitchen? What's your mother cooking?"

He smiled. "Pancakes," he said. "I can smell the pancakes. I think I could eat a million of them."

Smiling, I asked, "And where is your father?"

"He's in the family room watching TV, and Kathy is in her room playing."

"Well, just stay with those pictures inside your mind. Smell those good smells and surround yourself with all those good feelings. Forget about anything bad. Right now, everything you have is good."

With those images he drifted in and out of sleep. After a few hours, he woke up crying for his mother.

"She's not here now, Paul. She'll be back soon." He was holding on to his baseball mitt like a pillow, rocking back and forth, calling again and again for his mother.

My mind flashed to the scarf still on top of the dresser. It must be his mother's, I thought. I went to get it and unfolded it. It was a large square scarf, exactly the right size for what I had in mind. I took Paul's pillow and wrapped the scarf around it, tying the ends at the back. Paul noticed the faint scent immediately.

"Mommy? Are you here? Is that you?"

"Here she is, Paul. Can you feel her now?" I put the pillow up against his side.

He grabbed the pillow and pulled it to himself, crying, "Mommy, Mommy, what took you so long?"

The scent of the scarf seemed to be all he needed. I sat beside him, knowing that for this moment, he was with his mother in the only way he could be. It was safe for Paul to die now.

There is no death. There is only me . . . me . . . me . . .
who is going to die.
—ANDRÉ MALRAUX
The Royal Way

Western Society Today

IN DAYS GONE by and in different cultures around the world, generations grew up in a society where families stayed intact and always lived nearby. Children never moved far from their homes, and when it was time for the older generation to retire, they did so in their lifelong setting. If they needed care, their children were close at hand. If there was someone in the family who was disabled or unable to care for himself, family members were usually the ones who sacrificed themselves to do it. Illness and dying were family affairs. No one was left to die alone. You knew you had a place to be and someone to care for you.

This is no longer the case. Families and communities have become transient. People leave their community of birth for many reasons. Children grow up and move out into the wider world. Parents retire and move away. Hundreds of miles often separate the generations, and we find that people in their forties and fifties who are at the peak of family responsibilities are also dealing long distance with parents who are elderly, ailing, or dying. Men and women across the country are overwhelmed with these double family responsibilities. This has left many elderly and infirm people alone, without community or family.

Because we place such a high value on work-oriented aspects of our lives, we look at those who are ill or elderly as drains on our society. We don't know what to do with those who need care, and because of the high cost of health care, we label them as burdens and cast them aside.

For Those Who Are Alone and Dying

THOSE WHO ARE alone and dying have a difficult time navigating the health care system or the daunting logistics of social services. The elderly, especially, are most vulnerable. But anyone, regardless of age, is at a disadvantage if she faces a life-threatening illness alone. For example, in San Francisco there is a large population facing AIDS. Many of these men and women are alone in their struggle. If they have been alienated from their families because of their sexuality, they have the double burden of facing illness in the midst of strangers. Illness means loss of work, and the resulting poverty often makes it impossible to meet the challenges of finding care and simply staying alive. No one wants to provide help for those who are destitute and dying, and there are very few places to turn for those who cannot survive on their own.

At a recent conference a woman asked me about my work. As I was explaining it to her, she said, "But what do you do if you have to die all by yourself?"

I looked at her and asked, "Are you dying?"

She nodded yes.

I pointed to some chairs along the wall and said, "Let's go sit and talk."

She explained to me that she had cancer and that she lived by herself. She had some friends, and they were a help sometimes, but most of the time she had to take care of herself. She was plugged into social services, so a visiting nurse came by periodically. And when the situation worsened, she explained, the nurse would come more often.

"It's not the same as having someone around all the time, though," she continued. "I guess it's up to me how I want to do this."

"What are your friends willing to do?" I asked.

"Oh, they sometimes help when I need a ride to the doctor's office, or they'll pick up some food for me when I can't get to the store. But they all have their own lives and their own families. It's catch as catch can."

"What about a religious connection? Do you belong to a church or synagogue?" I asked.

She nodded. "I go to a Buddhist church, and I'm on their prayer list. Sometimes one of the members comes over after services. I never know when, though, so I can't really count on anything there."

"Okay. I think I get the picture," I said. "Tell me what's the most important thing for you as you go through this. What do you want to happen? Realistically."

She thought for a moment. "I want to feel safe. I want to be able to have something there so I won't get really panicked at the end. I don't want to die in the hospital; I hate it there. I don't mind being alone as much as I mind being scared."

"What makes you feel safe?" I asked.

She smiled. "I want my things around me, and I want my own bed. And when the time comes, I just want to go to sleep and die. None of those crazy medical heroics. I'm tired of my body hurting so much and I'm tired of watching it fall apart. Just give me a couple of days to put my things in order and let me fall asleep and not wake up. That's how I want to die."

"Where do you have control? What can you do now?" I asked.

"Well," she replied, "I guess I can begin sorting out my things. I still have some time; I don't think it will get bad again for a month or so."

"Right," I said. "You can make your will and sort through your papers so they're in order. You can put your relationships in order too. Talk to friends and let them know what you're doing."

"Yes," she said, "I can do that. I can also let them know that I am getting myself ready. Maybe that will help me not be so afraid."

"You know, even if they can't be with you every day, I am sure they want to check in with you when they can. Is there someone who might be able to organize a phone tree? That way they know someone is checking in on you each day," I suggested.

"Well, most of them don't really know each other very well," she said slowly.

"So here's a chance for them to come together for a common purpose," I said. "If one person can organize the logistics, then I am sure everyone would be willing to do their part. It might give them an opportunity to face some hard things in their own lives too. You aren't asking them to come take care of you—I'm only talking about a check-in phone call every day and perhaps occasional errands or help with food. But at least you can try to have one person whose responsibility it is to see what you need each day."

"Then no one person would feel overwhelmed. There would be a back-up system," she smiled. "I have this fear of being too much of a burden."

I took her hand. "Maybe they want to help but don't know how."

"I think this could work. I'll ask my friend Nancy if she could manage the schedule. She'd be good at that. And she could even check in with my visiting nurse if there was a problem. You know, if someone had a conflict or something, they could work it out with Nancy and not me. That way they wouldn't worry about letting me down."

"Exactly," I said. "You shouldn't be the one to arrange all this. Don't put yourself in that position. Now what about when the time comes for you to die? What do you want to do there?"

"Well, if I know that someone is looking in on me every day, then I won't be quite so scared." She looked as if half her worries just flew out the window. "But," her eyes got dark for a minute, "I still have to think about dying all alone."

"But there is a way to prepare for that too," I suggested.

She looked at me questioningly.

"Can you think about what you need to do to give yourself comfort and safety? What can you bring into your room to help you?"

"You mean as in physical things?"

"Yes," I replied.

She thought for a few minutes.

"The things around me are really important. I guess I want some music and my favorite books. Maybe even some of my favorite clothes. And I have this doll . . . ," she blushed in embarrassment.

I smiled and asked her if it was an old doll.

"Yes," she replied. "I got her when I was about four from my grandmother. She's always been in my room. I've had her my whole life." Her eyes began tearing up. "Do you think it's childish to want her there with me when I die?"

"No, not at all," I replied gently. "You love her and she helps take care of you."

The woman nodded, staring at her hands folded in her lap.

"Maybe you could go home and think about gathering all the things that help take care of you and begin getting them ready," I suggested.

She nodded again, brushing the tears from her eyes, and then walked away.

I don't know what happened to her, or how and when she died, but I think she was able to see how to take some control while there was still time. I think she began to understand how to create her own care system and to know what was important to her in the end. I hope that someone was with her. But if not, I am sure her much-loved doll was not far away.

Bringing in Support

If you are facing death on your own, there are ways to be less isolated and more supported that won't leave you feeling that you will be a burden to any one person or group. The most crucial thing is to identify the things that are important to you and to take control and make them happen. This means creating an environment and support system that will honor your process of sacred dying.

FRIENDS AND ACQUAINTANCES

Even though most people cannot offer large amounts of time and energy to assist during this time, most people are willing to help in small ways. There may be no one person who can facilitate all the arrangements, but various people can attend to small needs. Combine forces; ask each one to do a small amount. When people stop in to visit, ask for specific things that cannot be handled alone. If you tell people what you need, they are more likely to respond than if they have to second-guess.

Ask friends to help move furniture so you're more comfortable and can function more easily. Ask for help in preparing food. Ask them to bring you certain meaningful items. Ask them to set up music so it is nearby or to find books on tape for you to listen to.

If certain friends are spiritually connected, ask them to pray or meditate with you. If you want to sanctify the bedroom and dedicate it to having a peaceful death, then ask those who have a strong spiritual basis to help. They may help with cleansing rituals, things you cannot do by yourself, things that require a level of stamina, energy, and strength that you no longer have.

Many communities are defined by ethnic ties. In our multicultural world, our closest-knit ties are often ethnic. In urban areas, racial and ethnic communities are set up to help others in need. If the tie is there, even when you thought it had been broken long ago, there may be help.

RELIGIOUS SUPPORT

Houses of worship are generally not social service agencies, but most have volunteers to help with shut-ins and those who are dying. Contact the institution where you have membership, but if you have none, contact a neighborhood congregation and see if they can help. Well-established congregations with a reputation for outreach ministries offer the best chance for arranging visits to nonmembers. Each faith community and congregation handles pastoral concerns in different ways, but compassionate outreach is a part of virtually every religious congregation. That being said, it is also true that they're not usually a source of consistent care. However, if you go to them with specific needs, most congregations will respond. Asking for help is almost always the hardest part, but remember, providing for the spiritual is what congregations and clergy are about, and most people really do want to help. They only want to know what is most needed.

Sometimes a pastoral visit will be arranged. What can you expect from a pastoral visit? You can ask for time to talk about the illness and issues around dying, both practical and spiritual. The clergy or lay visitors know how to address the spiritual dynamics of death and the afterlife. You can ask for support, both emotionally and spiritually, as you go through this difficult experience. You can ask for prayers, and it is appropriate to request any specific rituals the faith offers, like communion, baptism, anointing, or laying on of hands. You can also ask for assistance in funeral and burial planning.

RELIGIOUS SOCIAL SERVICES

In many major cities there are religious social services agencies. Catholic Charities and Jewish Social Services are nationally known.

A national organization called Stephen Ministries, used by many Christian churches, enables congregations of all denominations to train church members to go into the community with care and support for those in need. These church members are not counselors or social workers, but they do minister on a regular basis to people who are ill or infirm. They are trained to know how to listen and care and most of all to be of spiritual help. Many congregations across the country take part in the Stephen Ministries and let their communities know they are involved in this way. A Stephen Ministries church will have the resources and training to assist people who are alone and dying.[1]

Massage Therapists

Many professional therapists provide massages to the sick and the dying. They come into the hospital or home and work with patients to relieve pain and stress. This is a good support for those on their own, those who have no one to count on for physical comfort. Your social services network or local hospital may know how to find therapists, or a traditional massage therapist may know of someone who does this specialized work.

Music Therapists

A growing number of music therapists work with the ill and the dying. They are musicians who visit patients and play music to help soothe and comfort or to aid in meditation. There are organizations with both trained music thanatologists and volunteers practicing in scattered parts of the country. If no one knows about such practitioners locally, check the yellow pages or try calling a local music therapist for names of people who do this particular work.

Network of "Midwives"

Many people sit with the dying as part of their volunteer work. Some of them are known as "Midwives for the Dying." Your local hospice association may offer referrals for these specialized volunteers. These volunteers are usually not trained health care professionals and should not be considered substitutes for

---

1. The Stephen Ministries headquarters is located in St. Louis, Missouri. The Web address is www.stephenministries.com.

medical providers. Rather, midwives sit and watch, to comfort and be a presence with those who are dying. They usually have a strong sense of the spiritual and can help bring prayer and peacefulness into the experience.

Creating a Sacred Experience

There are numerous practical ways to make dying alone a sacred experience.

RITUALS OF SACRED SPACE AND PROTECTION

It is not always easy to create sacred space by oneself for such a major transition as death, but it is possible. It is important to bring into the room as much of the sacred as possible. Some people like to have protection around the room. One woman had some holy water and each night, before turning off her light, would sprinkle it around the room asking for divine protection as she slept. Another kept sage by her bedside, and when she could, she would burn some as a cleansing.

PRAYER

Prayer is something each person can do alone. It can be extensive, or it can be simple. It can be extemporaneous, or it can be a prayer from a book. It only requires a heart turned toward the divine, boldly or hesitantly. There are many prayers from different faith traditions cited in the appendix. A particularly poignant prayer I use is Marianne Williamson's "A Prayer for a Peaceful Death," from her book of prayers, *Illuminata*.

> *Dear God,*
> *I think that I am going to die.*
> *I think I'm going to leave this world.*
> *Give me the strength, Lord, that I might not fear.*

To read the rest of the prayer, please turn to page 314–315 in the appendix.

Practical Planning

Making funeral and burial plans are practical necessities, even though emotionally it may be extremely difficult. Many prefer to make these decisions on their own; others want help from friends or social services. Regardless, making these preparations is a way of taking control and seeing that your death and burial are handled in a way you want. There are many books available about the necessary legal requirements, and each state and county is different in how it handles death certificates and burial necessities.

Some things you may wish to consider are a will, a living will, the executor of your affairs, burial or cremation (if there is no money for a burial, the county of residence provides that service), and a funeral or memorial service. Some people prefer to leave detailed instructions; others prefer to leave it open.

For Those Who Wish to Help People Dying Alone

YOU MAY KNOW someone who lives alone and is ill and may be dying. He may be a client, a neighbor, or someone from your religious congregation. You can help the person in many small ways. It does not have to be a full-time commitment; any small offering makes a difference.

Someone who is dying alone feels as if the world has no place for him. It feels as if every connection to friends or family has been severed. That may be true for the most part, but there is usually something, an association somewhere, that can be made, even if it is only through memory. When I speak with those who are alone, I ask about any connection I can think of, like family, friends, animals, special interests.

When you offer your time to someone dying, consider the following.

Be present.

Even if you cannot spend much time with the person, use the encounter you do have to be fully there. This time is not about you or your needs. Leave everything else outside the door and respond to what the person needs and wants at that particular moment. Listen to what the dying person is asking for and try to respond the best you can. The person may need to talk about what is happening to her. Or she may need some very practical solutions, like help with food or transportation. If you are offering spiritual assistance, be open to what the person truly needs for the journey.

Be consistent.

If you promise to show up or to do something for the person, do it. Often you are his only resource for help. He is counting on you. Don't let him down. Even if you can come only once every few weeks, be there consistently and reliably. You are a strong link to the outside world, and it is important to be reliable.

Offer practical help.

Try to anticipate what the person may need, but always ask. Make suggestions. Can you do something around the house? Can you help straighten up the room? Vacuum or do dishes? Laundry? Errands are always difficult for someone housebound. Offer to go to the pharmacy or to buy groceries and make meals that can be reheated.

Find the right community or link.

Find the connections the person has to any community, religion, family, neighborhood, activity, and so on, and follow up. People from the most unlikely sources may be willing to assist in providing a support for this person. If there is truly no connection to a community, then help find whatever unseen link there is to assure the person of a loving presence. Like Paul in the story above, the love may have to be pulled in from symbolic sources. There is always a path to love, although you may have to search hard to find it.

Here are some ways to incorporate links to help someone feel less alienated:

- *Photos*
Photographs are links to other people and experiences. They often represent whatever connections the person has to love and concern.

- *Mementos*
Mementos are another link, through memories, to people or things that mean a lot to the individual. They often bring comfort as well as reassurance.

- *Senses*
Use the senses to evoke memories. Paul responded very strongly to the sense of smell. Be creative and use what is around you. Let the dying person lead you to his connection to love.

Enlist the aid of animals.

Many times people who are alone have pets. Animals provide an enormous amount of love and support.[2] Frequently during visiting hours at local hospitals, backpacks have been used surreptitiously to smuggle in a much loved pet. I have been present at many vigils where a cat or dog has curled up with the person dying. Animals have a strong intuitive sense of what is happening; they know that love is needed now more than ever before. I have seen people reach out and cling to their longtime animal companions, petting them and crying into their fur, letting out all of the pain and fear, knowing that the animal will hold it for them and give back unconditional love and comfort.

I sat with Michael in the AIDS ward of the hospital. A neighbor was there and had brought in Michael's cat, Lucy. She was mostly white with a few red spots around her face. Michael held Lucy tightly to his chest. She burrowed into him, licking his chin now and then. Michael's hands could not stay still; he

2. There are organizations that facilitate the use of pets to visit the sick and the dying. One is called Therapy Dogs, Inc.

kept petting her and stroking her fur. I could hear her deep purr all the way across the room.

As we prayed for Michael, we asked that Lucy help ease him into death. We knew that she was the one who could give him the most comfort. I watched both Michael and Lucy as the sun began to set. His hands began to fall from her body, and at that moment Lucy stood and butted her head against his face. He did not move, but she continued to nudge him, back and forth. Finally, realizing that he was not going to respond, she stood on his chest, raised her head, and began to cry. It was a terrible wail. It was a wail that I think all humans should know how to do. It was a wail of death.

Loneliness Versus Solitude

There is a difference between being alone because of a personal desire for a solitary experience and being forced to live in loneliness and isolation. Living a solitary life has many rewards, and one must always respect the other's privacy. On the other hand, when a person is dying, there are many things that cannot be managed alone. Also, the more lonely a person is, the more difficult it is for her to accept help. Helpers must walk a fine line in that situation.

When someone is forced into isolation, for whatever reason, loneliness can become overwhelming. The act of your reaching out and trying to help in any way possible is an act of love.

Conclusion

WHETHER YOU ARE the person faced with dying alone or are the one who helps provide support and care to someone, there are ways to make dying less frightening and isolating. There are practical ways of inviting the larger community to help, and there are ways of making this difficult journey a bit more intimate and comforting, and certainly more sacred. Finding where the love is, seen and unseen—and therefore where the sacredness is—is the ultimate solution.

CHAPTER 11

Intentional Death:
Ending Life Support

I DREADED CALLS LIKE this. A family at the hospital needed help when the doctors stopped life support for their little boy.

David and Susie were in their late thirties, and this was their younger child, Christopher, who was not quite two. He had come down with a bad case of pneumonia several months before and had eventually gone into a coma. By the third day the doctors told them he was brain dead and put him on life support. He had been like that for about six weeks. Everyone was convinced there was no hope. It was time to let him die.

The decision to end life support had already been made, so all I needed to do was to help them create some rituals while the machines were being turned off. We had some time in which to talk it through and do some planning.

"Tell me about Christopher," I said.

"He was such a good baby," Susie replied. She was composed for the moment but clearly on the edge of falling apart.

"He's our second child so we knew a bit more about what to expect. He's always into something. I guess that's a stage he's in—almost two—I have to keep an eye on him all the time. He is so curious. Or was. I don't know if I should talk about him as if he is still alive or as if he is already dead."

"It's neither one, is it?" I said.

She looked at me and nodded. "Yes, exactly."

"Then why don't we talk about him for the moment as if he was still with us. He is, in a way."

David interjected, "But we have to get used to thinking about him dying."

"Well," I considered the situation carefully, "perhaps the rituals we do together can help make that transition. We can create rituals for Christopher to let go of this life and to help you let go of him too."

Susie and David told me about Christopher's love for living and for learning new things and about his older sister, Emma, who was almost five. They talked about their religious beliefs. David was born and raised Lutheran, but they only went to church now and then. Susie was Chinese-American and grew up with a mixture of Protestantism and Buddhism. Susie was closer to her Buddhist grandmother than to anyone else in her family and wanted her to be with them as they ended Christopher's life. Other relatives would join them later for the funeral.

"Let's talk for a minute about why rituals help," I said. "They can take us from one level of understanding or awareness to the next. Christopher is in a kind of limbo right now. His body is alive, but his soul doesn't know where to go. He can't move into death because those machines are still holding him in his body. On the other hand, his soul cannot return to you and to his life as a two-year-old little boy because his body just can't support that on its own. So he's stuck."

"You know, my grandmother said the exact same thing,"

said Susie. "She talked about his soul not being able to travel on, that he was caught in the middle between two worlds."

"Right. The rituals we do can help him gently move out of that middle place. We can prepare him, rather than just turning off the machines suddenly. That way the transition will be more peaceful for him." I touched Susie's hand lightly.

"We can almost carry him from life into death with our prayers."

We talked for a few more minutes and then arranged to meet again the next morning. I asked them to bring a few things with them, and they went home seeming a little more secure in their decision and how it would be carried out.

> "HIS BODY IS *alive, but his soul doesn't know where to go. He can't move into death because those machines are still holding him in his body."*

The next morning I met Susie and David at the hospital. Susie's grandmother was there, and in a corner by herself was Emma. She was tiny and looking more like her Chinese mother than her German father. She was beautiful. I knelt down and introduced myself to her. She was silent, but her eyes were wide, taking in everything around her.

We walked into Christopher's room and began. The family wanted to be with him for a few minutes before the medical staff joined us.

The room was filled with machines making all sorts of pumping and beeping and swooshing sounds. In the middle of all that was a huge crib, and in that crib was a very small boy. He had black hair and very pale skin, and he seemed to be swallowed up by all the tubes and monitors.

We began by gathering around Christopher's crib. I opened in prayer, asking God to be present in the room and with all the people there. I asked that special help be given to us in this very difficult thing we needed to do. Susie's grandmother prayed in Chinese, and Susie smiled, telling us that her grandmother asked especially that the good spirits come down to assist us. Emma looked up to the ceiling, hoping, I imagined, to see an angel or two.

We then began to make Christopher feel more comfortable. David rearranged his bed sheets. Susie put some new socks on his feet. They had each brought in something he was attached to, and, in turn, each member of the family placed it next to him.

Susie leaned into the crib and put in a stuffed rabbit. David placed Christopher's favorite bowl and spoon beside him and then laid a very worn-out copy of *Goodnight Moon* beside his hand. The grandmother had a red jacket she made for him and tried putting it on him around all the tubes and monitors. And then David lifted up Emma so she could give him his pillow from home. They lifted his head and put it under him.

"Let's take a few minutes and tell Christopher thank you for being here with us during his short life," I said.

David began, taking Christopher's small hand in his. "Son, I remember when you were born. I was so very happy. You brought such joy to me. I would look into your eyes and see all the things you were going to do when you grew up. Well, I guess you won't get a chance now. But we will always remember all the things you *did* do. You loved to dig. Remember when you dug up all those flower bulbs your mother had just planted?" He looked over at his wife who was crying now.

"And remember last Christmas when we played all afternoon with your new train set? I'll keep it for you, Chris. I'll keep it going for you. Thank you, son. Thank you for being our baby."

"I want to go next, Daddy," Emma said, looking back and forth from her father to her mother.

"Sure, honey."

"Can I get into the crib with him?"

David looked at me, questioningly.

"I don't see why not," I said.

He picked her up and swung her over the bars of the bed. Emma sat cross-legged next to her brother and began.

"Christopher, it's me, Emma. Can you hear me?" She waited a moment. "Okay. I'm going to go next." She began stroking his hair, combing it with her fingers back from his forehead.

"Chrisser, Mommy and Daddy told me that it was time for you to leave. You are going to die. I really don't want you to go, but they say you have to. Will you remember me in heaven? Will you wait for me to get there too, so we can play together? I'm not sure when I can come, so watch for me, okay?"

Her parents' eyes were wide.

"I will help you paint when we both are in heaven. Just let me know what you want to play with and I will help. I like helping you. I'll even bring your red jacket if it gets cold there."

"Why don't you tell him thank you for being your brother, Emma?" asked David.

"Okay," replied Emma. "I like having a little brother. Thank you for being mine. I remember when you were a baby and cried a lot. I still liked you even then. Remember when you fell out of your crib and I helped pick you up? Or when I tried teaching you how to brush your hair? Or when I showed you how to flush the toilet?" She giggled. "You did that all day long."

Emma looked up at her parents with a grin on her face and then back at her brother. She leaned over and began whispering in his ear, giggling and babbling at the same time. None of us could make out what she was saying, but that was exactly the way it should have been. The look of conspiracy in her eyes was delightful.

"'Bye, Chrisser," she finally said as she began to stand up. "I'll see you when I get to heaven. Wait for me there." She lifted her arms up to her father, and he gently brought her out of the crib.

We all stood there quietly for a moment, and then the grandmother leaned over the bars and began talking, half in English and half in Chinese. She stroked his arm and his face over and over again. She clearly loved this little boy, this great-grandson of hers.

As she stepped back, we each looked at Susie. This was going to be the hardest.

"My baby," she cried. "You're my baby. Thank you for coming to us. I love you so much, and you were such a good baby. You made me so happy. I wish I could make this all better, but I can't. I'm your mother, and I can't make it go away. I'm sorry, sweetheart." She burst into tears and fell into David's arms.

"Darling, tell him thank you for being here with us this long."

"Yes, all right." she said. "Chrisser, thank you for being my little boy. We will always remember you and keep you alive in our hearts. You're my baby and I love you."

That was as much as she could say.

"Let's give him our gifts now to let him know how much you love him and to help him feel strong for his journey," I said.

They each in turn placed something special into his crib. The grandmother offered a beautiful red chrysanthemum and placed it on his chest. David gave him a little locomotive. Emma reached in and handed him her rag doll. And Susie placed a beautiful quilt around his feet.

"Oh," said Emma, "I forgot. This is for you too." She reached into her pocket and pulled out a little chocolate bar and put it beside her brother's hand.

I looked over and saw the doctor and nurses peering through the window. I invited them to join us. They entered the room, but I asked them to wait just another moment.

I rested my hand on Christopher's chest and began talking to him.

"Christopher, we are going to stop the machines now. That means you can begin to let go. You won't have to work so hard anymore to stay with us. You can move on. It will be all right. Your mommy and daddy will hold you while they do it. You will go to a wonderful place, and God will be there waiting for you. It will be just fine. Are you ready, sweetie?"

I motioned to Susie to pick him up, and she reached in to bring him into her arms. The nurse beside me helped her, rearranging all the tubes. I pulled over a chair for her to sit in.

"Talk to him. Tell him it's all right. Tell him how much you love him and will miss him. It's time to do this."

Susie sat with her child in her arms. David knelt beside her and held him too. The doctor began turning off the machines, one by one.

The grandmother began crying loudly, and Emma turned very pale. I picked up a Bible and began reading,

The Lord is my shepherd, I shall not want;
He maketh me lie down in green pastures. . . .

Both Susie and David continued to talk to the baby, telling him how much they loved him. I heard Susie say to him, "It's hard, Baby, but you can let go now. It will be all right. We'll hold you until you go."

Suddenly the room was quiet. I had not realized how loud the machines were until they were silent. Then the heart monitor squealed. I looked up and saw a flat line. Susie buried her face in his body and wept.

The doctor left, but one of the nurses stayed, and we stood quietly for a few more minutes.

The grandmother came over and touched the baby's feet. She murmured something in Chinese and then looked up into the sky and said a prayer. She went over to the window and opened it a crack. Later I found out that she was asking his soul to move onward.

We all stayed in the room until David lifted his son's body and put it back into the crib.

"Let's have some silent time now," I suggested, "to help Christopher's soul find its new home. I'm sure he wants to stay with you, but we need to give him our blessing. Maybe you can each picture God waiting for him, wanting to take care of him now. Can we do that?"

They all nodded.

"Remember, give him your love and your blessing to do what he needs to do."

We sat in silence around the crib. I could feel all their grief, but I could also feel a sense of release. Christopher's transition into death was indeed a good one.

After a while, I spoke up again. "You have decided to follow the Buddhist custom of washing the body and preparing it for burial. Grandmother, do you have all the things you need?"

She nodded.

"Why don't you and Susie begin then?"

The two women took the basin and cloths and began washing the tiny body. I thought about reading out loud some more Bible stories, but decided instead that they needed silence.

Many of the machines were now gone from the room, so it didn't seem quite so impersonal. Because the family did not want to take the body home and the funeral parlor did not seem the right place for the long watch either, I had arranged for the hospital to give us a small nursery room for the night.

After Susie and her grandmother had washed Christopher, they wrapped him in a white cloth. Susie picked him up in her arms, and the nurse escorted us to the new room. It was bright and cheery and somehow very comforting.

They would take turns sitting beside him all night long. The next day they would bury him. We put a candle beside the bed, and the room took on a hushed feeling. The toys and gifts were all spread out around him as Christopher lay peacefully in his white shroud.

I said a few prayers and then I excused myself. As David walked me to the door, I heard Susie quietly reading from *Goodnight Moon,*

Goodnight stars . . . goodnight air . . .
goodnight noises everywhere.

As we stood just outside the room, David said to me with a tone of bittersweetness in his voice, "He made that transition you were talking about, didn't he?"

I nodded.

"I can feel it too. I know he's gone now. We'll have to grieve, but I do know he's where he's supposed to be. I felt it immediately."

Emma then came over and reached up. I picked her up and held her in my arms. She spoke softly in my ear, "He told me something. He told me he was glad."

We hugged, and I left the family to grieve.

***

Be careful, then, and be gentle about death.
For it is hard to die, it is difficult to go through
the door, even when it opens.
—D. H. LAWRENCE
"All Souls' Day"

FAMILY MEMBERS HAVE been faced with horrendous choices. Do they take their loved one off life support, or do they put him on the machines in the first place? Should heroic measures be taken? Or should the medical crisis just be allowed to play itself out? All things have been considered, and now the decision is made. It is time to stop. This usually means that the decision is for the loved one to die.

Such decisions are agonizing for anyone. Once the decision is made, though, what happens? It is a significant moment when life support is stopped. It has been decided upon not by the powers of nature or by the divine, but by human choice.

Our society provides very little emotional support when there is intentional death. There is always a level of agony as family members ask themselves if they are doing the right thing. Life is literally on hold as the questions are debated. And then when the intentional decision is made, all the medical people have to do is turn off the machines, and life is suddenly ended. It can seem extremely orchestrated.

Turning off machines and watching death happen feels cold and uncaring. It is an experience few of us know how to handle. No one has guidance on what to do and how to do it. But we know we do need structure and the presence of the sacred. Technology needs to be put aside so the loved ones can make the process of intentional death something they can live with. It does not have to be about machines taking control. It can be about sanctifying a tragic experience.

The one helpful thing about intentional death is that there is a level of control in the situation. Family members can take whatever action they feel necessary, and they can act in their own particular time. They can perform rituals in the way they desire, and they can proceed when it feels absolutely right. The entire external situation can be decided upon and controlled by the loved ones.

THOSE I LEAVE *behind, I love.*
I hope I will remain in their hearts
as they will in mine. . . .
Thank you for taking such good care
of me. . . .
And all of you who have been my
friends,
thank you for teaching me about love.

—KAREN VERVAET
"Karen's Journal," 3 April 1993

When I meet with people who have a loved one on life support, the circumstances have usually been tragic. There has often been an accident or an illness that has left the loved one brain dead. Medical people involved in the life-or-death decision have usually told the family that there is no hope of recovery, that the physical body has no chance of existing on its own.

I believe that in such situations the soul is trapped in the body, unable to be fully alive and yet unable to die, and because machines are keeping the heart and lungs going, it cannot do either. Christopher was neither dead nor alive. His soul was in neither place. The rituals we performed helped him let go of the last thread that kept him hanging on. There was a strong sense of relief, and I think everyone felt it. Rituals can help immensely in this situation. They generally fall into two categories:

- Rituals that express love and acknowledge and honor the life that has been led

- Rituals that give permission and strength to let go and die completely

In addition, I include whatever rituals seem appropriate from the family's faith tradition to help ease the way. These may include prayers, anointing, meditation, readings, and so on. Acknowledging the sacred experience of the moment is extremely important.

Create the sacred space.
The ICU is not a pleasant place to be. It is full of high-tech machines. The first thing to do is bring a sense of intimacy to the space. Try to create a bond where the loved one knows you are all with him in the room. Create as much warmth and familiarity as possible. Bring in familiar objects from home. Bring in things that alert the senses to family ties.

Rearrange furniture so that everyone feels comfortable. Ask the nurses to take away any superfluous items. It's important to create a warm, loving feeling inside the room. Make sure that everyone feels included. Have everyone form a circle around the bed. Create a sense of privacy by closing the doors and draping something over the windows. The noise level in the common area and nurses station is often disruptive and annoying, and anything you can do to muffle the noise is helpful. Chapter 5 gives more suggestions on creating sacred space in general.

Address the dying person.

TALK TO THE LOVED ONE AND EXPLAIN EVERYTHING
THAT IS BEING DONE.

Usually the person on life support is unconscious and is seldom addressed personally. No matter what the outward signs, she should be treated with respect. Tell her that you are sorry that a decision like this had to be made. Share some of your concerns or regrets about making the decision. Explain that you want it to be the right decision.

THANK THE PERSON FOR EVERYTHING SHE DID
OR FOR WHAT SHE MEANS TO YOU.

You can make offerings of thanksgiving here—presents or significant items that evoke memories. The offerings can be religious or personal or both.

MAKE PERSONAL AMENDS.

If anything has been left unsaid, this is the time to tend to it. If privacy is needed, ask other members of the family to excuse themselves.

HONOR THE PERSON'S LIFE.

Talk about what the life held, about the people in the person's life, about joys and happy events. Give the person a chance to reflect on what is now drawing to an end. Even children, as in the case of Christopher, have a wonderful history, and it needs to be celebrated.

Permit the person dying to let go.

The person attached to the machines has been looking for a way either to return to life or to cut the cord from the body and let the soul move on. Once the decision is made to allow the person to die, explain that it is now time to move on. There has to be a moment when the trapped person realizes that he is free and that the machines or the family are no longer holding him back. Giving permission to die is always hard, but it must come from the loved ones.

Rituals at this moment are always poignant, and they are as much for the surviving family as for the patient. Allowing the physical cords to be severed feels like losing your last connection to the person. This is when it is important to realize that love and memories remain the strongest bond.

> WE NEED, IN LOVE,
> *to practice only this:*
> *letting each other go.*
> *For holding on comes easily; we do*
> *not need to learn it.*
>
> —RAINER MARIA RILKE
> *"Requiem"*

One family was having a hard time letting go of their teenage boy after a car accident. When his whole life was in front of him, they couldn't understand why he had to die. It was a terribly emotional time, but we had to find a way to help them accept this death and to let Joshua die. They had filled his room with all his things, hoping to pull him back to life. There were things from school and his sports equipment, his favorite music, and photographs of his friends and family.

As we prepared to terminate life support, I asked his family to begin removing all the items, one by one. I asked them to talk to him, to tell him what they were holding and why they were taking it home.

"Tell him why he won't need it anymore," I said. "Help him begin to detach from his life here."

As the room emptied out, I asked his parents to help prepare Josh for his difficult task of dying.

"Tell him how strong he is and how brave he is," I told them.

As they told their son how strong he was, I noticed how it gave them in turn the strength they themselves needed to let him go.

Find strength.

Emotional and spiritual strength is needed at this time. This is a huge transition to undergo. Reading from hymns or scripture is always helpful. Find other ways to build on that strength. I once visited a mother who was sitting with her very tiny premature baby. The baby girl had struggled for days, but she had gone into a coma, and it was clear she was not going to live. The doctors recommended not taking any further measures. The mother saw how fragile the baby was and agreed. The one remaining thing was to help the baby shift the strength she had used in fighting to live and use it to learn how to die. The mother took the baby from the incubator, wrapped her in a blanket, and held her in her arms. She sat and rocked and rocked, singing all the songs she could remember. The strength to die is a different kind of strength than we normally call upon. It requires courage to go into the dark unknown. But what is so wonderful about the first step is that, once it is taken, the dark becomes light.

Create sacred moments.

Once the decision is made on how and when the death is going to occur, it is easier to arrange for a service, short prayers, or a time with clergy. If rituals are part of a religious ceremony, then they can be incorporated into the medical procedure. Just before life support is shut off, the patient can be anointed or even baptized or given communion. I watched a priest baptize an infant who was still in the incubator.

Being present while life is shutting down, machine by machine, is difficult. But if the focus is on the sacred moment of releasing a soul into death and into the presence of the divine, or even simply moving into a new state of being, it becomes easier for those who are witnesses to it. Once I walked in on such an experience, quite by accident. The woman, who was witnessing her father's death, was weeping uncontrollably. She was so distraught that one of the nurses had to hold her back. She was the only family member there, and I was sure she felt horribly guilty about making the decision to stop his life support.

I asked the nurses to hold everything for just a few minutes while I took the woman into the hallway. I took her by the shoulders and spoke to her very firmly.

"I know this is a horrible experience for you, but let's think for a moment about your father. He's hearing everything going on around him. Do you really want the last thing he hears to be a hysterical daughter? Why don't you talk to him as this is happening? Tell him how much you love him. You might even sing to him!"

Her eyes grew round in amazement.

"I never thought about it that way," she said through tears and hiccups.

The woman took a deep breath and marched back in. She took his hand and said, "Daddy, I'm sorry I behaved that way. I was thinking about me more than I was thinking about you."

She sniffled, wiped her eyes with the back of her hand, and then began singing to him in the most extraordinary voice.

Amazing grace! how sweet the sound,
that saved a wretch like me!
I once was lost but now am found,
was blind but now I see.

I stared at the woman. Five minutes before, she was hysterical, almost having to be restrained, and now she was sitting here with a beautiful glow on her face. Her voice was pure and exquisite. The nurses were transfixed as they listened to her sing through three or four verses of that beautiful song. I watched people from the hallway stop and then come to the door of the room, listening.

The nurse at the machines had tears in her eyes as she sang softly with the daughter. Then, quiet. We let the echoes stay with us a bit longer, and the nurse came over to the bed and unhooked tubes and monitors. She looked at the daughter and nodded, without saying anything. We both left the room, allowing privacy for father and daughter in those moments. I didn't see her again, but I know that her father heard every single verse of that hymn as he was being escorted into death.

Hold your loved one.

If the person dying has been hooked up for a long time to machines working as an extension of the body, the separation can be particularly difficult. Treat his body with loving care.

Ask the medical personnel to disengage the person as much as possible from the machinery so that you can hold the one who is dying. That way body contact becomes much easier and the loved one can begin relating to the person in the bed. It becomes possible to massage his hands and feet as they grow colder, to stroke the forehead, even to get into the bed with the person.

The soul is also going through a difficult transition at this time. Remember that the body has been traumatized and the soul is looking for release. Prayers or meditations are helpful here.

Making it possible for the soul to let go is an extremely important part of intentional death, regardless of religious belief. There are blessings, poems, or songs that enable the process to take place. This will help the person on life support and can aid in creating a peaceful death.

Afterwards: The Hard Transition

UNDERSTANDABLY, THE TRANSITION of intentional death is particularly difficult emotionally. There may be extra rituals or prayers needed after the actual death. I recommend that the family spend at least a few hours with the undisturbed body before anything more is done to it. The body has gone through as much trauma as the soul has and will undoubtedly need the added peacefulness. If the hospital can provide another room, that would be ideal, especially if death has taken place in a busy room like a nursery or an ICU unit. If not, try to find a quiet area that is undisturbed.

Conclusion

IT IS IMPORTANT to realize that stopping life support is much more than just turning off switches in an intensive care unit. Even though the medical personnel have the controls to terminate life support, death is still taking place, and the need for an atmosphere conducive to sacred dying is just as important. The loved ones have the control in saying when and how life support is to be terminated and, more important, the way in which it is done. This time can be used to express love and understanding, as the person dying is freed from the constraints of the machines. It can be used to bless and to release rather than to break down and give in to tragic circumstances. The blessing needs to come from the family, though. And the release will follow.

CHAPTER 12

After Death: Until the Funeral

ARCUS WAS SITTING in the waiting area when I arrived at the hospital. He looked as if the world was falling down around him. When I introduced myself he could barely speak without crying.

"Thank you for coming," he said. "I appreciate your help in this. I really don't know how to handle everything."

"Tell me what happened," I said.

"It has been a couple of days now," Marcus explained. "Gabby—my wife—was driving home from work and was sideswiped by a huge semi. The car was crushed instantly and we were lucky she didn't die right there. Well, I guess we were lucky. Maybe not. They've done two operations already but it doesn't look good. I have a feeling she isn't going to pull through this."

"How awful," I exclaimed. "Do you have children?"

"Yes," he said. "We have two girls and a boy. They're all

teenagers. Justin is sixteen, and the girls are thirteen and fourteen."

I looked into his sad eyes. There was nothing to say. I took his hand.

"What do you want me to do?" I asked.

"Gabrielle was from Costa Rica, and she was always doing rituals around the house. I guess she grew up with that. I know she would want someone who knew about rituals to help her now."

"Do you have any idea what faith her family practiced?"

"No," he replied. "She has an elderly aunt back in Costa Rica, and her sister is here—she's on her way now with the kids. But that's all the family that she has left."

"And you?" I asked.

"I'm not sure where God is in all of this." Tears slipped down his cheeks; then he continued. "God doesn't seem to be around much right now."

He was silent.

Then he said quietly, "Her birthday is tomorrow. She's going to be forty."

I saw a tall, handsome black woman with three teenagers coming off the elevator, and Marcus rose to greet them. They all hugged, and I could tell that the girls had been crying. Just as we were being introduced, a nurse came to find the family. She took Marcus aside, and I knew then that his wife had just died.

The woman, Gabby's sister, knew it too and exclaimed through her tears, "I can't believe we weren't here in time. After all we've gone through these past two days, we weren't with her when she died!"

The boy, Justin, walked over to a chair and began kicking it, while his two sisters held each other crying. I stood in the midst of the grief, not knowing what to say.

Marcus came to me and began apologizing. "I'm sorry we got you here for nothing. It's all over. We can't do anything any more."

"I am so sorry," I offered. He looked so awful and confused.

"You know, maybe there is something you can do after all. If you want, we can talk about some rituals to help now, even at this point. I know she is dead, but I think her soul is still with us, don't you? And I think she may need you to be with her now."

He looked at me, thought a moment, and said, "Tell me what you mean."

"Marcus, no one knows what happens after we die, but most people believe that we continue in some way in the afterlife."

He nodded. "I believe in heaven. And I know Gabby does too."

"So when we die, something happens to release our soul so that it can move on to wherever it goes. When death has been so sudden and tragic, like Gabby's, I think separating from the body is very difficult. Many religions believe that the soul stays near the body immediately after death, that the person's soul doesn't move on for several days or perhaps even longer.

"Haven't you heard stories," I asked him, "of people who have lost someone and they feel as if that person is in the room, really close by?"

By this time, the children were listening to our conversation.

"I have," exclaimed Tonia. "I hear them all the time!"

I continued, "I imagine that if someone hasn't had time to say good-bye or to work things out with everyone in the family, she would want to stay around just a little bit longer to see that everything is all right."

Justin asked hesitantly, "So then what do you think we should do? Mom certainly didn't have a chance to say good-bye. And we didn't either."

"There are a number of things you could do. Why don't we sit and talk about different choices?" I suggested.

We were all standing in the waiting room, and the children pulled up chairs around me.

"First," I began, "it's important to make some practical arrangements with a funeral home. But you also have to let the hospital know what you want to do." I paused.

"Spiritually, you can try a couple of things. Most people just let the funeral home take care of everything, and then you have the funeral and that's it. If you want to do things differently, perhaps you might like some time with your mom right here, while she is still in her hospital bed. Her body is just beginning to change, but she is still warm and recognizable. Many religions have a custom where you sit with the body all night long in a vigil. It gives the family a chance to begin to let go, to make peace with the knowledge that the person they love is dead. It's good to have quiet time before all the confusion of the funeral."

The family looked at each other.

I continued, "I know a lot of people feel nervous about it beforehand, but afterward they say it was the best thing they have ever done."

"Would we have to stay here at the hospital?" asked Marcus.

"You could do it anywhere you want. Here, if they let you, or at the funeral home, or even at your own house," I replied.

Gabby's sister, Maria, spoke up. "Marcus, I remember when Mama and Papa died, when we were just kids. They had us pray all nightlong in the front room. There were candles everywhere and even a little altar. Everything was done at home back in Costa Rica. I will never forget that night. At first it was kind of eerie, but there was something very peaceful about it too. I remember going up to Mama in the middle of the night, holding her hand, and it was very cold by then, and telling her everything in my heart." Tears started forming in Maria's eyes. "I wasn't afraid of death anymore after that. Truly I wasn't."

Marcus looked at his children. "What would you like to do? Jenny? Justin? Tonia?"

Tonia was the first one to speak. "I didn't have a chance to say good-bye to Mommy. If we can do it now, I want to."

Jenny agreed. "I think we should do something all night."

Justin nodded and replied, "I agree."

"Well, that's decided then," Marcus said. "Why don't I talk to the nurse and the funeral home to see what I can work out?"

I hesitated, "Do you want me to help with some rituals here by her bed at the hospital?"

They all nodded.

Marcus spoke to the nurse, and he told us that we had a couple of hours before the people from the mortuary would pick up Gabby's body and take her to the funeral home where there would be a private room for the night.

> "MANY RELIGIONS HAVE *a custom where you sit with the body all nightlong in a vigil. It gives the family a chance to begin to let go, to make peace with knowing the person they love is dead. It's good to have quiet time before all the confusion of the funeral."*

We went into the hospital room where Gabby was still lying in her bed. I suggested that the family stand in a circle around Gabby and have a moment of silence. I began to pray for a feeling of peace and a chance to feel Gabby's presence and love. There was a stillness in the room as we stood there.

I asked each member of the family to rearrange some part of her bed or her body to make her more comfortable. One of the girls smoothed her hair, another tucked the sheet all around her body. Her husband laid her arms across her chest, and her son put her slippers on her feet. That got them comfortable with approaching her body and not being afraid of it.

"What is her favorite song?" I asked. "Maybe if you sing it to her, she will know you are all present and want to help her."

Marcus was the one to answer. "It's 'The Rose.' You know, Bette Midler sang it."

I smiled. "Do you remember the words to it, Marcus?"

"Yes, ma'am," he replied. "I sure do."

He began singing it hesitantly,

Some say love it is a river that drowns a tender reed.
Some say love it is a razor that leaves your soul to
*   bleed. . . .*

And as he continued, everyone was crying and holding on to each other.

> *When the night has been too lonely and the road has been*
> *   too long,*
> *and you think that love is only for the lucky and the strong,*
> *Just remember in the winter far beneath the bitter snows*
> *Lies the seed that with the sun's love in the spring becomes*
> *   the rose.*

I left the family. They knew what they wanted to do and didn't need me to help. I told them I would see them later that day at the funeral home.

When I met the family later, they were all waiting in the lobby of the funeral home.

"They are bringing her back now," Marcus said. "The funeral director wanted to talk about all the arrangements, like the coffin and services and everything, but I told him we needed time to think about it."

The children all looked quiet and forlorn.

"Well, do you have any idea what you want to do?" I asked. There was more silence.

Justin spoke out, "I hate it here. They wanted us to buy this fancy casket for thousands of dollars, and all they could talk about were bronze handles and satin linings and stuff. It's stupid. Like it's going to matter when she is buried in the ground. We should get something that is biodegradable."

Marcus gave him a parental look and said, "Justin is our environmental activist."

I smiled. "There is something to be said for respecting the environment, you know. Earth to earth and all that."

Marcus replied, "I guess we need to make some decisions here, folks."

"You have a little bit of time," I said. "Have you thought about the vigil and what you want to do?"

The younger daughter, Jenny, said, "I don't like it here. I think I want to stay home tonight. Is that okay, Daddy?"

"Of course it is, sweetie," Marcus said, putting his arm around her. "I told you that whatever you wanted to do is fine with me."

"Daddy, I think I want to stay home with Jenny too," Tonia said. "You know, maybe we can do some special ceremonies there, instead of being with Mommy here. Would that be okay to do?"

"What were you thinking of?" asked Maria.

"I'm not sure," replied Tonia.

"May I offer some ideas?" I interjected.

Everyone looked at me expectantly.

"Why don't you do some rituals in a few of her favorite places? I am sure that her spirit is certainly in your home, where she lived and worked and enjoyed you all so much. Isn't her studio there too?" I asked.

They all nodded.

"So go into her studio and gather her paintings or take some of her favorite things and be with her that way. I don't think you need to sit with her body to feel her presence, do you?"

"Hey, I have an idea," exclaimed Tonia. "We could put on her favorite music and get out some of her clothes and put them all in her studio. And we could light some of her candles and have our own vigil there. I'd rather be there than this creepy place."

Marcus looked at his children and smiled. "I think that's a great idea. Are you okay with my being here, though?"

The girls looked at each other. "All night?" they asked. Their dad nodded.

"Maria and I are going to be here the whole time," he said.

"Is there some other family member who might stay at the house with the girls?" I asked.

He thought and then replied, "No, but I'll bet Olivia will come and be with them. She's Gabby's best friend."

"Oh, yes, Daddy, will you call and ask her?" the girls both exclaimed excitedly.

He smiled and nodded and then turned to Justin. "What would you like to do, son?"

Justin thought for a moment and then said, "I don't really know, Dad. I don't think I want to stay here much longer. Those rituals and everything at home sound like girl stuff. I want to do something. I can't just sit here much longer. I need to do something."

Maria reached out and touched his shoulder. "It's okay, Justin."

"Justin," I asked, "what kinds of things do you want to do? Is there something you can help with? Or can you be with your mom in a special way? What makes you feel better?"

Tonia replied, "He's always going into the garage and sawing and pounding away and making things."

"Yeah, he's really good at building stuff. He's made a whole bunch of things," said Jenny.

I asked him, "Can you build something for your mom tonight?"

With that question, Justin gave me the most penetrating look I have ever experienced. All of a sudden I knew exactly what was occurring in his mind. It was totally absurd, but I knew he had to do it. Our eyes met, and I was sure he knew I knew what he was thinking.

I took a deep breath and said to everyone, "I think Justin should build his mother's coffin."

The looks on their faces were incredulous, and Justin sat up straight and looked poised for battle.

"Whoa. I don't know, Justin," said Marcus finally.

"Dad, think about it. I'm sure I can make one. Easy. And it would save all that money on those stupid caskets with silk pillows and fancy handles. You know Mom would much rather have something plain and simple."

"And you know," I added, "I think this could be Justin's way of vigiling with his mother too. Only he would be doing something, like he said. I am sure her presence will be with him in the garage as he makes this for her."

"Yeah, Dad, like when we were out there last week building all those frames for her paintings. We spent all day Saturday there. It was great." Justin's voice began to break.

Marcus thought and then said, "All right, son, you build your mother's coffin. I'll tell Mr. Thompson we won't need any of his." And under his breath, I heard him say, "And he's not going to like that."

At that moment the funeral director walked into the room to announce that the "viewing room" had been set up. As everyone rose, I said, "Remember as you each vigil in your own way that this time is about being with Gabrielle. Her spirit is still here, and you want to have that chance to talk to her and get used to her being gone. She wants to say good-bye to you too, so try to listen as well as to talk."

I left them as they all went into the room where her body was. The children would stay a little while and then leave and spend the night at home. I told them I would check in with them in the morning.

"I THINK THIS *could be Justin's way of vigiling with his mother too. Only he would be doing something, like he said. I am sure her presence will be with him in the garage as he makes this for her.*"

When I arrived at the funeral home the next morning, the entire family was sitting around the body. Gabby was dressed in a beautiful robe and head scarf. She looked much more at peace than yesterday at the hospital, and the rest of the family, although tired, looked happy and peaceful too. They couldn't wait to tell me what had happened.

The girls went first. "Olivia came over, and we went into Mommy's bedroom to get some of her clothes. We took them into her studio and started rearranging things."

Jenny took over the telling, "I got all of Mom's scarves, and there must have been a hundred of them, and we began tying the ends together. It was so cool. We had one long strand of all these scarves. Olivia suggested tacking them to the walls, so we did.

We went round and round, just above the doorway and then across the windows and on top of her paintings and everything! We circled the room about five times I think!"

Tonia piped in, "And then we put on some music and got out all the paintings Mom was working on and put them up against the walls and on the easels so we could see everything. I lit Mom's candles and put them in front of the pictures too. It was way cool."

"And what rituals did you do?" I asked.

"Well, we said some prayers," Tonia explained. "But then we mostly just sat in the middle of the room and talked. At first it seemed weird to talk to an empty room, but Olivia had the idea of putting Mom's palette with all the colors in the center of the room, and we kind of talked to that. Was that an okay thing?"

I smiled. "Of course it was."

She continued. "We spent the night mostly looking at Mom's things and talking to her. But then Justin came in to tell us her coffin was ready, and Olivia had the best idea ever. Tell her, Justin!"

Justin blushed slightly and began, "Well, I was in the garage most of the night, making the coffin for Mom. I got my friend Donald to take me to get the lumber and all—he has a pickup. Well, it felt kind of good to be in there sawing and getting things just right. When I finished, the girls were in the studio so I told them it was all ready. They were kind of messing with Mom's paints, and I got the idea to paint the coffin. We took all her stuff out to the garage and we spent the rest of the night painting. We did all sorts of designs on it, both inside and out. We used really bright colors too. It's kind of cool, actually."

Marcus looked at his children with pride. "Yes, it's beautiful. I know Gabby would be very, very happy."

I chuckled. "What did the funeral director say when you brought it in?"

Justin smiled. "Donnie loaned me his truck, and we just carried the coffin right through that door. The director looked kind of surprised, but he didn't say a word. I guess maybe other people have had the same idea."

I laughed out loud. "Don't count on it," I replied. "Maybe he was just so overwhelmed at how beautiful it was that he was speechless!"

Maria, who was sitting in a corner, began talking. "When we got the coffin, we began getting Gabby ready to be laid in it. The girls brought in all of her scarves and one of her robes from Costa Rica. We filled the box with the scarves, like multicolored cushions, and then we put the robe on her body. She'll go into the ground surrounded by all her colors and silks."

"Did you have a good vigil last night?" I asked.

She was quiet for a moment and then replied, "Yes, it was good, wasn't it, Marcus? We traded off sitting with her and then sleeping a bit. I know I had some time to think and to talk to her. And I prayed for the first time in a long time."

Marcus nodded. He remained silent.

Tonia piped in, "When we came in this morning with all of Mom's things, it felt good. We all sat with her for an hour or so. I liked it. It didn't feel creepy here anymore. Then by the time we dressed her and got her scarves ready, I was ready to think about the funeral and all."

Marcus told me what they had planned for the funeral and that they felt good as a family.

"I think we're ready now to get on with the funeral and being with all the people who are starting to arrive," he said.

I could see in their faces that they would get through this. The mourning would come, and getting used to a new life without Gabby would take time, but they would be fine.

Before I left, we gathered in a circle around Gabby once again, and I offered a prayer of thanksgiving that Gabby had left a big part of herself behind. Her family would go on, living the lessons she had taught them.

꿍

The soul lives after the body dies. The soul
passes through the Great Gate and makes
a way in the darkness to its source.
Let this soul pass on.
— *The Egyptian Book of the Dead*

"DYING IS LIKE shutting down a large factory," writes David Kessler, "filled with engines and assembly lines and giant boilers. Everything does not suddenly go quiet when the 'off' switch is pushed. Instead, the machinery creaks and moans as it slows to a halt. Unless suddenly felled by an accident, a heart attack, or other sudden trauma, most of our bodies are like those factories, creaking and moaning as they shut down. . . .

"Whenever I have seen someone who has just passed away, it seems to me as if their body has been turned off. The intangible current of life is most obvious when it is no longer present."[1]

I remember being with a family as their elderly mother died. First, she stopped breathing. The next moment, the heart monitor showed a flat line, and the nurse recorded the time of her clinical death. However, the mother's body did not relax for several minutes, and the room, which seemed to be alive with electricity, stayed that way for at least ten or fifteen minutes.

A distinct process was happening to the woman who was dying, to the family involved, and to the space around us. It did not subside for quite some time after the physical death was declared.

Many people talk about death taking place over a period of time; it is not just a medical pronouncement. Many unseen things happen as it occurs.

If this process is more than just a medical pronouncement, what else is happening? Most faith traditions believe that what

1. David Kessler, *The Rights of the Dying: A Companion for Life's Final Moments* (New York: HarperCollins Publishers, 1997), pp. 130, 146.

is really happening is that the soul gradually moves from the body to the afterlife. It is a process, and it takes time and attention to happen peacefully.

People who have studied the afterlife say that the soul, according to most belief systems, goes through various stages. The stages involve an in-between state or transition, a time of judgment or waiting, and then an eventual arrival at the place of destination, whether that be a reincarnated life or the final resting place.[2]

In my own experience, however, most people in the West believe that the body and soul have no connection with each other after death. When a person is alive, he is living and breathing and therefore exists as a human being. When the body ceases to function, it no longer matters; it is an empty shell. The lifeless body is, in fact, often something to be afraid of or shunned. It feels scary and somehow dirty.

When a body dies, we want it to be taken away by the hospital or the funeral home before we have to really look at it or deal with our loved one being physically dead. The mortuary people prepare it, making the body lifelike and presentable for the funeral service. If we believe in heaven, we are often reassured in our state of mourning that our loved one has now gone to heaven to be with God.

Most people assume that their responsibility to the person who has died ceases as soon as death occurs and the only things left to handle are the practical funeral arrangements. Mourning begins immediately, taking the emphasis away from the person—except in memorializing his life—and shifts the focus to the survivors and their grief.

Most faith traditions, especially non-Western cultures, believe and practice a very different view of the body and soul after death. The marked differences in the East are:

2. See especially Suki Miller's *After Death: Mapping the Journey* (Simon & Schuster, 1997).

- Once the body ceases to live, there is a specific progression as the soul separates from the body. The soul gradually detaches from its familiar home and moves on to its final resting place. This progression takes time.

- The soul is in a state of extreme flux during this detaching period, which may last from a few hours before the body actually ceases to function to several days or even longer after the death. The soul is extremely vulnerable and needs help from the living to move on. If the death has been tragic, there are additional concerns to be addressed.

- The body is sacred and needs to be honored and purified before preparing for the funeral.

- The people present at the death and the location where the death took place have also been changed by virtue of the death. Certain things must be done to the room to signify that the death has occurred, and the people involved are also marked as having come into contact with death.

- The body is attended to in prayer and vigil, both privately at first and then publicly, never being left alone until the funeral.

- Grief and mourning become the primary concern only after the rituals are complete. Taking care of the body comes first.

- The funeral is performed only after these rituals are done.

There are specific rituals, depending on the religion, to aid in this progression of the soul. They may vary in order or emphasis, but the progression from one level to the next is distinct. Rituals for caring for the body are also extremely important. Because Western Christianity is the only exception among all the religions in foregoing ritual care for the body, many of us are concerned with the overall attitude and customs regarding death in our society.

Creative Rituals from the Traditional Faiths

GIVEN OUR SOCIETY'S taboos, it is not easy introducing the possibility of attending to the body and soul of the person who has just died. Most people do not want to face this unfamiliar work. Moreover, our standard way of handling the time immediately after death has not always been healthy. One friend, Daphne, in talking about the death of her baby daughter from SIDS, said that as soon as the paramedics were called in and had determined that the baby was dead, they escorted her out of the room, immediately taking the baby from the house. There was no time to say good-bye, to hold the baby, change the baby's clothes, or to have any say in what was to be done. All this amplified the trauma and horror of the situation, and Daphne never recovered from the grief. For those, however, who have broken tradition and tried new ways of handling the after-death experience, it has been life-changing.

In considering creative rituals for our time, I suggest practices based on customs that already exist in various traditions. It is possible to elaborate or to make variations on them. This does not mean adopting a particular faith or usurping its customs; it just means that if we look at traditional wisdom, it may help us know what to do and why and therefore help in the grief and mourning process.

Consider three purposes for possible rituals:

Helping the Soul
- Acknowledge the change in soul status.
- Make symbolic changes in the room.

Honoring the Body
- Wash and purify the body.
- Clothe the body.
- Vigil with the body—this involves only the closest family or loved ones.
- Prepare the body for the funeral.

Beginning the Mourning
- Plan prefuneral ceremonies (wakes, public viewings, and so on)—this involves the greater community and family.

Each faith tradition has different rituals for these categories, and I advise using them as guidelines or for creating other ideas. Because the rituals I suggest here are an extreme departure from standard procedures in Western society, I am not recommending that everyone take on the entire scope of after-death rituals. Examine them, however, and see if any feel appropriate.

Prayers to God: Acknowledgment of
Divine Action and Presence at the Moment of Death

Most faiths have a very brief prayer that is recited when a person dies physically. It usually honors God and the divine command over life and death. There is also some symbol recognizing that, despite this painful act, God's presence has not departed. In Hinduism, Judaism, and Islam it is often the custom for a light to be placed at the head of the person who has just died or even around the entire body. In Hinduism flowers are placed on the body.

I have seen people place holy objects in the hands of the

deceased, such as a cross or a rosary. I have also been present where an entire rosary was prayed. It gave the loved ones time to focus their attention on God, acknowledging God's power over life and over death.

I have also seen people recite a prayer to God, first acknowledging the divine dominion over life and death and then expressing anger or even rage at why this happened at this time and in this way. Some may think this is a very human reaction to death. Some may think that God cannot contain anger, while others find our human response offensive to whatever divine plan is in place. There is no one answer to these dilemmas. Nor is there a right way or a wrong way to meet the moment.

FATHER OF COMPASSION, *shelter them under the shadow of your wings for ever and let their souls be bound in the bundle of life.*

—TRADITIONAL JEWISH PRAYER

Acknowledgment of the Physical Death

When thinking about rituals to help mark the change in the status of the body, loved ones can make a difference by relaxing or covering the body, such as the extremities and the face, and by somehow changing the location or position of the body to signify the difference.

In many faith traditions the body is moved, often to the floor or sometimes just turned in a different direction, symbolizing the different state it is now in. Out of respect it is covered with a sheet, and the eyes and mouth are closed and sometimes bound. Hindus sometimes place offerings of flowers or sandalwood on the body.

Some questions to ask are: Do you want the body to stay in the deathbed room? If so, do you want the room changed in any way? Is there another room where preparations will be made? Realizing that the person has moved from one state to another, what symbols can best represent the change?

Helping the Soul

This is the hardest area for Western people to understand. We assume that everything is automatic when a person dies. Death, judgment, off to the afterlife. Traditional wisdom says this is not the case. We can and should participate in the journey of the soul, just as we helped prepare it before death. Our responsibilities are not over.

Acknowledging the Change in Soul Status

Once physical death is ritually marked, the survivors can then participate in the process of the soul leaving the body and moving on. Prayers, poems, or songs might be used for the release of the soul.

Protecting and Changing the Room

Some customs call for covering mirrors or making other changes in the physical location. These customs are based on folklore as well as traditions about the soul as it leaves the body.

Honoring the Body
Washing and Purifying the Body

There are formalized rituals in virtually every religion for washing and purifying the body. Sometimes family members perform them, and sometimes outside community members wash the body, realizing that it may be too difficult for the immediate mourners. Most traditions are gender sensitive; males wash males, females wash females. There are prayers and specific instructions for these rites.

It is not difficult to follow the logic and reasoning for rituals concerning washing and preparing the body. When my women's group washed Sarah's body that last time, it was a very loving tribute to her life and her presence among us. We honored each part of her body as we washed it, from her mind and intellect to the feet that carried her. It was a wonderful time of remembering and paying tribute.

A prayer I particularly like honors each part of the body as it is blessed, washed, and prepared for the funeral.

I bless your hair
  that the wind has played with.
I bless your brow,
  your thoughts.
I bless your eyes
  that have looked on us with love.
I bless your ears
  that listened for our voices.
I bless your nostrils,
  gateway of breath.
I bless your lips
  that have spoken truth.
I bless your neck and throat;
  we will remember your voice.
I bless your shoulders
  that have borne burdens with strength.
I bless your arms
  that have embraced us.
I bless your hands
  that have shaped wonders.
I bless your breasts
  that nurtured us,
  formed in strength and beauty.
I bless your heart
  that loved us.
I bless your ribs and lungs
  that sustained your life.
I bless your solar plexus,
  seat of power.
I bless your belly,
  sacred storehouse of the body.

I bless your thighs,
  strong foundation.
I bless your knees
  that knelt at the sacred altars.
I bless your legs
  that carried you.
I bless your feet
  that walked your own path through life.[3]

I have seen people offer prayers of thanksgiving for the body left behind and its legacies; for instance, the children that were born, or the fruit of the hands and of the mind.

Some find that they need to thank the body that has just died. Others offer sympathy for all the pain it was caused. This is especially true of those who have died of AIDS or other degenerative diseases.

CLOTHING THE BODY

In some cultures the person is buried in formal clothing, and in others the clothing is changed immediately before burial to a simple shroud.

In some faith traditions the body is clothed in ritually pure garments, perhaps only until the funeral, and other times through burial and cremation. In Hinduism women are dressed in beautiful saris specifically intended for the funeral. There are different kinds of clothing for the status of the person, whether she is widowed or whether her husband is still alive. In both Judaism and Islam the clothing is usually a ritually pure, white shroud. Many times Jewish people are buried with a prayer shawl wrapped around them.

In Western culture we tend to choose the favorite clothing of the person who has died and ask the funeral parlor to dress the

3. Starhawk and M. Macha NightMare, *Pagan Book of the Living and Dying* (San Francisco: HarperSanFrancisco, 1997), pp. 152–3.

loved one. In most religions the clothing is a symbolic garment rather than everyday wear. In the gay community many ask to be buried in costumes representing their life and identity.

Instead of assuming that the loved one should be buried in a plain black suit or in a dress, you might like to think of symbols that can be used: a robe or a costume. Or just the opposite can be used, a very simple gown or shroud. Pure and clean, without much form, it wraps the body beautifully.

Some customs dress the body in very elaborate clothing first so that those family members and friends who come to pay respects and to sit vigil until the funeral can see the person in full honor. At the funeral of the mother of a Korean friend, the dead woman was dressed in her most beautiful traditional gown. It showed her status in the community and in her family.

I once sat with a mother who dressed her child one last time before releasing him to be buried. There was such tenderness to her movements. It was an absolute act of love to put clothing on him for the last time. Another mother told me, after she dressed her dead five-year-old son, that she had held each item to her face and whispered his name into the piece of the clothing and asked it to take care of him now for her.

Vigiling with the Body

The vigil is the time when the closest family members are able to sit with the body privately for a period of time. It is a time for people to be with their loved one in an extremely intimate way. Everything is over now; the death has occurred. Someone else usually takes responsibility for the practical funeral arrangements, so what is left is the opportunity for quiet and reflection time with the loved one. This is extremely important.

I have found there are many things that happen to the family members who vigil after death. They have a chance to say good-bye. They have a chance to come to terms with the fact that the death has actually occurred. There is time to feel emotion, whether it be grief, anger, disappointment, or even relief.

A vigil provides the opportunity for the family members to sit with each other without the stress of medical decisions or the fear and anxiety that comes with not knowing when death will occur. A vigil creates time and space for the loved ones to make the transition into a state of mourning.

For the person who has just died, the vigil gives space for the soul to move peacefully from the body. Many faiths believe that the soul needs this time to make a smooth transition from its longtime home. Hinduism teaches that the soul's inclination is to return to the body rather than seek a new home, so prayers and meditations must be said to encourage the soul to move on. No one can fully explain what happens when the body and the soul separate, but we do know that many people experience the soul in a very distinct and immediate way.

"I knew that Lew was with me in the room," a friend told me about her husband. "I sat with his body for a few hours after he died, and I felt his presence right there. Sometimes he was sitting with me, sometimes I felt he was floating just above me. But there was no doubt whatsoever that his soul was there."

Paul recounted that when he sat with Kurt for a period of almost eighteen hours, he watched the body go from being warm to the moment when the soul clearly left and all that remained was a cold body. He knew the exact moment when it happened and that Kurt no longer needed his body. That separation is powerful, especially when you see it before your eyes. Suddenly you don't need to cling to the empty body anymore. Your loved one is no longer there.

Debbie told me that as she vigiled with her mother, she experienced a myriad of emotions. "I was upset, I was angry, and I was just plain exhausted. I remember, though, feeling really abandoned. My mother was gone now; one moment I had a mother and then, poof! I didn't have one. I sat there crying and crying. Well, something happened, and all of a sudden I knew that my mother was sitting there beside me. 'Now Debbie,' she said. 'Why do you think I've gone away? You know that I'll always be right here with you.' She told me that everything was fine and that I shouldn't worry.

"I really understood then," Debbie explained, "that my mom was being taken care of and that I should go on with my life. I was sad, of course. I kept feeling that emptiness inside me, but I felt reassured that it was okay. I wouldn't have given up that experience for anything in the world."

Most people I know who have made the decision to keep a vigil had to be convinced that it would help. They were extremely skeptical. Most had never heard of sitting with a dead body for a period of time. But everyone, once it was over, felt that they had a chance to say their good-byes and to be assured that their loved one was ready to move on to the afterlife. It provided a deep and profound spiritual experience.

Practicalities of Vigiling

The practice of vigiling with a body is not normally done in our society, so arrangements need to be made as well as explanations given to other family members and the community. There are many options for doing this. Buddhists generally vigil through one sunset and the following sunrise. Traditional Judaism requires that someone sit with the body until the funeral, which is usually the next day. Hindus also have the funeral as soon as possible.

If you are choosing to create your own vigil, there is no set time or length. I would recommend strongly, though, to have it be throughout the night. Nighttime presents its own particular emotions and spiritual opportunities.

Some things to do during the vigil are:

- Read.
- Listen to music.
- Pray/meditate.
- Write in a journal.
- Be silent.

- Feel your emotions.
- Share quietly with others memories and stories about the loved one.
- Be open to what the experience brings.

This is a time for the immediate family, and the vigil should never be more than a few people at a time. There can be shifts so that people can sleep, but the purpose is for quiet reflection and not for social activities.

Beginning the Mourning—Prefuneral Ceremonies

AFTER THE FIRST night's vigil, the public mourning rituals now take over. The family moves from their private time with the loved one into the community. Many Christian churches have prayer services before the funeral, with or without the body present. In Judaism preparation begins for sitting *shiva*, which is the seven-day period of mourning after the interment and has specific rituals and traditions. It is a time for family and friends to show their respect both to the living and to the one who has died. Focus is on the mourners, and the community supports them in whatever way seems appropriate.

I have found that people are much more able to handle this time of public mourning if they have just come through their own personal vigil where many issues and feelings have been expressed.

The Shift to a State of Mourning

GRIEF AND MOURNING are powerful human emotions. When a loved one is dying, all one's feelings of loss come forward. These feelings often overwhelm and paralyze. They are normal, and each culture and religious tradition has specific ways for a person to mourn.

In some Asian cultures, such as the Japanese, stoic silence is considered the most dignified and appropriate. Korean culture, on the other hand, traditionally includes an elaborate display of wailing and tears. Arabic women from the Middle East have a unique high-pitched cry of mourning. How we act really depends on not only our individual personality but also the culture and society in which we live.

Conclusion

OUR RESPONSIBILITY TO our loved one is just as critical immediately after death as it is before the transition. Because there are few Western traditions to assist us, we can look to other religious beliefs and practices for guidance. Honoring the body and preparing it for its transition to the afterlife is not only important for our loved ones in the midst of this great journey, but it also helps us as survivors as we mourn and grieve our loss.

CHAPTER 13

The Soul's Journey

TWO FUNERALS IN one day. That was a first for me, but I knew I needed to attend both. Luckily, one was in the morning and the other in the afternoon. I was sure they would also be different as night and day. The two women, Sophie and Virginia, certainly were.

Sophie was an elderly woman, and her death was almost a relief. She told me that she was tired of waiting to die.

"I want to go home now," she said. "All I do is sit here and wait to die. It's time for me to go."

The two of us spent some time together talking. I asked her one day if she had all her funeral plans written out.

"Of course I do!" she snapped at me. "What else do I have to think about? The food in this place?"

I laughed. I had seen what they served for lunch at the nursing home. It wasn't inspiring, to say the least.

"So what kind of service do you want to have?" I asked her.

I knew her daughter was about an hour away, and I thought there was a son somewhere, too, although he didn't appear to be in the picture much.

"I want something short and to the point," she said. "No fuss, no bother. I can't stand it when people fuss. Get it over with and get me buried. That's it."

I thought for a moment. Then I asked, "So what do you think is the point of the funeral?"

She nodded her head as she considered her answer. "All I care about is that the coffin goes into the grave. I don't care about anything else. I don't think my daughter will care about anything else either. We're all tired of each other anyway." I thought I heard a harummph as we closed the discussion.

That was the last conversation I had with Sophie. A few months later, I got a call that she had died and her funeral was to be Tuesday morning at the local funeral home.

As I sat in the chapel, waiting for the funeral to begin, I noticed that most of the people there were friends of her daughter. They came up to her in an impromptu receiving line and were chatting away. I heard someone comment about looking forward to the catered luncheon afterward. I saw the son and his wife sitting quietly alone, near the front.

Sophie's casket was quite elegant—probably her daughter's taste—and elaborate flower arrangements were spread all around it. The casket was open, although most people clearly stayed as far away as possible. The pre-recorded organ music was playing in the background, and it softened as the minister approached the podium. People took their seats and listened to a reading from the Bible. Then he began to talk about how wonderful Sophie's life must have been.

"Although I personally never met Sophie, I am sure she lived a long and fruitful life. Her daughter tells me that she was active in the Red Cross for many years. She raised two wonderful children and had three grandchildren. She lived a quiet life after her husband died, and now the two of them can be with each other for all eternity."

The minister shuffled some papers for a moment, and then asked if the grandchildren were ready to read their poems.

I groaned to myself and wondered if that was going to be the whole content of the funeral. Certainly the family could do better than this. Is this what they thought "no fuss" was about? As two young children read some poems, I wondered what Sophie was thinking that very moment.

Ten minutes later, the service was over. The casket was closed and the funeral director announced that the burial would be private, but that guests were invited to go to her daughter's home for a buffet luncheon. People jumped up out of their pews and scrambled toward the door. I heard murmurs of "I'm so sorry for your loss," as the daughter hurried to take her place at the beginning of the receiving line. She reveled in the attention.

"Good-bye, Sophie," I said softly, walking away from the chapel. "When I get home, I'll say some prayers for you on my own."

As I made my way across town to a lovely small church with a beautiful garden in the back, I thought of Virginia and the hours we spent together before she died. She was in her late 50s and determined to live as fully as she could while fighting ovarian cancer. We had spent hours together, talking about everything from God and the afterlife to what to do with her cats when she died. The day we talked about her funeral plans was among the hardest of our conversations.

"My friends are my family," she said. "I have to trust that they will do what I ask them."

"Do you have an executor?" I asked her.

"My friend Kathy," she replied. "Kathy knows what I want, but I feel bad that she'll have to take care of everything. It's asking a lot."

Virginia began to cry.

"This is what happens when you don't have family. There is no one who has to do this for you. No one has to care. I feel so alone right now."

We talked about how much her friends were helping during the treatments; they brought her food and supplies and often came over to help with chores and errands.

"They are doing everything they can," Virginia said, "but I really hate asking them to manage my affairs."

"Have you kept up with the paperwork?" I asked. "Is your will in order and all that?"

She nodded. "The only thing left is to plan out the funeral. It sounds really horrible, but I kind of want to do that now. It gives me a feeling of control. This is one of the last things I can do on my own. I get to choose what I want."

"It makes complete sense," I told her. "Do you want me to help you with it?"

"Well, if you could help answer some questions, that would be good." she said.

"I know I want to have the service at my church. Funeral homes are pretty awful, at least the ones I've been to. They feel so. . . . " she paused. "So . . . generic."

We both laughed.

"But my church has been home for me, and I know they will welcome my friends and make them feel included."

"Then go for it. Have you talked to the clergy there?"

Virginia nodded. "At least initially. They gave me a sheet of things to consider. I have it here."

We looked over the list of things to choose from—hymns, readings, did she want a communion service? did she want special people to offer a eulogy?

"I've decided to be cremated and then buried in their memorial garden. I don't want to be buried back where my parents are. There is no connection there anymore. I want to stay here."

"That makes sense," I said. "Your friends will have a place to come to then, when they want to be with you. And your church community will be happy to have you with them too. There is something very powerful about the concept of the Communion of the Saints—those of us who are alive here on earth and those of us who have joined God in heaven. We're all part of the same community."

"I like that."

She continued, "Maybe that is what I am really looking for. A way to say I know we are really going to miss each other, but we'll still be connected." There were tears in her eyes. "I don't want to die, but I'm getting tired of my body hurting so much. If I know I can be with everyone after I go, it just makes it a bit easier, I guess."

I took her hand and held it quietly for a few moments.

"There is one more thing," she said. "We have done some rituals over the past few weeks, and those have helped me a lot. I want to do one more, but I want it done at the funeral. Do you think it will be okay?"

We talked about what she wanted and how to make it happen, and I knew it would be more than okay. It would make her funeral very special.

It was just a month before that we had the conversation, and now I was headed to her actual funeral. Virginia had died three days previously, and her friends were with her until the end.

When I got to the church, the parking lot was already overflowing. I found a seat in the sanctuary and said hello to the people I knew. There was a lot of activity, and although people were crying, there was also a feeling of joy.

The music started, and people watched expectantly as the procession began. I saw the choir come down the aisle, then several clergy, and then, all dressed in white flowing dresses, were Virginia's friends. The last one was Kathy, and she held up something high in front of her as she walked down the aisle. Of course. It was Virginia's ashes. The urn was a beautiful golden box.

When the women got to the front of the church, Kathy put the urn on a large pedestal, and they all formed a circle around it. They circled and circled, until each of the women had one hand on the urn. It looked beautiful, almost like the spokes of a wheel.

The music stopped, and the women still stood surrounding their friend. The minister welcomed us and spoke beautifully about this being a time of tremendous grief, but also a time of celebrating community.

"We are human, and we seek solace together, in community. Virginia was loved by everyone here, and we are lucky that we have each other to cry with."

"We'll celebrate her life, and share stories about her, but then we have to let her go. We have to return her to the earth and to God."

We had some readings, and then people stood up and shared lovely stories about Virginia's life and the way in which she had died. There were a lot of tears, and I could tell how very much people loved her.

We then processed out into the memorial garden, led by the women in white carrying the urn. The urn was placed on a stand in front of a small open grave. The stand was surrounded by beautiful, deep-red rose petals, hundreds of them. The minister asked us to gather around the grave.

"Virginia," she said, addressing the urn. "We have to say good-bye now. You have shared your life here on earth with us, and now we have to let you go. Your life is with God. Watch over us, and bless us. We will remember you as one of our saints in heaven."

"WE'LL CELEBRATE HER *life, and share stories about her, but then we have to let her go. We have to return her to the earth and to God.*"

She lifted the urn and placed it in the hole. Then she took a handful of rose petals and threw them into the grave. She invited us all to do the same.

One by one, people came up to the flowers and placed them on top of the urn. Many said good-bye, many just cried. Then the women in white began singing something quietly. It took me a moment to recognize it as Virginia's favorite song.

"When you're weary, feeling small,
When tears are in your eyes, I will dry them all . . .
Like a bridge over troubled water,
I will lay me down."

The minister began throwing dirt into the hole, covering up all those beautiful petals, and people circled the grave, arms around each other, singing softly.

I thought about family and community, about being in a better place, away from pain, yet never really leaving the circle that love creates.

⁂

"Take care with the end
as you do with the beginning."
—LAO TZU
Tao Te Ching

I ONCE STOOD in a 19th century graveyard, watching a funeral procession approach a newly dug gravesite. I didn't know the family, but I was drawn into the somber procession of cars, and then people gathering around the grave. As the mourners drew closer to the mound of soil, I could see the casket being lowered gently into the earth. Some prayers were said and then people took turns throwing clumps of dirt into the grave, weeping quietly.

"Earth to earth, ashes to ashes, dust to dust."

As men in black suits took shovels and filled in the rest of the hole, I felt myself shudder involuntarily. There was a body in that hole, I thought, and the body was being buried under a mound of dirt. The reality of it all hit me for the first time.

Death is more than losing someone we love. It is more than just absence. It is the stark realization that we are mortal. Our lives have a beginning, and they have an end.

Many people, when they speak of their own funeral, say jokingly, "Do what you want. I won't be there to enjoy it." In some sense, that is absolutely correct. The funeral is primarily for the living, an opportunity to remember, a chance to grieve, a time for the community to gather and mourn their loss. But the funeral also serves another purpose, one which I think we have mostly forgotten in contemporary society. The funeral is a time when we must let the soul truly and completely depart from the body. We must return the body to the elements, whether that be to the earth, or fire, or water, and encourage the soul to move onward.

The soul's final separation from the body.

It is not easy being in the presence of a body. We are not used to it. The funeral is our one chance to cut the cords and say our final good-bye to the person we knew on earth, to remember that the soul has departed. Yet we also focus on expressing the loss we feel as survivors. I believe such balance is necessary, both emotionally and spiritually. We cannot have one without the other.

Our culture has become very good at creating memorial services. We gather as a community when someone has died or when tragedy has occurred. We come together as a community to express how much pain we feel. We honor those who have died with photographs and mementoes. We hold them high for the world to see: "I loved this person, and now he is gone."

We cry together as we listen to stories. We sometimes ask, "Why did this happen?" We celebrate a life lived. All that is absolutely essential, and we do it well. However, we have forgotten for the most part to perform rituals for the final disposal of the body.

Most services these days are memorial services, without the body present. There is a disconnect from what is really happening. We focus on the loss of the survivors, forgetting the need of a ritual for the person who has died, completing the cycle of life, from birth to death.

I once spoke to a hospice worker who was attending the funeral of a patient, a man who had been born and raised in India. The family gathered together for the event, as did the entire local community, most of them practicing Hindus. The hospice worker sat in the back of the chapel, wanting to be inconspicuous as the family grieved their patriarch. There were prayers said and family stories recounted. Then, instead of ending the ceremony there, they processed out of the chapel and into another part of the funeral home. The hospice worker followed the family, suddenly finding herself at the front of the procession. She was totally unprepared for what happened next, and as she recounted the story to me, I could see her face go pale as she remembered the event.

"We crammed into a small room," she said, "and as I looked around me I realized it was the crematorium. The crowd was pushing me toward a large, open oven door. The body was laid out on a platform, wrapped in a shroud, and it was ready to go into the oven.

"Here I was, in a ringside seat, watching a body being cremated.

"The son moved toward the oven, and a hush took over the room. I wanted to escape, but there was no way. I was right there, like it or not.

"The son reached over and pressed a button. The body went into the oven, the door closed. Then he pressed another button, and I could tell that the fire was starting. I almost fainted."

She explained that later she discovered that this was a traditional Hindu funeral, one outside of India, that is.

If the family were in India, the community would process through the streets with the body perched high on a bier. At the place of cremation, always outdoors, there would be a huge pyre. The eldest son would place the body on top of the pyre and then light the fire. The community would gather round the fire until the body was burned. Fire is the great purifier in Hindu belief.

The traditional funeral in India doesn't work well logistically in the West. American funeral homes have had to adapt to meet the needs of this culture, especially where there are large communities of immigrants. American law doesn't permit open aired burning of bodies, so instead, funeral homes with crematoria have adapted their service to allow the eldest son to symbolically "light" the fire.

The reality of the body needing to be purified still remains. The fire is still present, and the event remains an integral part of community ritual.

Preparing the Body

HONORING THE BODY by washing it and preparing it for the community gathering is only one piece of the entire drama that occurs before the actual funeral. It is part of a greater whole.

Most religious traditions recognize that the body, devoid of the soul, is empty and no longer pure. Both Judaism and Islam consider the body to be ritually impure, requiring both immediate cleansing and then burial. Traditions that believe in reincarnation, predominantly Hinduism and Buddhism, also have funerals almost immediately after death. The soul wants so desperately to return to the familiar body that it must be encouraged to move on. By burying or cremating the body, there is nowhere to return. The soul has to find its way ahead.

Symbolically as well as religiously, it is important to care for the body. Whether our beliefs reside in reincarnation or in a final resting place in heaven, honoring the body and letting it return to the elements is important. Emotionally, seeing the body actually reach its resting place helps us understand that death is indeed a closing of this cycle. Mortality is real. Our bodies die.

Finding the Balance

THE MOURNING HAS begun. Family and loved ones are grieving the loss of someone who has been a part of their lives. How do we create a balance which allows for attention to be paid to all their needs?

Sometimes it is helpful to make a clear distinction between what is necessary for the person himself and the journey of his soul, and what the living need for comfort. Just as the dying process is about the person going through it, not about the loved ones, the burial or cremation completes the cycle. We finish what has been started. There is finality.

In the midst of burial, however, is mourning. The two are now intertwined.

1. Honor the body

The first thing we can do to honor the body is to have it present. In the U.S., we have traditions of both open-casket and a closed-casket funerals. If there is to be an open casket, the funeral home usually prepares the body so that people see a "natural" appearance. If there is to be a closed casket, it is usually draped in some sort of pall as it resides in the midst of the people who are gathered.

If the person wants to be cremated, there are various ways for the body to be present. The ashes might already be in an urn, and the urn can be present on an altar or table in the midst of the gathering. Another alternative is for the body to be in the casket and present during the funeral. Cremation and interment would take place afterward.

There is something very profound about having the body present as people gather in mourning. It makes the death of someone we love both real and tangible.

In previous generations, when death occurred in the home, it was a natural part of the process for family members to wash and dress the body for burial. These days, the body disappears almost immediately, and strangers care for it out of sight. Funerals have turned into memorial services for the most part, again with no body present.

Try to find a ritual that lets you honor the body and incorporate it into your funeral arrangements. Even if burial or cremation is to be performed at a later time, or at another location, there are ways to have the body present, physically or symbolically.

"His Maker kissed his soul away, And laid his flesh to rest."
—Isaac Watts

I once attended a funeral in the person's home, casket and all. It startled a good many people to see a homemade casket in the middle of the living room, but it turned out to be a very moving ceremony. The woman died at home, cared for by her family, and she wanted to stay there as long as she could. The funeral home came to the house to escort the body to the grave and we all followed the hearse. It was a very genuine experience.

I know that many people have misgivings about open caskets and displays of the body. Different families and cultures have different practices. If the casket is to be closed, there are still ways to acknowledge that the body is present. Have the casket in the midst of the people, rather than discretely placed in a corner. Cover the casket with personal items, such as scarves or clothing. Place photographs of the person on it so that mourners may have a point of focus.

2. Move the body from the community to the place of rest

Virtually every culture throughout history has understood that the living reside within the walls of the community, and the dead reside "apart," outside of the walls. There is always a sense of being "apart." In death, we make a voyage from the activity of life and community to that outside place.

Whether it be crossing the river Styx or the river Jordan, the journey is important. It is also important that the living help prepare both the soul and the body for that journey. Funeral processions are ancient symbols. We travel with the body as far as we can and then we help place it in its earthly resting place.

Not too long ago, funeral processions going through a city or town would stop traffic, and cars would pull over out of respect. Some observers would cross themselves or say a prayer for the repose of the departed soul. Others would take off hats as a sign of respect.

I have a video recording of the funeral of a friend's mother in Korea. The entire extended family as well as neighboring friends made the long procession from the house to the family burial ground, drums beating, priests chanting, and women wailing. It was heart wrenching, but there is no doubt that the beloved mother was coming home to rest with her ancestors.

The symbol of making that journey is easy to put into ritual form. If the funeral cannot be concluded by immediate burial or interment, there are rituals that can symbolize the journey.

One family took a special object belonging to their father and buried it in the yard. I knew a woman who had the entire funeral congregation walk from the chapel to the park where she scattered her husband's ashes. It gave us time to reflect as well as recognize the journey we all have to make.

3. Create a sense of place to mark the focus of grief

Human beings often need someplace physical to direct grief and loss. We have cemeteries with headstones in order to mark the place where each person now resides. A sense of place is important.

More and more, people are deciding to be cremated, with their ashes spread at sea, or over special places on land. This is a wonderful way to acknowledge both the specialness of one particular place, as well as the reality that land is at a premium. Ecology speaks strongly.

If there is no grave, or place in a columbarium, consider finding a place where the person's name is marked, and family members and loved ones can return and grieve. It can be anywhere—in a back yard, or perhaps at a favorite landmark. Having a physical place lets the mourners find a home for rituals and emotions.

It is also helpful to actually see the body being buried. In the Jewish tradition, mourners almost always follow the body to the cemetery, where family members shovel dirt into the grave. The hollow sound of "thud, thud, thud" creates an almost a visceral feeling of finality. The soul is no longer in this body, which is destined to become earth once more. Such finality is important in letting go.

Markers which say, "Here is where I remember you" allow those of us who are living to focus our grief. It is not uncommon for us to have conversations with the dead at the place of burial. We need that sense of place and of connection.

When I was in London, I went to Westminster Abbey to visit the Poet's Corner, where many famous people are laid to rest. I stood at the place where T.S. Eliot, one of my favorite poets, was buried. I found myself totally overwhelmed with emotion. I wanted to touch the place where he lay, connecting my self to something that remained of him. It was a very powerful moment.

Even if there is no body to be buried, find a connecting point and make it tangible. To create a place where the living intersect with the dead is a very strong need.

4. Speak of the afterlife and what is happening on the other side

In all the deaths I have witnessed, virtually every person who was able to communicate has asked me "What is going to happen when I die?" Yet, in this day and age, people are quite hesitant to bring up the topic of afterlife beliefs. Beliefs are not as uniform as they once seemed to be. People come from very diverse backgrounds, and being raised in a particular faith tradition does not mean specific beliefs follow. More often than not, I hear, "I don't know what to believe."

There is no right or wrong answer here. Just as I speak of the afterlife to people who are dying, it seems equally as important to honor the images of the afterlife during funerals. It gives comfort and even a feeling of safety not only to visualize but also to speak of our loved one in a safe and peaceful place.

One of the most beautiful prayers I have ever read is filled with wonderful images. It is part of the commendation service for several Christian denominations, and is called *In Paradisum*. It reads:

> *"Into paradise may the angels lead you;*
> *and at your coming may the martyrs receive you,*
> *and bring you into the Holy City Jerusalem."*

5. Offer rituals to cut the cords and say goodbye

Many faith traditions believe that the soul takes many days, even weeks, to move on. There are ways to help that process during a funeral or memorial service. Funerals are times when the living are asked to say good-bye. We are the ones left behind, and it becomes our responsibility to "take care" of the dead.

I once attended a Chinese Buddhist ceremony conducted in a funeral home. Many of the symbols and traditions were foreign to me (like the very apparent pig's head on a platter), but one of the things I found soothing was that the family felt responsible for the grandfather's journey to the afterlife. They were doing everything they could to insure his happiness and prosperity in heaven.

Grandfather had his own responsibilities too, I am sure, moving into the land of his ancestors. He would watch out for his family, making sure that they, too, would prosper and grow. Despite the family's mourning and displayed grief, they knew that they were doing what was expected as a family member. This was more than their personal grief. This was about Grandfather's place in heaven.

In contemporary culture, our funerals and memorial services seem to be very one-sided. Our grief and loss are held up as the extreme sacrifice we must make. The service becomes a collection of stories and displays of our own loss. All of that is good and it is appropriate. I am suggesting that we balance the focus on ourselves with a ritual for cutting the cords of physical life and connection.

We bury our loved ones in a variety of ways. There is no right way, or wrong way. Most faith traditions teach that the spiritual links to the dead that we forge carry us through to death and beyond. We may believe that families reside together in the Mormon Spirit World, or perhaps the Buddhist Pure Land, or we may believe that our loved ones become part of the spiritual Communion of Saints, or that they reside forever in the Land of the Ancestors. Regardless, when we say goodbye, we hope that they are in a place surrounded by a more perfect love. Perhaps the greatest gift we can give them is to ask for their blessing, and offer to keep them alive in our memories.

Scriptures and Sacred Texts

Hebrew Bible

The Twenty-Third Psalm

The Lord is my shepherd; I shall not want.
He maketh me to lie down in green pastures:
He leadeth me beside the still waters.
He restoreth my soul:
He leadeth me in the paths of righteousness
for his name's sake.

Yea, though I walk through the valley of the shadow
    of death,
I will fear no evil:
for thou art with me;
thy rod and thy staff they comfort me.

Thou preparest a table before me in the presence
    of mine enemies;
thou anointest my head with oil;
my cup runneth over.
Surely goodness and mercy shall follow me
all the days of my life:
and I will dwell in the house of the Lord forever.

KING JAMES VERSION

Psalm 139

O Lord, thou hast searched me and known me,
You know when I sit down and when I rise up;
   you discern my thoughts from far away.
You search out my path and my lying down,
   and are acquainted with all my ways.
Even before a word is on my tongue, O Lord,
   you know it completely.
You hem me in, behind and before, and lay your hand
   upon me.
Such knowledge is too wonderful for me;
   it is so high that I cannot attain it.

Where can I go from your spirit?
Or where can I flee from your presence?
If I ascend to heaven, you are there;
   if I make my bed in Sheol, you are there.
If I take the wings of the morning
   and settle at the farthest limits of the sea,
   even there your hand shall lead me,
   and your right hand shall hold me fast.
If I say, "Surely the darkness shall cover me,
   and the light around me become night,"
even the darkness is not dark to you;
   the night is as bright as the day,
   for darkness is as light to you.
For it was you who formed my inward parts;
   you knit me together in my mother's womb.
I praise you, for I am fearfully and wonderfully made.
Wonderful are your works; that I know very well.
My frame was not hidden from you,
   when I was being made in secret,
   intricately woven in the depths of the earth.
Your eyes beheld my unformed substance.

In your book were written all the days that
    were formed for me,
      when none of them as yet existed.
How weighty to me are your thoughts, O God!
How vast is the sum of them!
I try to count them—they are more than the sand;
    I come to the end—I am still with you . . .

Search me, O God, and know my heart;
    test me and know my thoughts.
See if there is any wicked way in me,
    and lead me in the way everlasting.

NRSV

I have taken you by the hand and kept you. . . .

Thus says God, the Lord,
    who created the heavens and stretched them out,
    who spread out the earth and what comes from it,
    who gives breath to the people upon it
    and spirit to those who walk in it:
I am the Lord, I have called you in righteousness,
    I have taken you by the hand and kept you;
    I have given you as a covenant to the people,
    a light to the nations, to open the eyes that are blind,
    to bring out the prisoners from the dungeon,
    from the prison those who sit in darkness.

ISAIAH 42: 5–7
NRSV

Do not fear, for I am with you. . . .

> But you, Israel, my servant, Jacob, whom I have chosen,
>> the offspring of Abraham, my friend;
>> you whom I took from the ends of the earth,
>> and called from its farthest corners,
>> saying to you, "You are my servant,
>> I have chosen you and not cast you off;"
> Do not fear, for I am with you,
>> do not be afraid, for I am your God;
> I will strengthen you, I will help you,
>> I will uphold you with my victorious right hand. . . .
>
> For I, the Lord your God, hold your right hand;
>> it is I who say to you, "Do not fear,
>> I will help you."

ISAIAH 41:8–13
NRSV

♐

> Heal me, O Lord, and I shall be healed;
> save me, and I shall be saved;
> for you are my praise.

JEREMIAH 17:14
NRSV

Do not fear . . . I have called you by name, you are mine.

> But now thus says the Lord, he who created you, O Jacob,
>   he who formed you, O Israel:
> Do not fear, for I have redeemed you;
>   I have called you by name, you are mine.
> When you pass through the waters, I will be with you;
>   and through the rivers, they shall not overwhelm you;
> When you walk through fire you shall not be burned,
>   and the flame shall not consume you.
> For I am the Lord your God,
>   the Holy One of Israel, your Saviour. . . .
> Because you are precious in my sight,
>   and honored, and I love you,
> I give people in return for you,
>   nations in exchange for your life.
> Do not fear, for I am with you;
>   . . . everyone who is called by my name,
>   whom I created for my glory,
>   whom I formed and made.

ISAIAH 43:1–7
NRSV

The Death of Jacob

After this Joseph was told, "Behold, your father is ill"; so he took with him his two sons, Manasseh and Ephraim. And it was told to Jacob, "Your son Joseph has come to you"; then Israel summoned his strength, and sat up in bed. . . .

When Israel saw Joseph's sons, he said, "Who are these?" Joseph said to his father, "They are my sons, whom God has given me here." And he said, "Bring them to me, I pray you, that I may bless them." Now the eyes of Israel were dim with age, so that he could not see. So Joseph brought them near him; and he kissed them and embraced them. And Israel said to Joseph, "I had not thought to see your face; and lo, God has let me see your children also." Then Joseph removed them from his knees, and he bowed himself with his face to the earth. . . .

Then Israel said to Joseph, "Behold, I am about to die, but God will be with you, and will bring you again to the land of your fathers."

. . . Jacob drew up his feet into the bed, and breathed his last, and was gathered to his people. Then Joseph fell on his father's face, and wept over him, and kissed him.

FROM GENESIS 48–50
RSV

Christian New Testament

Do not let your hearts be troubled.

> Do not let your hearts be troubled. Believe in God,
>   believe also in me.
> In my Father's house there are many dwelling places.
> If it were not so, would I have told you that I go to
>   prepare a place for you?
> And if I go and prepare a place for you, I will come again
> and will take you to myself, so that where I am, there
>   you may be also.
> And you know the way to the place where I am going.

JOHN 14:1–4
NRSV

⨭

The Peace of God which surpasses all understanding,
will guard your hearts and your minds in Christ Jesus.

> Rejoice in the Lord always; again I will say, Rejoice.
> Let your gentleness be known to everyone. The Lord is near.
> Do not worry about anything,
> but in everything by prayer and supplication
>   with thanksgiving
> let your requests be made known to God.
> And the peace of God, which surpasses all understanding,
> will guard your hearts and your minds in Christ Jesus.

PHILIPPIANS 4:4–7
NRSV

Peace I leave with you; my peace I give to you.

I have said these things to you while I am still with you.
But the Advocate, the Holy Spirit, whom the Father will
　　send in my name,
will teach you everything, and remind you of all that I
　　have said to you.
Peace I leave with you; my peace I give to you.
I do not give to you as the world gives.
Do not let your hearts be troubled, and do not let them
　　be afraid.
You heard me say to you, "I am going away, and I am
　　coming to you."
If you loved me, you would rejoice that I am going to
　　the Father,
because the Father is greater than I.
And now I have told you this before it occurs, so that
　　when it does occur, you may believe.
I will no longer talk much with you, for the ruler of this
　　world is coming.
He has no power over me; but I do as the Father has
　　commanded me,
so that the world may know that I love the Father.
Rise, let us be on our way.

JOHN 14:25–31
NRSV

Neither death, nor life, nor angels, nor rulers . . .
will be able to separate us from the love of God. . . .

> No, in all these things we are more than conquerors
> through him who loved us.
> For I am convinced that neither death, nor life, nor
> angels, nor rulers,
> nor things present, nor things to come, nor powers, nor
> height, nor depth,
> nor anything else in all creation,
> will be able to separate us from the love of God in Christ
> Jesus our Lord.

ROMANS 8:37–39
NRSV

God, who is rich in mercy,
out of the great love with which he loved us . . .
made us alive together with Christ. . . .

But God, who is rich in mercy, out of the great love with
which he loved us
even when we were dead through our trespasses,
made us alive together with Christ—by grace you have
been saved—
and raised us up with him and seated us with him in the
heavenly places in Christ Jesus, so that in the ages to
come he might show the immeasurable riches of his grace
in kindness toward us in Christ Jesus.

For by grace you have been saved through faith, and this
is not your own doing;
it is the gift of God—not the result of works, so that no
one may boast.
For we are what he has made us, created in Christ Jesus
for good works,
which God prepared beforehand to be our way of life.

EPHESIANS 2:4–10
NRSV

He will wipe away every tear from their eyes. . . .

> Then I saw a new heaven and a new earth;
> for the first heaven and the first earth had passed away,
>   and the sea was no more.
> And I saw the holy city, new Jerusalem, coming down
>   out of heaven from God,
> prepared as a bride adorned for her husband;
> and I heard a loud voice from the throne saying,
> "Behold, the dwelling of God is with men.
> He will dwell with them, and they shall be his people,
>   and God himself will be with them;
> and he will wipe away every tear from their eyes, and
>   death shall be no more,
> neither shall there be mourning nor crying nor pain
>   any more,
> for the former things have passed away."

REVELATION 21:1–4

RSV

Listen, I will tell you a mystery!

Listen, I will tell you a mystery! We will not all die, but
we will all be changed, in a moment, in the twinkling of
an eye, at the last trumpet.
For the trumpet will sound, and the dead will be raised
imperishable, and we will be changed.

For this perishable body must put on imperishability,
    and this mortal body must put on immortality.
When this perishable body puts on imperishability,
and this mortal body puts on immortality,
then the saying that is written will be fulfilled:
"Death has been swallowed up in victory."

I CORINTHIANS 15:51–55
NRSV

The Muslim Qur'an

"What is there but our life in this world?
We shall die and we live, and nothing but Time can
    destroy us."
But of that they have no knowledge: they mearly conjecture:

And when Our Clear Signs are rehearsed to them,
their argument is nothing but this:
They say: "Bring back our forefathers, if what you say
    is true!"

Say: "It is Allah who gives you life, then gives you death;
then He will gather you together for the Day of Judgment
About which there is no doubt": but most men
    do not know. . . .

Then Praise be to Allah, Lord of the heavens and Lord of
    the earth,
Lord and Cherisher of all the worlds!

And unto Him alone belongeth Majesty in the heavens
    and the earth:
and He is Exalted in Power, and Full of Wisdom!

Sura Al-Jathiya 45:24–26, 36–37

On the Day of Judgment the whole of the earth will be
    but His handful,
and the heavens will be rolled up in His right hand:
Glory to Him!
High is He above the Partners they attribute to Him!

The Trumpet will be sounded, when all that are in the
    heavens and on earth will swoon,
Except such as it will please Allah.
Then will a second one be sounded, when, behold, they
    will be standing and looking on!

And the Earth will shine with the light of its Lord:
The Record of Deeds will be placed open;
The prophets and the witnesses will be brought forward;
And a just decision pronounced between them;
And they will not be wronged in the least.

And to every soul will be paid in full the fruit of its deeds;
and Allah knoweth best all that they do.

Sura Az-Zumar 39:67–70

And those foremost in faith will be foremost in the
hereafter.
These will be nearest to Allah in the Garden of Bliss:
A number of people from those of old,
and a few from those of later times.
They will be on couches encrusted with gold and precious
stones,
Reclining on them, facing each other.

Round about them will serve youths of perpetual freshness,
with goblets, shining beakers, and cups filled out the
clear-flowing fountains:
No after-ache will they receive therefrom,
nor will they suffer from intoxication:

And with fruits, any that they may select;
and the flesh of fowls, any that they may desire.

And there will be virgin companions with beautiful, big,
and lustrous eyes,
like unto pearls well-guarded.
A reward for the deed of their past Life.

SURA AL-WAQI'A 56:10–24

The Hindu Upanishads

Neither by breathing in nor yet by breathing out
Lives any mortal man:
By something else they live
On which the two [breaths] depend.

Lo! I will declare to thee this mystery
Of Brahman never-failing,
And of what the self becomes
When it comes to [the hour of] death.

Some to the womb return—
Embodied souls, to receive another body;
Others pass into a lifeless stone (sthanu)
In accordance with their works (karma),
In accordance with [the tradition] they had heard (sruta).

When all things sleep, [that] Person is awake,
Assessing all desires:
That is the Pure, that Brahman,
That is the Immortal, so they say:
In It all the worlds are established;
Beyond it none can pass.
    This in truth is That.

KATHA UPANISHAD V:5–8

As a caterpillar, drawing near to the tip of a blade of grass,
prepares its next step and draws itself up towards it,
so does this self,
striking the body aside and dispelling ignorance,
prepare its next step and draw itself up
(for its plunge into the Brahman-world).

As a goldsmith, making use of the material of a
    golden object,
forges another new and more beautiful form,
so does this self,
striking the body aside and dispelling ignorance,
devise another new and more beautiful form, —
be it the form of one of the ancestors
or of a Gandharva (heavenly angels) or of a god
or of one in the Prajapati [world]
or of one in the Brahman [world]
or of any other being. . . .

As a man acts [karma], as he behaves,
so does he become.
Whoso does good, becomes good:
Whose does evil, becomes evil.
By good works a man becomes holy,
by evil [works] he becomes evil. . . .

This indeed, the great, unborn Self, that knows neither
    age nor death
nor fear, is Brahman—yes, Brahman, free from fear!
Who knows this becomes Brahman, free from fear!

BRHADARANYAKA UPANISHAD IV:3–5, 25

The Bhagavad Gita

Never was there a time when I was not,
Nor thou, nor yet these lords of men;
Nor will there be a time when we shall cease to be—
All of us hereafter.

Just as in this body the embodied soul
Must pass through childhood, youth and age,
So too [at death] will he take another body up:
In this a thoughtful man is not perplexed. . . .

Of what is not there is no becoming;
Of what is there is no ceasing to be:
For the boundary-line between the two
Is seen by men who see things as they really are.

Indestructable [alone] is That—know this—
By Which this whole [universe] was spun.
No one at all can bring destruction
On This which passes not away. . . .

Finite, they say, are these [our] bodies
[Indwelt] by an eternal embodied soul—
[A soul] indestructable, incommensurable.
Fight then, O scion of Bharata!

. . . As a man casts off his worn-out clothes
And takes on other new ones [in their place],
So does the embodied soul cast off his worn-out bodies
And enters others new.

II. 12–13, 16–18, 22

Buddhist Sutras

There is a sphere where there is neither earth nor water
    nor heat nor air,
for it is beyond the field of matter;
nor is it the sphere of infinite space, or consciousness,
for it is beyond the field of mind.
There is not the condition of nothingness,
neither is there the state of this world or another world,
nor sun nor moon. This is the uncreated.
This condition I call neither arising nor passing away,
neither dying nor being born. It is without form and
    without change.
It is the eternal, which never originates and never passes
    away.
To find it is the end of sorrow.

There is this unborn, uncreated, unformed, and
    unconditioned.
Were there not this unborn, uncreated, unformed, and
    unconditioned,
there would be no transcendence from the world
of the born, created, formed, and conditioned.
But since, monks, there is the unborn, uncreated,
    unformed, and unconditioned,
therefore there can be transcendence for the born,
    created, formed, and conditioned.

UDANA SUTRA

Buddha's Farewell

My age is now full ripe, my life draws to its close:
I leave you, I depart, relying on myself alone!
Be earnest then, O brethren, holy, full of thought!
Be steadfast in resolve! Keep watch o'er your own hearts!
Who wearies not, but holds fast to his truth and law,
Shall cross this sea of life, shall make an end of grief.

MAHAPARINIRVANA SUTRA

The Pure Land

There ne'er was a country so brightened with gladness
As the Land of the Pure far off to the West.
There stands Amitabha with shining adornments,
He makes all things ready for the Eternal Feast.
He draws every burdened soul up from the depths
And lifts them into his peaceful abode.
The great transformation is accomplished for the worm
Who is freed from the body's oppressive sorrows.
It receives as a gift a spiritual body,
A body which shines in the sea of spirits.

And who indeed is it with grace in his tones,
Who sends his smile out to the dwellings of the suffering;
And who indeed is it whose glance is like the sun
Who shows his compassion on life and is victor?
Yes, it is God himself, who sits on the throne
And, by his Law, redeems from all need.
With gold-adorned arm, with crown of bright jewels,
With power over sin, over grief, over death.
None other is like to our God in his greatness,
And none can requite his compassion's great power!

THE WHITE LOTUS ODE

The Tibetan Book of the Dead

O son of noble family, now what is called death has arrived. You are not alone in leaving this world, it happens to everyone, so do not feel desire and yearning for this life. Even if you feel desire and yearning you cannot stay, you can only wander in samsara [the wheel of life]. Do not desire, do not yearn. Remember the Three Jewels. . . .

O son of noble family, when your body and mind separate, the dharmata will appear, pure and clear yet hard to discern, luminous and brilliant, with terrifying brightness, shimmering like a mirage on a plain in spring. Do not be afraid of it, do not be bewildered. This is the natural radiance of your own dharmata, therefore recognize it.

TRANSLATED BY FRANCESCA FREMANTLE &
CHÖGYAM TRUNGPA

Poetry

Star Light

Perhaps
    after death
the strange timelessness, matterlessness,
    absolute differentness
        of eternity
will be shot through
like a starry night
with islands of familiar and beautiful
joys.

For I should like
to spend a star
sitting beside Grandpapa Bach
at the organ, learning, at last, to play
    the C minor fugue as he, essentially,
    heard it burst into creation;

and another star
    of moor and mist, and through the shadows
    the cold muzzle of the dog against my hand,

and walk with Emily. We would not need to
talk, nor ever go back to the damp of
Haworth parsonage for tea.

I should like to eat a golden meal
    with my brothers Gregory and Basil,
    and my sister Macrina. We would raise
    our voices and laugh and be a little drunk
    with love and joy.

I should like a theatre star,
    and Will yelling, "No! No! that's not
    how I wrote it! but perhaps it's better
    that way: 'To be or not to be:' All
    right, then! Let it stand!"

And I should like
    another table
    —Yes, Plato, please come, and you, too,
Socrates, for this is the essential table
of which all other tables are only
flickering shadows on the wall.
This is the heavenly banquet,
(Oh, come!)
the eternal convivium.

The sky blazes with stars!

MADELEINE L'ENGLE
from *The Weather of the Heart*

I don't know which is wearier,
my body or my spirit.
The disease eats at my bones,
the medicines wipe me out.
But missing you
is the heavier burden.
When I feel that my pains are your will,
something you want to redeem,
they are not hard to carry.
When I find in them no sense,
they seem only destructive.
I want to cry out in frustration
for all the wrong in the world.
We are small people, God,
as easily rolled up and crushed as paper.
The longest of our lives
does not last one of your seconds.
Hold us close then in your meaning
lest we feel terribly badly made.
Help us to believe
deep in our souls
that you have purposes for our dying
and you let nothing decent be lost.

JOHN TULLY CARMODY
God Is No Illusion: Meditations on the End of Life
Poem No. 24

I am learning
that I must let myself go,
drift out on your darkness,
sail along by the stars.
Nothing and no one
can assure me about you.
You have to be
your own guarantor.
So I pray:
Do not baby me
but remember my weakness,
giving me the diet
my soul needs each now.
Sharpen my mind,
anneal my soul,
stimulate my endorphins
to hold off my pain.
I know that I am dying
and I want to go well
but not without carrying
her whom I love.
So grant in your heaven
loving and marrying
an endless unfolding
of what began well
in flesh you took to yourself
to dwell among us
and die to defeat our death.

JOHN TULLY CARMODY
God Is No Illusion: Meditations of the End of Life
Poem No. 31

I died a mineral and became a plant.
I died a plant and rose an animal.
I died an animal and I was a man.
Why should I fear? When was I less by dying?
Yet once more I shall die as a man, to soar
With the blessed angels; but even from angelhood
I must pass on. All except God perishes.
When I have sacrificed my angel soul,
I shall become that which no mind ever conceived.
O, let me not exist! for Non-Existence proclaims,
"To Him we shall return."

JALAL AL-DIN RUMI (1207–1273)
Muslim poet and mystic

We shall not cease from exploration

We shall not cease from exploration
And the end of all our exploring
Will be to arrive where we started
And know the place for the first time.
Through the unknown, remembered gate
When the last of earth left to discover
Is that which was the beginning;
At the source of the longest river
The voice of the hidden waterfall
And the children in the apple-tree
Not known, because not looked for
But heard, half-heard, in the stillness
Between two waves of the sea.
Quick now, here, now, always—
A condition of complete simplicity
(Costing not less than everything)
And all shall be well and
All manner of thing shall be well
When the tongues of flame are in-folded
Into the crowned knot of fire
And the fire and the rose are one.

T. S. ELIOT (1888–1965)
from "Little Gidding" in *Four Quartets*

Home is where one starts from.

Home is where one starts from. As we grow older
The world becomes stranger, the pattern more complicated
Of dead and living. Not the intense moment
Isolated, with no before and after,
But a lifetime burning in every moment
And not the lifetime of one man only
But of old stones that cannot be deciphered.
There is a time for the evening under starlight,
A time for the evening under lamplight
(The evening with the photograph album).
Love is most nearly itself
When here and now cease to matter.
Old men ought to be explorers
Here and there does not matter
We must be still and still moving
Into another intensity
For a further union, a deeper communion
Through the dark cold and the empty desolation,
The wave cry, the wind cry, the vast waters
Of the petrel and the porpoise. In my end is my beginning.

T. S. Eliot (1888–1965)
From "East Coker" in *Four Quartets*

So I turn my head and look towards death now.
Feeling my way through the tunnel with the space of
emptiness and quiet.
That shimmering silence that awaits me.

I do not have a passion to remain, but a willingness to go.
My body is tired and my soul longs to fly free to the
shores of no pain.

Thoughts clutch at my gown as I make my way down
the stony corridors.
Holding me, pulling me back to concerns I am
finished with.

A breath . . . a pause.
I relax, and then float on toward the opening awaiting me.
This place of peace resides so deep inside me;
It is one, huge and all encompassing.

In the quiet of my mind I find the greatest Truth, the
great Mother/Father.
This is the Hail Mary, the Rod and Staff of Comfort,
The Kingdom and the Glory.

Yea, though I walk through the valley of death, I will
fear no evil.

This is my direction now; inward to the green pastures,
to the great light of divine love, the great peace of
All Knowing.

KAREN PAINE-GERNEE
(written shortly before her death)
from *Life Prayers from Around the World*

Entry

This long shift at the hospital behind,
and reaching this point after midnight,

such a simple thing, it seems.
Turn the key in the light of a moon so bright
that I can see the fading grey-blue paint
on the sturdy wooden door of my own home.

Such a simple thing, it seems,
opening that door,
and having entered, closing it behind.
I stand there in the chill air at the bottom of the stairs.

And as I climb
the room grows warm, and
it seems such a simple thing as I turn on the light
and smell the shadows of this morning's incense.
My hesitation falls like laundry on the floor.

Such a simple thing, it seems,
just being peaceful here,

at home at last,
yet for the first time, home,

alone.

The silence welcomes me.
The solitude within the solitude calls out a warm salute.
Such a simple thing.

It seems it has been waiting here,

forever.

Waiting to embrace me like a brother.
It seems such a simple thing.

CHRISTOPHER CARSTENS
Contemporary poet

You waited until you were alone.
Death is a private thing.
You knew your last act
was to a different audience.

As it entered you—
oh how you must have danced!
curving toward God,
elegant and alone.

Dear one, what is it like?
Tell us! What is death?

Birth,
you say, your voice swathed in wings.
I am born in the endless beginning.
I am not. I am.

You start turning into us,
we who love you.
You weep in our sadness,

you laugh when we do,
you greet each moment fresh,
when we do.

So may your gift of loving enter our own
and be with us that way, forever.

ELIAS AMIDON
from *Life Prayers from Around the World*

⁊

Inside this new love, die.
Your way begins on the other side.
Become the sky.
Take an axe to the prison wall.
Escape.
Walk out like someone suddenly born into color.
Do it now.
You're covered with thick cloud.
Slide out the side. Die,
and be quiet. Quietness is the surest sign
that you've died.
Your old life was a frantic running
from silence.

The speechless full moon
comes out now.

JALAL AL-DIN RUMI (1207–1273)
Muslim poet and mystic

All Souls' Day

Be careful, then, and be gentle about death.
For it is hard to die, it is difficult to go through
the door, even when it opens.
And the poor dead, when they have left the walled
and silvery city of the now hopeless body
where are they to go, Oh where are they to go?

They linger in the shadow of the earth.
The earth's long conical shadow is full of souls
that cannot find the way across the sea of change.
Be kind, Oh be kind to your dead
and give them a little encouragement
and help them to build their little ship of death.

For the soul has a long, long journey after death
to the sweet home of pure oblivion.
Each needs a little ship, a little ship
and the proper store of meal for the longest journey.
Oh, from out of your heart
provide for your dead once more, equip them
like departing mariners, lovingly.

D. H. LAWRENCE (1885–1930)

When Lilacs Last in the Dooryard Bloomed

Come, lovely and soothing Death,
Undulate round the world, serenely arriving, arriving,
In the day, in the night, to all, to each,
Sooner or later, delicate Death.

Praised be the fathomless universe
For life and joy, and for objects and knowledge curious;
And for love, sweet love—But praise! O praise and praise
For the sure-enwinding arms of cool-enfolding Death.

WALT WHITMAN (1819–1892)

If you would indeed behold the spirit
of death, open your heart wide
unto the body of life.
For life and death are one, even as the
river and the sea are one.

KAHLIL GIBRAN (1883–1931)

A Visitation

You told me of the cancer
your pain and fear . . .

A golden light filled the room
a miracle between us:

An angel
speaking of peace:

"Greater than Faith
Stronger than Hope
Deeper than Love
Peace is the water
In the River of Truth
And Truth is all that is"

I bowed to your pain
I took some into my flesh

I wept for you in your sorrow
I offered the Blue Buddha
Incense and Light
And I wept
because I forget and suffer

I too am a man, I am forgiving
and I am For

Giving

this gift to you and me:
the angel was
you and I . . . you see.

RAYN ROBERTS
Contemporary poet

Vigil strange I kept on the field one night

Vigil strange I kept on the field one night:

When you, my son and my comrade, dropt at my side
that day,

One look I but gave, which your dear eyes return'd, with
a look I shall never forget;

One touch of your hand to mine, O boy, reach'd up as
you lay on the ground;

. . . Then on the earth partially reclining, sat by your
side, leaning my chin in my hands;

Passing sweet hours, immortal and mystic hours with
you, dearest comrade—Not a tear, not a word;

Vigil of silence, love and death—vigil for you my son
and my soldier.

WALT WHITMAN (1819–1892)

I heard a Fly buzz—when I died—
The Stillness in the Room
Was like the Stillness in the Air—
Between the Heaves of Storm—

The Eyes around—had wrung them dry—
And Breaths were gathering firm
For that last Onset—when the King
Be witness—in the Room—

I willed my Keepsakes—Signed away
What portion of me be
Assignable—and then it was
There interposed a Fly—

With Blue—uncertain stumbling Buzz—
Between the light—and me—
And then the Windows failed—and then
I could not see to see—

EMILY DICKINSON (1830–1886)

Because I could not stop for Death—
He kindly stopped for me—
The Carriage held but just Ourselves—
And Immortality.

We slowly drove—He knew no haste
And I had put away
My labour and my leisure too,
For His Civility—

We passed the School, where Children strove
At Recess—in the Ring—
We passed the Fields of Gazing Grain—
We passed the Setting Sun—

Or rather—He passed Us—
The Dews drew quivering and chill—
For only Gossamer, my Gown—
My Tippet—only Tulle—

We paused before a House that seemed
A Swelling of the Ground—
The Roof was scarcely visible—
The Cornice—in the Ground—

Since then—'tis Centuries—and yet
Feels shorter than the Day
I first surmised the Horses' Heads
Were toward Eternity—

EMILY DICKINSON (1830–1886)

Readings

May we find the world in our lifetime,
our completion in the World to Come,
and our hopes realized in those who follow us.
May our hearts meditate in understanding,
our mouths speak wisdom,
our tongues sing songs of jubilation.
May our eyes look straight before us,
afire with the light of Torah,
our faces shining with a heavenly light.
May our lips utter knowledge,
and our inward parts rejoice.
May our footsteps hasten towards the words
of the Ancient of Days.

JEWISH TALMUD
B.BER.17A

What, I pray you, is dying? Just what it is to put off a garment. For the body is about the soul as a garment; and after laying this aside for a short time by means of death, we shall resume it again with more splendor.

St. John Chrysostom (347–407)
Early Christian saint

သို့

We rejoice over a birth and mourn over a death. But we should not. For when a man is born, who knows what he will do or how he will end? But when a man dies, we may rejoice—if left a good name and this world in peace.

Jewish Midrash
Ecclesiastes Rabbah 7:1, (4)

သို့

The first sign of love to God is not to be afraid of death, and to be always waiting for it. For death unites the friend to his friend—the seeker to the object which he seeks.

Al-Ghazali (1058–1111)
Muslim medieval mystic

The meaning of death is not the annihilation of the spirit, but its separation from the body, and that the resurrection and day of assembly do not mean a return to a new existence after annihilation, but the bestowal of a new form or frame to the spirit.

AL-GHAZALI (1058–1111), Muslim medieval mystic

I am that supreme and fiery force that sends forth all living sparks. Death hath no part in me, yet I bestow death, wherefore I am girt about with wisdom as with wings. . . . I am the source of the thundered word by which all creatures were made, I permeate all things that they may not die. I am life.

HILDEGARD OF BINGEN (1098–1179),
Medieval abbess and theologian
poet, artist, musician, scientist, and healer

The death of such souls is ever sweeter and gentler than was their whole life; for they die amid the delectable encounters and impulses of love, like the swan, which sings most sweetly when it is about to die and is at the point of death. For this reason David said: "Precious is the death of the just"; for at such a time the rivers of love of the soul are about to enter the sea, and they are so broad and dense and motionless that they seem to be seas already. The beginning and the end unite together to accompany the just man as he departs and goes forth to his kingdom, and praises are heard from the ends of the earth, which are the glory of the just man.

St. John of the Cross (1542–1591),
Medieval Christian mystic
from *Living Flame of Love*

The Rabbi who said, "Repent the day before thy death," was asked by his disciples how they could follow his advice, as man was unable to tell upon what day his death would occur. He answered, "Consider every day thy last; be ever ready with penitence and good deeds."

JEWISH TALMUD
Shabbat 153A

There once was a King who had a son dear to him,
yet the son was rebellious and went away.
The son took a servant and went on a journey of one
    hundred days.
The father grieved terribly.
Friends said to the son, "Return to your father, he
    loves you."
But the son replied, "I cannot do that."
The father sent a messenger and asked the son to return.
But the son said, "I cannot. I have not the strength."
So once again, a messenger was sent by the King to say,
    "Then return to me as far as you can,
    and the rest of the way I will come to you."

So the Master of the Universe says to each of us,
    "Come to me as far as you can,
    and I will meet you there."

PASIKTA RABBATI

In the great night my heart will go out;
Toward me the darkness comes rustling.
In the great night my heart will go out.

PAPAGO PRAYER

Of My Father's Cancer, and His Dreams

He'll soon give in to the rising pain
and crave the needle that will numb
his knowledge of a passing world,
and bring the consummating sleep
he knows will come.

JIMMY CARTER
Always a Reckoning

When I die if you need to weep
Cry for your brother or sister
Walking the street beside you
And when you need me put your arms around anyone
And give them what you need to give me.

I want to leave you something
Something better than words or sounds.

Look for me in the people I've known or loved
And if you cannot give me away
At least let me live in your eyes and not on your mind.

You can love me most be letting hands touch hands
By letting bodies touch bodies
And by letting go of children that need to be free.

Love doesn't die; people do
So when all that's left of me is love
Give me away.

ANONYMOUS
from *Life Prayers from Around the World*

Every day I will be on the watch for death, and will look about me that he take me not by surprise. I will learn how to die; I will turn my thoughts to yonder world. Lord, I see that there is no remaining here; Lord, in sooth, I will not save up my sorrow and repentance till death.

BLESSED HENRY SUSO (1295–1366)
German Christian mystic from *Eternal Wisdom*

Your essence was not born and will not die. It is neither being nor nonbeing. It is not a void nor does it have form. It experiences neither pleasure nor pain. If you ponder what it is in you that feels the pain of this sickness, and beyond that you do not think or desire or ask anything, and if your mind dissolves like vapour in the sky, then the path to rebirth is blocked and the moment of instant release has come.

BASSUI (1327–87)
Zen Buddhist

"So death will come to fetch you?" "No, not death, but God Himself. Death is not the horrible spectre we see represented in pictures. The catechism teaches that death is the separation of the soul from the body; that is all. I am not afraid of a separation which will unite me for ever with God."

From ST THERESE OF LISIEUX (1873–1897)
French nun and mystic from *Counsels and Memories*

Out of life comes death, and out of death, life,
Out of the young, the old, and out of the old, the young,
Out of waking, sleep, and out of sleep, waking,
the stream of creation and dissolution never stop.

HERACLEITUS (540–480 BCE)
Greek philosopher

Know, beloved that we cannot understand the future world
until we know what death is; and we cannot know what
death is until we know what life is; nor can we understand
what life is until we know what the spirit is—the seat of the
knowledge of God.

AL-GHAZALI (1058–1111)
Muslim medieval mystic

Prayers

The Prayer of St. Francis of Assisi

Lord, make me an instrument of your peace.
Where there is hatred, let me sow love;
where there is injury, pardon;
where there is discord, harmony;
where there is doubt, faith;
where there is despair, hope;
where there is darkness, light;
where there is sadness, joy.

Grant that I may not so much seek to be consoled
    as to console;
to be understood as to understand;
to be loved as to love.
For it is in giving that we receive;
it is in pardoning that we are pardoned;
and it is in dying that we are born to eternal life. Amen.

ST. FRANCIS OF ASSISI (1182–1226)

On Waking in Prison

O God, early in the morning I cry to you.
Help me to pray
And to concentrate my thoughts on you:
I cannot do this alone.
In me there is darkness,
But with you there is light;
I am lonely, but you do not leave me;
I am feeble in heart, but with you there is help;
I am restless, but with you there is peace.
In me there is bitterness, but with you there is patience;
I do not understand your ways,
But you know the way for me . . . .

DIETRICH BONHOEFFER (1906–1945)
Written while waiting execution in a Nazi prison

Lord Jesus Christ, you are the only source of health for the
living, and you promise eternal life to the dying. I entrust
myself to your holy will. If you wish me to stay longer in this
world, I pray that you will heal me of my present sickness. If
you wish me to leave this world, I readily lay aside this
mortal body, in the sure hope of receiving an immortal body
which shall enjoy everlasting health. I ask only that you
relieve me of pain, that whether I live or I die, I may rest
peaceful and contented.

ERASMUS (1469–1536)
Book of Prayers

For People Dying

God our creator and our end,
give us grace to bear bravely
the changes we must undergo,
the pain we may have to face
to come to our home with you.
Give us the courage to welcome
that unimaginable moment awaiting us;
give us trust and confidence;
and at the last give us peace.

from A New Zealand Prayer Book (Anglican)/
He Karakia Mihinare o Aotearoa

A Prayer for a Peaceful Death
    Dear God,
    I think that I am going to die.
    I think I'm going to leave this world.
    Give me strength, Lord, that I might not fear.
    I know, dear God, that when I leave I do not die, that
        when I die I shall continue to live in Your arms, in
        Your mind, in Your spirit forever.
    And yet, dear Lord, my heart beats wildly.
    I am so scared.
    My heart breaks to be leaving those I love: my friends,
        my mate, my children, my loves.
    And yet I know I shall not be leaving.
    Heal my heart that I might know this.

    Heal theirs also that they might know we are bound
        together forever, through Your power, which is
        greater than the power of death.
    For the arms of God are the arms of life.
    Dear God, I surrender my body to You.
    If it serves Your purpose, then may I live,
    And if the arc of destiny now calls me home, then let me
        die in peace, dear God.
    Send the Angel of Death to me when it is my time.
    Let me feel the Angel's tenderness as I exit this world
        and enter the next.
    Let me go from dark to light,
    Let me feel the love of God.

    Please comfort me and those I love.
    Now while I wait, now while I face my fears and my pain,
    Let me see the truth and know Your peace.
    May my family and friends now feel the same.
    For we shall not be torn asunder.
    Our love is larger than death,

Our bond is eternal.
Your life is with us always.
So I believe, so shall I feel, now and forever.

Hallelujah, Lord.
For Yours is the power and the glory and love.
You are with me as I am with You.

Thank you, God, for what has been.
Thank you, God, for what shall be.
Forgive me my darkness,
Reveal to me Your light.
Bless my family.
Take care of them, my darling ones.
Take me home.
I willingly surrender.
I shall not fear, for You are with me.

Thank you, Lord.
Thank you, Lord.
Thank you, Lord.
Amen.

MARIANNE WILLIAMSON
Illuminata

Bardo Protection from Fear

When the journey of my life has reached its end,
and since no relatives go with me from this world
I wander in the bardo state alone,
may the peaceful and wrathful buddhas send out the
    power of their compassion
and clear away the dense darkness of ignorance.

When parted from beloved friends, wandering alone,
my own projections' empty forms appear,
may the buddhas send out the power of their compassion
so that the bardo's terrors do not come. . . .

In all the stages of learning, high, middle and low,
may I understand just by hearing, thinking and seeing;
wherever I am born, may that land be blessed,
so that all sentient beings may be happy.

Translated by
FRANCESCA FREMANTLE & CHÖGYAM TRUNGPA
from *The Tibetan Book of the Dead*

Vidui: Jewish Prayer of Confession

O God, the God of my ancestors, hear my prayer. Forgive me for the sins I have committed during my lifetime. I am ashamed of all those things I have done wrong. Please accept my suffering and pain as an atonement and forgive me my sins, for I know it is against You that I have sinned.

O God, the God of my ancestors, may it be Your will that I sin no more. In Your Mercy, cleanse me of all my sins, but not through suffering and disease. Heal me and all those who are also ill.

I acknowledge before you, Lord, my God and the God of my ancestors, that my life is in Your hands. May You heal me completely, but if it is Your will that I die from this illness, then I accept Your decree.

May my death be an atonement for all the sins, errors, and transgressions that I have committed against You. May You grant me a portion in Gan Eden and in the world-to-come.

Protector of all widows and orphans, be with and watch over my loved ones, for our souls are bound together.

Into Your hands I commit my spirit, for you have redeemed me, O Lord God of truth.

Shema Yisrael, Adonai eloheinu, Adonai echad.
Hear, O Israel, the Lord our God, the Lord is One.

You are blessed in the Mother's eyes;
You are blessed in your children's eyes;
You are blessed in all your doings;
You are blessed in all your endings;
You are blessed and purified.
There is no pain where you are going;
There is no sadness where you are received;
There is only the happiness of going home;
There is only the bliss of having arrived.

ZAUZSANNA E. BUDAPEST
from *The Goddess in the Bedroom*

Hail to thee, mighty Lord, all-potent Vishnu!
Soul of the universe, unchangeable,
Holy, eternal, always one in nature,
whether revealed as Brahma, Hari, Siva—
Creator or Preserver or Destroyer—
Thou art the cause of final liberation;
Whose form is one, yet manifold; whose essence
Is one, yet diverse; tenuous, yet vast;
Discernible, yet indiscernible;
Root of the world, yet of the world composed;
Prop of the universe, yet more minute
Than earth's minutest particles; abiding
In every creature, yet without defilement,
Imperishable, one with perfect wisdom.

VISHNU PURANA

A Prayer from the Taizé Community

Holy Spirit, Spirit of the Living God,
you breathe in us
on all that is inadequate and fragile,
You make living water spring even
from our hurts themselves.
And through you, the valley of tears
becomes a place of wellsprings.
So, in an inner life
with neither beginning nor end,
your continual presence
makes new freshness break through. Amen.

BROTHER ROGER OF TAIZÉ

Bring us, O Lord God, at our last awakening into the
    house and gate of heaven;
to enter into that gate and dwell in that house,
where there shall be no darkness nor dazzling, but one
    equal light;
no noise nor silence, but one equal music,
no fears nor hopes, but one equal possession;
no ends, nor beginnings, but one equal eternity;
in the habitation of thy glory and dominion, world
    without end. Amen.

JOHN DONNE (1572–1631)

The Lord bless us, and keep us,
and shew the light of His countenance upon us,
And be merciful unto us,
And give us peace!
I commend to Thee, O Lord,
my soul, and my body,
my mind, and my thoughts,
my prayers, and my vows,
my senses, and my limbs,
my words, and my works,
my life, and my death;
my brothers, and my sisters,
and their children;
my friends, my benefactors, my well wishers,
those who have a claim on me;
my kindred, and my neighbours,
my country, and all Christendom.
I commend to Thee, Lord,
my impulses, and my startings,
my intentions, and my attempts,
my going out, and my coming in,
my sitting down, and my rising up.

LANCELOT ANDREWES (1555–1626)

in *Private Devotions*

A Buddhist Prayer

> Light without equal, so pure;
> Beauty without peer, so serene;
> We desire to be reborn with you.
> Power without limits, so strong;
> Glory without end, so majestic;
> We desire to be reborn with you.

Kayla's Prayer

Listen to my voice,
O Lord our God
and the God of my ancestors.

I lie here on the brink of life,
Seeking peace, seeking comfort, seeking You.
To You, O Lord, I call and to You, O Lord, I make
    my supplication.
Do not ignore my plea.
Let Your mercy flow over me like the waters,
Let the record of my life be a bond between us,
Listen to my voice when I call,
Be gracious to me and answer me.

I have tried, O Lord, to help You complete creation,
I have carried Your yoke my whole life.
I have tried to do my best.
Count my effort for the good of my soul,
Forgive me for when I have stumbled on Your path.
I can do no more, let my family carry on after me,
Let others carry on after me.

Protector of the helpless, healer of the brokenhearted,
Protect my beloved family with those whose soul my
    own soul is bound.
Their hearts depend on mine,
Heal their hearts when they come to depend on You.

Let my soul rest forever under the wings of Your presence,
Grant me a share in the world-to-come.
I have tried to love You with all my heart and with all
    my soul,
And even though You come to take my soul,

Even though I don't know why You come,
Even though I am angry at the way You take me,
For Your sake I will still proclaim:
Hear, O Israel, the Lord is our God, the Lord alone.
The Lord is with me, I shall not fear.

Bibliography and
Recommended Readings

General Death and Dying

Albom, Mitch. *Tuesdays with Morrie: An Old Man, a Young Man, and Life's Greatest Lesson.* New York: Doubleday, 1997.

Anderson, Patricia. *All of Us: Americans Talk About the Meaning of Death.* New York: Delacort Press, 1996.

Arnold, Johann Christoph. *Be Not Afraid: Overcoming the Fear of Death.* Farmington, PA: The Plough Publishing House, 2002.

Basta, L. L., MD. *Life and Death on Your Own Terms.* Amherst, N.Y.: Promethius Books, 2001.

Bernard, Jan Sellikan, and Miriam Schneider. *The True Work of Dying: A Practical and Compassionate Guide to Easing the Dying Process.* New York: Avon Books, 1996.

Buckman, Robert, MD. *"I Don't Know What to Say . . .": How to Help and Support Someone Who is Dying.* New York: Vintage Books, 1988.

Byock, Ira, MD. *Dying Well: The Prospect for Growth at the End of Life.* New York: Riverhead Books, 1997.

Callahan, Daniel. *The Troubled Dream of Life: In Search of a Peaceful Death.* Washington, D.C.: Georgetown University Press, 2000.

Callanan, Maggie, and Patricia Kelley. *Final Gifts.* New York: Bantam, 1993.

Carmody, John. *Conversations with a Dying Friend.* New York: Paulist Press, 1992.

Carroll, David. *Living with Dying: A Loving Guide for Family and Close Friends.* New York: McGraw Hill, 1986.

Coberly, Margaret, PhD. *Sacred Passage: How to Provide Fearless, Compassionate Care for the Dying*. Boston: Shambhala Publications, 2003.

DeSpelder, Lynne Ann, and Albert Lee Strickland. *The Last Dance: Encountering Death and Dying*. Boston: McGraw Hill, 2002 (6th Edition).

Eliade, Mircea, ed. *Death, Afterlife, and the Soul (Selections from The Encyclopedia of Religion)*. New York: Macmillan, 1987.

Green, Ron Wooten. *When the Dying Speak: How to Listen to and Learn from Those Facing Death*. Chicago: Loyola Press, 2001.

Grollman, Earl A. *Talking About Death: A Dialogue Between Parent and Child*. Boston: Beacon Press, 1990.

Guthrie, Alfred E. "Pastoral Care of the Sick and Dying." *Homiletic and Pastoral Review*. August–September (1996): 25–30.

Heinz, Donald. *The Last Passage: Recovering a Death of Our Own*. New York: Oxford University Press, 1999.

Johnson, Elizabeth A. *As Someone Dies: A Handbook for the Living*. Carson, Calif.: Hay House, Inc., 1995.

Kessler, David. *The Rights of the Dying: A Companion for Life's Final Moments*. New York: HarperCollins, 1997.

Klein, Allen. *The Courage to Laugh: Humor, Hope, and Healing in the Face of Death and Dying*. New York: Jeremy P. Tarcher/Putnam, 1998.

Kramer, Kenneth. *The Sacred Art of Dying*. New York: Paulist Press, 1988.

Kübler-Ross, Elisabeth. *Death: The Final Stage of Growth*. New York: Touchstone, 1975.

——. *On Life After Death*. Berkeley, Calif.: Celestial Arts, 1991.

——. *Living with Death and Dying*. New York: Touchstone, 1997.

——. *On Children and Death: How Children and Their Parents Can and Do Cope with Death*. New York: Collier Books, 1997.

——. *On Death and Dying*. New York: Touchstone, 1997.

——. *Questions and Answers on Death and Dying*. New York: Touchstone, 1997.

——. *To Live Until We Say Goodbye*. New York: Touchstone, 1997.

——. *The Wheel of Life: A Memoir of Living and Dying*. New York: Scribner, 1997.

——. *Working It Through: An Elisabeth Kübler-Ross Workshop on Life, Death and Transition*. New York: Touchstone, 1997.

——. *Death Is of Vital Importance: On Life, Death, and Life After Death*. Talman Co, 1998.

Kübler-Ross, Elisabeth and David Kessler. *Life Lessons*. New York: Scribner, 2000.

Kuhl, David, MD. *What Dying People Want: Practical Wisdom for the End of Life*. New York: PublicAffairs, 2002.

Levine, Stephen. *Meetings at the Edge: Dialogues with the Grieving and the Dying, the Healing and the Healed*. New York: Anchor Book, 1984.

———. Healing into Life and Death. New York: Anchor Book, 1987.

———. *A Year to Live: How to Live This Year As If It Were Your Last*. New York: Random House, 1997.

Levine, Stephen, and Ondrea Levine. *Who Dies? An Investigation of Conscious Living and Conscious Dying*. New York: Anchor Book, 1982.

Lynn, Joanna, MD, Joan Harrold, MD, and The Center to Improve Care of the Dying. *Handbook for Mortals: Guidance for People Facing Serious Illness*. New York: Oxford University Press. 1999.

Mitford, Jessica. *The American Way of Death*. New York: Simon & Schuster, 1963.

———. *The American Way of Death Revisited*. New York: Alfred Knopf, 1998.

Morris, Virginia. *Talking About Death Won't Kill You: Find Comfort and Control by Lifting the Cloud of Denial*. New York: Workman Publishing, 2001.

Nuland, Sherwin B. *How We Die: Reflections on Life's Final Chapter*. New York: Alfred Knopf, 1993.

Palmer, Greg. *Death: The Trip of a Lifetime*. San Francisco: HarperSanFrancisco, 1993.

Peck, M. Scott. *Denial of the Soul: Spiritual and Medical Perspectives on Euthanasia and Mortality*. New York: Harmony Books, 1997.

Singh, Kathleen Dowling. *The Grace in Dying: How We Are Transformed Spiritually As We Die*. San Francisco: HarperSanFrancisco, 1998.

Smith, Harold Ivan. *Finding Your Way to Say Good-bye: Comfort for the Dying and Those who Care for Them*. Notre Dame, Ind.: Ave Maria Press, 2002.

Smith, Rodney. *Lessons from the Dying*. Boston: Wisdom Publications, 1998.

Staton, Jana, Roger W. Shuy, and Ira A. Byock. *Few Months to Live: Different Paths to Life's End*. Washington, D.C.: Georgetown University Press, 2001.

Stillwater, Michael, and Gary Remal Malkin, eds. *Graceful Passages: A Companion for Living and Dying* (Book CD-ROM edition) Novato, Calif: New World Library; 2003.

Webb, Marilyn. *The Good Death: The New American Search to Reshape the End of Life.* New York: Bantam Books, 1997.

Weenolsen, Patricia. *The Art of Dying: How to Leave this World with Dignity and Grace, at Peace with Yourself and Your Loved Ones.* New York: St. Martin's Press, 1996.

Wilcock, Penelope. *Spiritual Care of Dying and Bereaved People.* Harrisburg, Pa.: Morehouse Publishing, 1996.

Wogrin, Carol. *Matters of Life and Death: Finding the Words to Say Goodbye.* New York: Broadway Books, 2001.

Spiritual Concerns and Readings

Ashcroft, Mary Ellen, and Holly Bridges Elliott. *Bearing our Sorrows: Christian Reflections for Courage, Hope and Healing.* San Francisco: HarperSanFrancisco, 1993.

Bane, J. Donald, et al., ed. *Death and Ministry: Pastoral Care of the Dying and the Bereaved.* New York: Seabury Press, 1975.

Bernardin, Joseph Cardinal. *The Gift of Peace.* Chicago: Loyola Press, 1997.

Carmody, John Tully. *God is No Illusion: Meditations on the End of Life.* Valley Forge, Pa.: Trinity Press International, 1997.

Carter, Jimmy. *Always a Reckoning.* New York: Times Books, 1995.

Dalai Lama, His Holiness. *Advice on Dying and Living a Better Life.* New York: Atria Books, 2002.

Hughes, Kathleen, and Joseph A. Favazza, eds. *A Reconciliation Sourcebook.* Chicago: Liturgy Training Publications, 1997.

Kalina, Kathy. *Midwife for Souls: Spiritual Care for the Dying.* Boston: Pauline Books and Media, 1993.

Longaker, Christine. *Facing Death and Finding Hope: A Guide to the Emotional and Spiritual Care of the Dying.* New York: Doubleday, 1997.

Remen, Rachel Naomi. *Kitchen Table Wisdom: Stories that Heal.* New York: Riverhead Books, 1996.

——. *My Grandfather's Blessings: Stories of Strength, Refuge, and Belonging.* New York: Riverhead Books, 2000.

Rinpoche, Sogyal. *The Tibetan Book of Living and Dying.* San Francisco: HarperSanFrancisco, 1993.

Sharp, Joseph. *Living Our Dying: A Way to the Sacred in Everyday Life.* New York: Hyperion, 1996.

Wilcock, Penelope. *Spiritual Care of Dying and Bereaved People.* Harrisburg, Pa.: Morehouse Publishing, 1996.

Caregiving and Hospice

Beresford, Larry. *The Hospice Handbook: A Complete Guide.* Boston: Little, Brown & Co., 1993.

Bernard, Jan Sellikan, and Miriam Schneider. *The True Work of Dying: A Practical and Compassionate Guide to Easing the Dying Process.* New York: Avon Books, 1996.

Boerstler, Richard W., and Hulen S. Kornfield. *Life to Death: Harmonizing the Transition.* Rochester, Vt.: Healing Arts Press, 1995.

Buckingham, Robert W. *The Handbook of Hospice Care.* Amherst, N.Y.: Prometheus Books, 1996.

Byock, Ira, MD. *Dying Well: The Prospect for Growth at the End of Life.* New York: Riverhead Books, 1997.

Collett, Merrill. *At Home with Dying: A Zen Hospice Approach.* Boston: Shambala, 1999.

Hoefler, James M. *Managing Death: The First Guide for Patients, Family Members, and Care Providers on Forgoing Treatment at the End of Life.* Boulder, Colo.: Westview Press, 1997.

Kalina, Kathy. *Midwife for Souls: Spiritual Care for the Dying.* Boston: Pauline Books and Media, 1993.

Lattanzi-Licht, Marcia, with John J. Mahoney and Galen W. Miller. *The Hospice Choice: In Pursuit of a Peaceful Death.* New York: Fireside Books, 1998.

McLeod, Beth Witrogen. *Caregiving: The Spiritual Journey of Love, Loss, and Renewal.* New York: John Wiley & Sons, Inc., 1999.

Rosen, Elliott J. *Families Facing Death: A Guide for Healthcare Professionals and Volunteers.* San Francisco: Jossey-Bass Publishers, 1998.

Smith, Douglas C. *Caregiving: Hospice-Proven Techniques for Healing Body and Soul.* New York: Macmillan, 1997.

Stoddard, Sandol. *The Hospice Movement: A Better Way of Caring for the Dying.* New York: Vintage Books, 1992.

Suttcliffe, Pauline; Guinevere Tufnell, and Ursula Cornesh, eds. *Working with the Dying and Bereaved.* New York: Routledge, 1998.

Visiting Nurses Association of America. *Caregiver's Handbook: A Complete Guide to Home Health Care.* New York: DK Publishing, Inc., 1998.

Grief and Mourning

Akner, Lois, and Catherine Whitney. *How to Survive the Loss of a Parent: A Guide for Adults.* New York: William Morrow & Co., 1993.

Ashcroft, Mary Ellen, and Holly Bridges Elliott. *Bearing Our Sorrows: Christian Reflections for Courage, Hope and Healing.* San Francisco: HarperSanFrancisco, 1993.

Becvar, Dorothy S. *In the Presence of Grief: Helping Family Members Resolve Death, Dying, and Bereavement Issues.* New York: The Guilford Press, 2001.

Boss, Pauline. *Ambiguous Loss: Learning to Live with Unresolved Grief.* Cambridge: Harvard University Press, 1999.

Childs-Gowell, Elaine. *Good Grief Rituals: Tools for Healing.* Barrtown, N.Y.: Station Hill Press, 1992.

Cobb, Nancy. *In Lieu of Flowers: A Conversation for the Living.* New York: Pantheon Books, 2000.

Crenshaw, David A., PhD. *Bereavement: Counseling the Grieving through the Life Cycle.* New York: Crossroad, 1990.

Davies, Phyllis. *Grief: Climbing Towards Understanding.* Secaucus, N.J.: Lyle Stuart Inc., 1988.

Davis, Deborah L., PhD. *Empty Cradle, Broken Heart: Surviving the Death of Your Baby.* Golden, Colo.: Fulcrum Publishing, 1996.

Edelman, Hope. *Motherless Daughters: The Legacy of Loss.* New York: Dell Publishing, 1994.

Elison, Jennifer, EdD, and Chris McGonigle, PhD. *Liberating Losses: When Death Brings Relief.* Cambridge, Mass.: Perseus Publishing, 2003.

Fitzgerald, Helen. *The Grieving Child: A Parent's Guide.* New York: Fireside Books, 1992.

——. *The Mourning Handbook.* New York: Simon & Schuster, 1994.

——. *The Grieving Teen: A Guide for Teenagers and Their Friends.* New York: Fireside Books, 2000.

Harris, Maxine, PhD. *The Loss That is Forever: The Lifelong Impact of the Early Death of a Mother or Father.* New York: Plume, 1996.

James, John W., and Frank Cherry. *The Grief Recovery Handbook.* New York: Harper Perennial, 1988.

Jeffreys, J. Sheppard. *Helping Grieving People: A Handbook for Care Providers.* New York: Brunner-Routledge, 2004.

Kelley, Patricia. *Companion for Grief: Finding Consolation When Someone You Love Has Died.* New York: Simon & Schuster, 1997.

Kennedy, Alexandra. *Losing a Parent: Passage to a New Way of Living.* San Francisco: HarperSanFrancisco, 1991.

Larson, Dale G. *The Helper's Journey: Working with People Facing Grief, Loss, and Life-Threatening Illness.* Champaign, Ill.: Research Press, 1993.

Lewis, C. S. *A Grief Observed.* San Francisco: HarperSanFrancisco, 1994.

Meeks, Blair Gilmer. *Standing in the Circle of Grief: Prayers and Liturgies for Death and Dying.* Minneapolis: Abingdon Press, 2002.

Neeld, Elizabeth Harper. *Seven Choices: Finding Daylight after Loss Shatters Your World.* New York: Warner Books, 2003.

Pogue, Carolyn. *Language of the Heart: Rituals, Stories and Information about Death.* Louiseville, Quebec: Northstone Publishing, Inc., 1998.

Rothman, Juliet Cassuto. *The Bereaved Parents' Survival Guide.* New York: Continuum, 1997.

Staudacher, Carol. *Beyond Grief: A Guide for Recovering from the Death of a Loved One.* Oakland, Calif.: New Harbinger Publications, 1987.

Van Praagh, James. *Healing Grief: Reclaiming Life After Any Loss.* New York: Dutton, 2000.

Walsh, Froma, and Monica McGoldrick. *Living Beyond Loss: Death in the Family.* New York: W. W. Norton, 1991.

Rituals

Anderson, Herbert, and Edward Foley. *Mighty Stories, Dangerous Rituals: Weaving Together the Human and the Divine.* San Francisco: Jossey-Bass, 1998.

Bass, Dorothy C., ed. *Practicing Our Faith: A Way of Life for Searching People.* San Francisco: Jossey-Bass, 1997.

Driver, Tom F. *Liberating Rites: Understanding the Transformative Power of Ritual,* formerly titled, *The Magic of Ritual: Our Need for Liberating Rites That Transform Our Lives and Our Communities.* San Francisco: HarperSanFrancisco, 1991.

Feinstein, David, and Peg Elliot Mayo. *Mortal Acts.* San Francisco: HarperSanFrancisco, 1993.

Gillis, John R. *A World of Their Own Making: Myth, Ritual and the Quest for Family Values.* New York: BasicBooks, 1996.

Grimes, Ronald L. *Beginnings in Ritual Studies.* Columbia: University of South Carolina Press, 1994.

———. *Readings in Ritual Studies.* Upper Saddle River, N.J.: Prentice Hall, 1996.

McCoy, Edain. *Entering the Summerland: Customs and Rituals of Transition into the Afterlife.* St. Paul, Minn.: Llewellyn Publications, 1996.

Pauw, Amy Plantinga. "Dying Well." *Practicing Our Faith.* (1997): 163–177.

Rathschmidt, Jack, OFM Cap; Gaynell Bordes Cronin. *Rituals for Home & Parish: Healing and Celebrating Our Families.* New York: Paulist Press, 1996.

Roose-Evans, James. *Passages of the Soul: Rediscovering the Importance of Rituals in Everyday Life.* Rockport, Mass.: Element Books, 1994.

Turner, Victor. *The Ritual Process: Structure and Anti-Structure.* New York: Aldine de Gruyter, 1969.

Vogel, Linda J. *Rituals for Resurrection: Celebrating Life and Death.* Nashville, Tenn.: Upper Room Books, 1996.

York, Sarah. *Remembering Well: Rituals for Celebrating Life and Mourning Death.* San Francisco: Jossey-Bass, 2000.

Religious Traditions

Badham, Paul, and Linda Badham, eds. *Death and Immortality in the Religions of the World.* New York: Paragon House, 1987.

Bowker, John. *The Meanings of Death.* Cambridge, U.K.: Cambridge University Press, 1993.

Cohn-Sherbok, Dan, and Christopher Lewis, eds. *Beyond Death: Theological and Philosophical Reflections on Life After Death.* New York: St. Martin's Press, 1995.

Coward, Harold, ed. *Life after Death in World Religions*. Maryknoll, N.Y.: Orbis Books, 1997.

Johnson, Christopher Jay, and Marsha G. McGee, eds. *How Different Religions View Death and Afterlife*. Philadelphia: Charles Press, 1998.

Kramer, Kenneth. *The Sacred Art of Dying*. New York: Paulist Press, 1988.

LaRue, Gerald A. *Playing God: 50 Religions' Views on Your Right to Die*. Wakefield, R.I.: Moyer Bell, 1996.

Ma'asùmián, Farnáz. *Life After Death: A Study of the Afterlife in World Religions*. London: Oneworld, 1995.

Obayashi, Hiroshi, ed. *Death and Afterlife: Perspectives of World Religions*. New York: Praeger, 1992.

Occhiogrosso, Peter. *The Joy of Sects*. New York: First Image Books, 1996.

Parry, Joan K., and Angela Shen Ryan. *A Cross-Cultural Look at Death, Dying, and Religion*. Chicago: Nelson-Hall Publishers, 1996.

Parkes, Colin Murray, Pittu Laungani, and Bill Young, eds. *Death and Bereavement Across Culture*. New York: Routledge, 1997.

Christianity

Ashcroft, Mary Ellen, and Holly Bridges Elliott. *Bearing Our Sorrows: Christian Reflections for Courage, Hope and Healing*. San Francisco: HarperSanFrancisco, 1993.

Bergenheim, Richard C. "Because God is Life," in "Life, Not Death." *Christian Science Sentinel* 99, No. 7 (1997): 3–7.

Carmody, John. *Conversations with a Dying Friend*. New York: Paulist Press, 1992.

Gleason, Edward S. *Dying We Live*. Cambridge, Mass.: Cowley Publications, 1990.

Guroian, Vigen. *Life's Living Toward Dying*. Grand Rapids, Mich.: William B. Eerdmans Publ. Co., 1996.

Kirven, Robert H. *A Book About Dying: Preparing for Eternal Life*. West Chester, Pa.: Crysalis Books, 1997.

——. *Now and At the Hour of Our Death: Instructions Concerning My Death and Funeral*. Chicago: Liturgical Training Publications, 1989.

Pauw, Amy Plantinga. "Dying Well." *Practicing our Faith* (1997): 163–177.

Vaux, Kenneth L., and Sara A. Vaux. *Dying Well.* Nashville: Abingdon Press, 1996.

Waters, Brent. *Dying and Death: A Resource for Christian Reflection.* Cleveland: United Church Press, 1996.

Judaism

Brener, Anne. *Mourning and Mitzvah.* Woodstock, Vt.: Jewish Lights Publishing, 1993.

Diamant, Anita. *Saying Kaddish: How to Comfort the Dying, Bury the Dead, and Mourn as a Jew.* New York: Schocken Books, 1998.

Dorff, Elliot N. *Matters of Life and Death: A Jewish Approach to Modern Medical Ethics.* Philadelphia: The Jewish Publication Society, 1998.

Gillman, Neil. *The Death of Death: Resurrection and Immortality in Jewish Thought.* Woodstock, Vt.: Jewish Lights Publishing, 1997.

Goldberg, Rabbi Chaim Binyamin. *Mourning in Halachah: The Laws and Customs of the Year of Mourning.* Brooklyn: Mesorah Publications, Ltd., 1994.

Grollman, Rabbi Earl A. *Living with Loss, Healing with Hope: A Jewish Perspective.* Boston: Beacon Press, 2000.

Harlow, Rabbi Jules, ed. *The Bond of Life: A Book for Mourners.* New York: Rabbinical Assembly, 1975.

Kamin, Rabbi Ben. *The Path of the Soul: Making Peace with Mortality.* New York: Plume, 1999.

Kolatch, Alfred J. *The Jewish Mourner's Book of Why.* Middle Village, N.Y.: Jonathan David Publishers, Inc., 1996.

Lamm, Maurice. *Jewish Way in Death and Mourning.* New York: Jonathan David Publishers, 1969.

Levine, Rabbi Aaron. *To Comfort the Bereaved: A Guide for Mourners and Those Who Visit Them.* Northvale, N.J. and London: Jason Aronson, Inc., 1994.

Ozarowski, Joseph S. *To Walk in God's Ways: Jewish Pastoral Perspectives on Illness and Bereavement.* Northvale, N.J.: Jason Aaronson, Inc., 1995.

Raphael, Simcha Paull. *Jewish Views of the Afterlife.* Northvale, N.J.: Jason Aronson, Inc., 1994.

Riemer, Jack. *Jewish Reflections on Death.* New York: Schocken Books, 1975.

——. *Wrestling with the Angel: Jewish Insights on Death and Mourning.* New York: Schocken Books, 1995.

Rozwaski, Chaim Z. *Jewish Meditations on the Meaning of Death.* Northvale, N.J.: Jason Aronson, Inc., 1994.

Shapiro, Rami M. *Last Breaths: A Guide to Easing Another's Dying.* Miami, Fl.: Temple Beth Or, 1993.

Solomon, Lewis D. *The Jewish Book of Living and Dying.* Northvale, N.J.: Jason Aronson, Inc., 1999.

Soncino, Rifat, and Daniel B. Syme. *What Happens After I Die? Jewish Views of the Life After Death.* New York: UAHC Press, 1990.

Spiro, Jack D. *A Time to Mourn: Judaism and the Psychology of Bereavement.* New York: Bloch Publishing Company, 1985.

Tuchazinsky, Yechiel Michel. *Gesher Hachaim: The Bridge of Life.* Brooklyn: Moznaim Publishing Corp., 1983.

Other Traditions

Dalai Lama, His Holiness. *The Joy of Living and Dying in Peace.* San Francisco: HarperSanFrancisco, 1997.

Evans-Wentz, W. Y., trans. *The Tibetan Book of the Dead.* London: Oxford University Press, 1960.

Fremantle, Francesca, and Chögyam Trungpa, trans. *The Tibetan Book of the Dead.* Boston: Shambala, 1975.

Kapleau, Philip. *The Wheel of Life and Death: A Practical and Spiritual Guide.* New York: Doubleday, 1989.

——. *The Zen of Living and Dying.* Boston and London: Shambala, 1998.

Lodo, Venerable Lama. *Bardo Teachings: The Way of Death and Rebirth.* San Francisco: KDK Publications, 1982.

Longaker, Christine. *Facing Death and Finding Hope: A Guide to the Emotional and Spiritual Care of the Dying.* New York: Doubleday, 1997.

McCoy, Edain. *Entering the Summerland: Customs and Rituals of Transition into the Afterlife.* St. Paul, Minn.: Llewellyn Publications, 1996.

Mullin, Glenn H. *Death and Dying: The Tibetan Tradition.* Boston: Arkana Paperbacks, 1986

Rinpoche, Bokar. *Death and the Art of Dying in Tibetan Buddhism*. San Francisco: Clear Point Press, 1993.

Rinpoche, Sogyal. *The Tibetan Book of Living and Dying*. San Francisco: HarperSanFrancisco, 1993.

Starhawk, M. Macha Nightmare, and the Reclaiming Collective. *The Pagan Book of Living and Dying: Practical Rituals, Prayers, Blessings, and Meditations on Crossing Over*. San Francisco: Harper SanFrancisco, 1997.

Thurman, Robert, trans. *The Tibetan Book of the Dead*. New York: Bantam Books, 1994.

Varela, Francisco J., ed. *Sleeping, Dreaming, and Dying: An Exploration of Consciousness with the Dalai Lama*. Boston: Wisdom Publications, 1997.

Multicultural Traditions

Berger, Arthur, et al., eds. *Perspectives on Death and Dying: Cross-Cultural and Multi-Disciplinary Views*. Philadelphia: The Charles Press, 1989.

Counts, David R., and Dorothy A Counts, eds. *Coping with the Final Tragedy: Cultural Variation in Dying and Grieving*. Amityville, N.Y.: Baywood Publishing Company, Inc, 1991.

Irish, Donald P., Kathleen F. Nelsen, and Vivian Jenkins Lundquist, eds. *Ethnic Variations in Dying, Death and Grief*. Washington, D.C.: Taylor & Francis, 1993.

The Afterlife

Cohn-Sherbok, Dan, and Christopher Lewis, eds. *Beyond Death: Theological and Philosophical Reflections of Life After Death*. New York: St. Martin's Press, 1995.

Coward, Harold, ed. *Life after Death in World Religions*. Maryknoll, N.Y.: Orbis Books, 1997.

Johnson, Christopher Jay, and Marsha G. McGee, eds. *How Different Religions View Death and Afterlife*. Philadelphia: Charles Press, 1991.

Ma'asùmián, Farnáz. *Life After Death: A Study of the Afterlife in World Religions*. London: Oneworld Publications, 1995.

Miller, Suki. *After Death: Mapping the Journey.* New York: Simon & Schuster, 1997.

Neiman, Carol, and Emily Goldman. *AfterLife.* New York: Viking Penguin Books, 1994.

Practical Concerns

Albery, Nicholas, Gil Elliot, and Joseph Elliot of the Natural Death Centre. *The New Natural Death Handbook.* London: Rider, 1997.

Anderson, Patricia. *Affairs in Order: A Complete Resource Guide to Death and Dying.* New York: Macmillan Publishing Company, 1991.

Carlson, Lisa. *Caring for the Dead: Your Final Acts of Love.* Hinesburg, Vt.: Upper Access Books, 1998.

Hoefler, James M. *Managing Death: The First Guide for Patients, Family Members, and Care Providers on Foregoing Treatment at the End of Life.* Boulder, Colo.: Westview Press, 1997.

Preston, Thomas A., MD. *Final Victory: Taking Charge of the Last Stages of Life, Facing Death on Your Own Terms.* Roseville, Calif.: Forum, 2000.

Tobin, Daniel R., with Karen Lindsey. *Peaceful Dying: The Step-by-Step Guide to Preserving Your Dignity, Your Choice, and Your Inner Peace at the End of Life.* Reading, Mass.: Perseus Books, 1999.

Wiskind, Julie, and Richard Spiegel. *Coming to Rest: A Guide to Caring for Our Own Dead.* Kamuela, Hawaii: Dovetail, 1998.

Ethical Issues

Beauchamp, Tom L., and Robert M. Veatch. *Ethical Issues in Death and Dying.* Upper Saddle River, N.J.: Prentice Hall, 1996.

Committee on Medical Ethics in the Episcopal Diocese of Washington. *Toward a Good Christian Death: Crucial Treatment Choices.* Harrisburg, Pa.: Morehouse Publishing, 1999.

Dorff, Elliot N. *Matters of Life and Death: A Jewish Approach to Modern Medical Ethics.* Philadelphia: The Jewish Publication Society, 1998.

LaRue, Gerald A. *Playing God: 50 Religions' Views on Your Right to Die.* Wakefield, R.I.: Moyer Bell, 1996.

Quill, Timothy E., M.D. *A Midwife Through the Dying Process: Stories of Healing & Hard Choices at the End of Life.* Baltimore: Johns Hopkins Press, 1996.

Singer, Peter. *Rethinking Life and Death: The Collapse of our Traditional Ethics.* New York: St. Martin's Griffin, 1994.

Vaux, Kenneth L., Sara A. Vaux. *Dying Well.* Nashville: Abingdon Press, 1996.

Music

Campbell, Don. *The Mozart Effect: Tapping the Power of Music to Heal the Body, Strengthen the Mind, and Unlock the Creative Spirit.* New York: Avon Books, 1997.

Lane, Deforia. *Music as Medicine.* Grand Rapids, Mich.: Zondervan Publishing House, 1994.

Paxton, Fred. "From Life to Death." *Connecticut College Magazine,* May/June 1994: 26–29.

Schroeder-Sheker, Therese. "Musical-Sacramental-Midwifery." *In Music and Miracles.* Wheaton, Ill.: Quest Books, 1992.

——. "Music for the Dying." *Journal of Holistic Nursing* 12, no. 1 (1994): 83–99.

——. "Music for the Dying: Using Prescriptive Music in the Death-Bed Vigil." *Noetic Sciences Review,* Autumn 1994: 32–36.

——. "Death and the Chalice of Repose Project: Prescriptive Music and the Art of Dying." *LAPIS.* Issue 2, 1995: 9–11.

Storr, Anthony. *Music and the Mind.* New York: Ballantine Books, 1992.

Psychology of Death

Kramer, Kenneth P. *Death Dreams: Unveiling Mysteries of the Unconscious Mind.* New York: Paulist Press, 1993.

Orbach, Ann. *Life, Psychotherapy and Death: The End of Our Exploring.* London and Philadelphia: Jessica Kingsley Publishers, 1999.

Singh, Kathleen Dowling. *The Grace in Dying: How We Are Transformed Spiritually As We Die.* San Francisco: HarperSanFrancisco, 1998.

Spiro, Jack D. *A Time to Mourn: Judaism and the Psychology of Bereavement*. New York: Bloch Publishing Company, 1985.

von Franz, Marie-Louise. *On Dreams and Death*. Boston: Shambala, 1986.

Historical Treatment of Death and Dying

Aries, Philippe. *The Hour of Our Death*. New York & Oxford: Oxford University Press, 1981.

Barley, Nigel. *Grave Matters: A Lively History of Death Around the World*. New York: Henry Holt and Company, 1995.

Beaty, Nancy Lee. *The Craft of Dying: The Literary Tradition of the Ars Moriendi in England*. New Haven and London: Yale University Press, 1970.

Binski, Paul. *Medieval Death: Ritual and Representation*. Ithaca, N.Y.: Cornell University Press, 1995.

Paxton, Frederick. *Christianizing Death: The Creation of a Ritual Process in Early Medieval Europe*. Ithaca, N.Y.: Cornell University Press, 1990.

Anthologies

Carmichael, Andrew, ed. *Carmina Gadelica: Hymns and Incantations*. Hudson, N.Y.: Lindisfarne Press, 1992.

Dunn, Philip, ed. *Prayer: Language of the Soul*. New York: Dell Publishing, 1997.

Enright, D. J., ed. *The Oxford Book of Death*. Oxford & New York: Oxford University Press, 1983.

McNees, Pat, ed. *Dying: A Book of Comfort*. New York: Warner Books, Inc., 1998.

Moffat, Mary Jane, ed. *In the Midst of Winter: Selections from the Literature of Mourning*. New York: Vintage Books, 1992.

Munro, Eleanor, ed. *Readings for Remembrance: A Collection for Funerals and Memorial Services*. New York: Penguin Books, 2000.

Nearing, Helen, ed. *Light on Aging and Dying: An Inspirational Gathering of Thoughts on Living a Good Old Age into Death*. San Diego: A Harvest Book, 1995.

Potter, Peter, comp. *All About Death*. New Canaan, Conn.: William Mulvey, Inc., 1988.

Roberts, Elizabeth, and Elias Amidon, eds. *Life Prayers from Around the World*. San Francisco: HarperSanFrancisco, 1996.

Sloyan, Virginia, ed. *Death: A Sourcebook about Christian Death*. Chicago: Liturgical Training Publications, 1990.

Ulanov, Barry, comp. *On Death: Wisdom and Consolation from the World's Great Writers*. Luguori, Mo: Triumph Books, 1996.

Van de Weyer, Robert, ed. *The HarperCollins Book of Prayers*. San Francisco: HarperSanFrancisco, 1993.

Permissions and Acknowledgments

The following translations of scriptures and sacred texts were used:

Selections from the Hebrew and Christian Bible were from the Authorized King James Version, the New Revised Standard Version, and the Revised Standard Version.

Selections from the Qur'an, from The Presidency of Islamic Researches, IFTA and King Fahd Ibn Abdul-Aziz of the Kingdom of Saudi Arabia.

Selections from the Upanishads were translated by Dominic Goodall in *Hindu Scriptures.*

Selections from the Bhagavad Gita were translated by Dominic Goodall in *Hindu Scriptures.*

The Buddhist Sutras were from the following sources:

Udama Sutra. As cited in *The Buddha Speaks,* edited by Anne Bancroft. Boston: Shambhala, 2000.

Mahaparinirvana Sutra. As cited in *The Teachings of the Compassionate Buddha,* edited E. A. Burtt. New York:New American Library, 2000.

White Lotus. As cited in The Teachings of the Compassionate Buddha, edited E. A. Burtt. New York: New American Library, 2000.

The Tibetan Book of the Dead, translated by Francesca Fremantle and Chögyam Trungpa. Boston: Shambhala, 1975.

The following passages (in the order that they appear in the book) were used with permission:

Blessing the Body from *The Pagan Book of Living and Dying: Practical Rituals, Prayers, Blessings and Meditations on Crossing Over* by Starhawk, M. Macha Nightmare and The Reclaiming Collective. Copyright © 1997 by Miriam Simos a.k.a. Starhawk and Aline O'Brien a.k.a. M. Macha NightMare. Reprinted by permission of HarperCollins Publishers, Inc.

Star Light by Madeleine L'Engle. Reprinted from *The Weather of the Heart*. Copyright © 1978 by Madeleine L'Engle. Used by permission of WaterBrook Press, Colorado Springs, Colo. All rights reserved.

Poems numbered 24 and 31 from *God Is No Illusion: Meditations on the End of Life* by John Tully Carmody. Published by Trinity Press International, 1997.

Excerpt from "Little Gidding" in *Four Quartets*, copyright 1942 by T. S. Eliot and renewed 1970 by Esme Valerie Eliot, reprinted by permission of Harcourt, Inc.

Excerpt from "East Coker" in *Four Quartets*, copyright 1940 by T. S. Eliot and renewed 1968 by Esme Valerie Eliot, reprinted by permission of Harcourt, Inc.

Entry by Christopher Carstens. Used with permission from author.

Quietness by Jalal al-Din Rumi, from *The Essential Rumi*. Originally published by Threshold Books.

All Souls' Day by D. H. Lawrence. From *The Complete Poems of D. H. Lawrence*, published by Oxford University Press. Special acknowledgments to Laurence Pollinger Limited and the Estate of Frieda Lawrence Ravagli.

A Visitation by Rayn Roberts. Used with permission from the author.

Poems by Emily Dickinson. Reprinted by permission of the publishers and Trustees of Amherst College from *The Poems of Emily Dickinson*, Thomas H. Johnson, ed., Cambridge, Mass.: The Belknap Press of Harvard University Press, Copyright © 1951, 1955, 1979 by the President and Fellows of Harvard College.

On Waking in Prison, by Deitrich Bonhoeffer. From The Oxford Book of Prayer, edited by George Appleton. Published by Oxford University Press, 1985.

Papago Prayer. Reprinted from the Bureau of American Ethnology #22. Washington, D.C.: Smithsonian Institution Press, 1996.

A Prayer for a Peaceful Death, by Marianne Williamson. From Illuminata by Marianne Williamson, copyright © 1994 Marianne Williamson. Used by permission of Random House, Inc.

For People Dying. Copyright material taken from *A New Zealand Prayer Book—He Karakia Mihinare o Aotearoa* is used with permission.

You Are Blessed In the Mother's Eyes from *The Goddess in the Bedroom* by Zsuzsanna E. Budapest. Copyright © 1993 by Zsuzsanna E. Budapest. Reprinted by permission of HarperCollins Publishers, Inc.

The author wishes to thank Christopher Carstens and Eileen Walsh for their original contributions to this book, *Entry* found on page 293, and "Altars" found on pages 92 and 93. Thank you also to Marianne Williamson for graciously granting permission to use *A Prayer for a Peaceful Death* found on pages 313 and 314.

Thanks to the Central Conference of American Rabbis for permission to use *Kayla's Prayer* found on pages 321 and 322.

CPSIA information can be obtained at www.ICGtesting.com
Printed in the USA
BVOW08s1031040913

330216BV00002B/156/A